Nonviolence and the Theo-Drama of Peace

Anabaptist Ethics and the
Catholic Christology of
Hans Urs von Balthasar

Layton Boyd Friesen

t&tclark
LONDON • NEW YORK • OXFORD • NEW DELHI • SYDNEY

T&T CLARK
Bloomsbury Publishing Plc
50 Bedford Square, London, WC1B 3DP, UK
1385 Broadway, New York, NY 10018, USA
29 Earlsfort Terrace, Dublin 2, Ireland

BLOOMSBURY, T&T CLARK and the T&T Clark logo are trademarks of
Bloomsbury Publishing Plc

First published in Great Britain 2022

Cover image: kevron2001/iStockphoto

A catalogue record for this book is available from the British Library.

Library of Congress Cataloging-in-Publication Data
Names: Friesen, Layton Boyd, author.
Title: Secular nonviolence and the theo-drama of peace : anabaptist ethics
and the Catholic Christology of Hans Urs von Balthasar / Layton Boyd Friesen.
Description: London ; New York : T&T Clark, 2022. |
Includes bibliographical references and index. |
Identifiers: LCCN 2021035291 (print) | LCCN 2021035292 (ebook) |
ISBN 9780567704030 (pb) | ISBN 9780567704047 (hb) |
ISBN 9780567704054 (epub) | ISBN 9780567704061 (epdf)
Subjects: LCSH: Balthasar, Hans Urs von, 1905–1988. | Jesus Christ–History
of doctrines–Early church, ca. 30–600. | Pacifism–Religious
aspects–Mennonites. | Anabaptists–Doctrines. | Mennonites–Doctrines.
Classification: LCC BX4705.B163 F75 2022 (print) | LCC BX4705.B163 (ebook) |
DDC 230.209–dc23
LC record available at https://lccn.loc.gov/2021035291
LC ebook record available at https://lccn.loc.gov/2021035292

ISBN: HB: 978-0-5677-0404-7
PB: 978-0-5677-0403-0
ePDF: 978-0-5677-0406-1
ePUB: 978-0-5677-0405-4

Series: T&T Clark Studies in Anabaptist Theology and Ethics

Typeset by Newgen KnowledgeWorks Pvt. Ltd., Chennai, India
Printed and bound in Great Britain

To find out more about our authors and books visit www.bloomsbury.com
and sign up for our newsletters.

Secular Nonviolence and the Theo-Drama of Peace

T&T CLARK STUDIES IN ANABAPTIST
THEOLOGY AND ETHICS

Series editors
Malinda Berry
Paul Martens

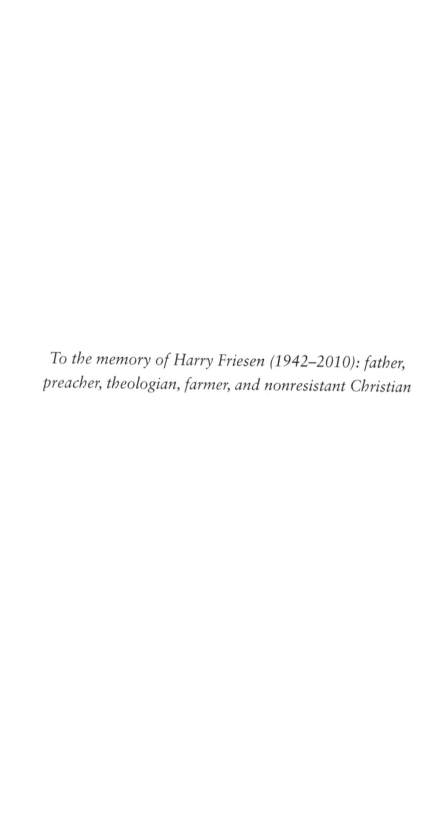

To the memory of Harry Friesen (1942–2010): father, preacher, theologian, farmer, and nonresistant Christian

CONTENTS

SERIES PREFACE

T&T Clark Studies in Anabaptist Theology and Ethics is dedicated to displaying the vibrant global resurgence of theological reflection and praxis in and adjacent to the Anabaptist tradition. In a world that is fraught with overt and covert forms of violence, this series provides a platform for new ways of seeing, understanding, and living what it means to love one's enemy and one's neighbor with the peace of God that surpasses much of the wisdom of the day.

With debts to the New Testament, the early church, and late-medieval reformers, Anabaptism emerged as a loosely organized Christian movement in sixteenth-century Europe. Today the heirs of this continually evolving and sometimes highly contested tradition—whether called Mennonite, Brethren, Hutterite, Amish, or any number of other designations—are scattered around the world and especially the Global South. Therefore, while recognizing that the preponderance of academic theology in the peace church tradition still occurs in North America and Europe, this series is committed to publishing voices that represent the theological imaginations, concerns, heartbreaks, and convictions of the entire global Anabaptist family. To that end, volumes draw from established and emerging voices and take a variety of forms, including but not limited to monographs, case studies, and edited collections.

T&T Clark Studies in Anabaptist Theology and Ethics is published under the editorial direction of the Institute of Mennonite Studies, the research and publication agency of Anabaptist Mennonite Biblical Seminary in Elkhart, Indiana. The Institute of Mennonite Studies was founded in 1958 to promote and create opportunities for research, conversation, and publication on topics and issues vital to the Anabaptist faith tradition. For more information or to submit a proposal to the series, please visit www.ambs.edu/ims.

Malinda Berry, Anabaptist Mennonite Biblical Seminary
Paul Martens, Baylor University

ACKNOWLEDGMENTS

The project of this book now stretches back nine years. It had its birth in the fires of my doctoral work at Wycliffe College at the University of Toronto. There are more people to thank than I can remember. Joseph Mangina, my doctoral supervisor, has been an early and enthusiastic supporter of the basic convictions expressed in this work. He helped me banish many of the foggy and nameless notions that drift around a project like this, wanting entrance. Sr. Gill Goulding C.J.'s course on Balthasar at Regis College introduced me to the vast depths of Balthasar's spirituality. I also benefited from the perceptive comments and questions given by my defense committee: John Rempel, John Berkman, Ephraim Radner, and Peter Erb. David Cramer, managing editor at the Institute of Mennonite Studies, helped me in the process of reimagining and reworking this work as a book. I thank the editors at T&T Clark, especially Anna Turton, for taking on this project and improving its style. They know how to make better writers.

My family, Glenda, Carmen, and Marcus, has lived costly love while I wrote about it. Glenda, my wife, walked me out of the slough of despair on too many occasions to number as I struggled through Balthasar's theology. Her glad friendship and love have been simply heroic. I love you three to the moon and back.

I have no doubt that what attracts me to Hans Urs von Balthasar has much to do with how he returns me to the faith of my father, Harry Friesen.

Introduction: Anabaptist Ethics and Hans Urs von Balthasar's Christology

In the fall of 1968, the "Concern Group" was in no mood for a merry Christmas. This was a group of young, radical Mennonite theologians disturbed by the complicity of "bourgeois" Mennonites, seen to be assimilated, prosperous, and comfortable in America. The Concern Group had joined their prophetic voices in a series of pamphlets known as *Concern*. In the fall of 1968, the editorial board decided that, for its next issue, the way to address the nest of problems the nation faced ("Vietnam, the urban crisis, or communism")[1] was to attack Christmas.

Of course, it was 1968; Bohemian subculture was in full flower; the Tet offensive of that year signaled the failure of the United States in Vietnam and the vindication of anti-war agitation; the assassination of Martin Luther King Jr. symbolized a martyr in the cause of nonviolent cultural change. Revolution was in the air across the nation and the time was ripe for Mennonites to shake off their bucolic lethargy and raise an assertive resistance.

The pamphlet begins with a poem titled "Nasty Noel"[2] and Marlin Jeschke's piece "Getting Christ Back Out of Christmas," leaving little doubt about where the Concern Group stood on the Yule: Christ has no place in Christmas and none should be sought. There were the boilerplate criticisms one often hears of Christmas;

---

[1] Virgil Vogt, "Marginalia," *Concern* 16 (November 1968): 22–4.
[2] Henderson Nylrod, "Nasty Noel," *Concern* 16 (November 1968): 2–3.

it is sentimental syrup, it is crassly pagan, it tames Jesus, it is consumerism, it misreads the Gospels, and so on. But then John Howard Yoder ties in with a deeper connection:

> Christmas is typical of a strategy of cultural accommodation. All the dates on the liturgical year have been diluted by an element of accommodation to pre-Christian cult patterns, but only Christmas, of the major feasts recognized by most Christians, has no base either in the early church or in Israel. ... Thus it is only Christmas which must be explained primarily as an assimilation or displacement of its pagan predecessors in the age of Constantine. It thereby represents in a quintessential way the issue of accommodation versus iconoclasm in Christian cultural strategy.[3]

Christmas stands "at the intersection of two competing conceptions of what the Christian faith is all about."[4] A church that is "religious," "established," and committed to "responsibility" seeks to "add depth or meaning to the world as it is, by giving a dimension of transcendence" to its natural wisdom.[5] It exists to bless the cycles of harvest and fertility.

> The other type of faith we may call "historical" or "covenantal." Here the focus is on events in this world which change it. "Transcendence" means not a dimension "beyond" this world but a power active within it. The cycle of life and of the year are broken through by a history which is linear, which is going somewhere. The given unities of family, class, nation are broken up by two new loyalties: by a visible, voluntary new community of those who respond in faith to what God has done, and by the vision of the stranger, the enemy, the outsider, the ends of the earth as the measure of the extent of that God's purposes.[6]

Christmas and all its Constantinian acclimatization is to be contrasted with Anabaptism, a believers church determined in its

---

[3]John Howard Yoder, "On the Meaning of Christmas," *Concern* 16 (November 1968): 21–2.
[4]Ibid., 14.
[5]Ibid.
[6]Ibid.

visibility by the transforming power of the Christ in history—a faith that stands in opposition "to every religious sacramentalizing of natural relationships that tends to undermine the importance of the church."[7]

Why do I raise here this rather hyperbolic, 1960s dispatch against Christmas? It's a quick bath in the modern Mennonite struggle to find a place for the Anabaptist ethic in this world without becoming worldly. At one level, these iconoclasts are sure that the American status quo badly needs to be contradicted and interrupted. Christ's community must be forever setting out, departing like Abram from hearth and home. The old Mennonite concern about worldliness is still sharply evident. And yet at the same time, this is no call for withdrawal from the world in traditional Mennonite terms. These are men of the world, fresh into their Mennonite communities from the universities of Europe. They are drinking in the spirit of the sixties; antiestablishment, antiauthoritarian, and de-ceremonializing. Rather than viewing farming as the vocation best suited to Mennonite world resistance, this is an urban faith that uses agricultural metaphors as symbols of complacency and complicity.[8] Their concern is to recover communities of countercultural discipleship modeled after Jesus, and yet this piece is clearly also a child of its era.

And it is interesting that all this revolves around a celebration of the incarnation. Yoder at this stage is suspicious of it:

What fourth-century Christendom celebrated was not an event but a doctrine, not a life breaking into the world but the miracle of incarnation transforming it. If in the effort to save Christmas, we bring to it the full weight of the miracle of God-made-infant, we fall into the docetic heresy, affirming the full divine presence apart from the story of the man.[9]

Here, Yoder sees "incarnation" as another word for liberal Protestants' attempt to impart a divine hue to the world that might illuminate our otherwise arid rationalistic existence. It is a Constantinian word, a word that tames Christ's intent to establish

[7]Marlin Jeschke, "Getting Christ Back Out of Christmas," *Concern* 16 (November 1968): 9–13.
[8]Yoder, "On the Meaning of Christmas," 14, 17.
[9]Ibid., 19.

God-sent but still verily human sociopolitical outposts in the world which interrupt the numbing cycles of time. "Incarnation," as Yoder and company perceived it in 1968, suffers from the collapse of holy difference into compromising unity. In Chalcedonian terms, it named a divine/human mixture that nevertheless prioritized the divine and ultimately left humanity untransformed. Rather than raising a resistance against the violence enshrined in the world's political ideology, this mixture compromised Christ's plan to found a counterculture of peace.

All of this forms a backdrop to this work on the relationship between incarnation, unity in difference, and gospel pacifism in Mennonite theology.[10] Immediately, I need to say a word about the term "unity in difference." Sometimes this phrase refers to how the church can remain united in spite of differences. That is not how I use it. It is used here to refer to questions all Christians must answer about the unity in difference between God and the world, and the unity in difference Christians then also must have with the world.

Mennonites have spent much time in their history talking about unity in difference. What is worldliness? What lifestyles mark believers as children of God set apart from the world? Who are the pure and unstained, yielded only to God? Is it possible for the church to be in the world but not of it? In this study I intend to look at gospel pacifism as both a form of difference from the world and as a form of unity with the world. It can certainly be the life of a believer lived in union with Christ, but it can also become a common-sense posture not needing Christ at all.

As the Concern Group intuited, a central locus for the Christian answer to the question of unity in difference is the incarnation, the event in which God entered the world and accomplished reconciliation with his creation. This was done not in spite of his difference with the world, but through it, gaining thus a covenant

---

[10] A note about my use of the terms *pacifism*, *nonviolence*, and *nonresistance*: Generally, "pacifism" refers to all absolute refusals of violence, whether religiously or secularly based. I affix *gospel* to "pacifism" when I refer specifically to a Christian faith-based ethic. *Nonresistance* is an older word that I make much use of because it seems to me to retain a spirituality that "pacifism" lacks. "Nonviolence" is used for a more general attempt to abandon violence in society, and need not indicate complete pacifism.

of love between the Creator and the creation.[11] My argument will seek to show that the incarnation, when interpreted rightly, not only describes the act of God's unity in difference but also draws the church into participation with Christ, thus showing it to be not "merely" a doctrine but a doctrine glimpsing an event in history. I will argue that when the incarnation is interpreted and entered into according to the Chalcedonian tradition of the church, it is deeply twined with a gospel pacifism, or a Christ-formed intent to address evil without violence, through love.

In the descent of Christ into human flesh, in the relation Christ maintained with the Father during his sojourn, and in the ways in which he invited the church to participate in his relationship with the Father through the Spirit, we find a social vision. This could be compared to twentieth-century proposals about the Trinity being our social program or vision.[12] I am arguing, in a sense, that the incarnation is our social vision. It is this "incarnational social program" that provides a dynamic for gospel pacifism. Miroslav Volf distinguishes his version of the "trinity as social program" in a way that highlights the incarnation's special relation to enemy love:

> It is not so much the [divine] giving that feeds on and delights in love's reciprocities that the disciples are called to emulate … [but rather] the kind that seeks to elicit the non-existent response of love in those who practice the very opposite of love. Jesus demanded not so much that we imitate the divine dance of love's freedom and trust, but the divine labor of love's suffering and risk.[13]

We turn to the incarnation for our social vision because it is here that God's love for enemies is shown in a way that invites our participation and discipleship. It is here that the church's unity in difference with God and the world is figured as enemy love. Gospel

---

[11]In the twenty-first century, one is conscious of how divine pronouns are used. Though I am comfortable with the masculine pronoun for the deity, I recognize this is a contested question in academic theology. I will use the masculine pronouns for God. In other matters, I try to be as gender-neutral as possible.

[12]See Miroslav Volf, "'The Trinity Is Our Social Program': The Doctrine of the Trinity and the Shape of Social Engagement," *Modern Theology* 14, no. 3 (July 1998): 403–23.

[13]Ibid., 413.

pacifism, I believe, is the attempt to describe unity in difference in a way that participates in the incarnation of the Word of God. The pacifist church gazes into the mystery of God's encounter with a good but evil world and seeks to extend the incarnation by its own relation to the world in the form of enemy love, and it does all this through the transforming work of the Spirit.

To the ongoing struggles of Mennonites with worldliness, I would like to offer some key aspects of Hans Urs von Balthasar's Christology to see if incarnation might yet be the dogmatic undercarriage needed for a theology of peace lived within a secular age. I am seeking a pacifist ethic that is linked dramatically, mystically, and personally to the descent of Christ into the conditions of human life. This calls for a pacifism that is contemplative, calibrated by the real-time movements of Christ in the Spirit. It must be scriptural, attentive to and imitative of the decisions of Christ in his earthly sojourn. It shall be eschatological, lived in patient expectancy under the conditions of this world. It must also be contextual, taking up the language, wary of the hazards, and attuned to the possibilities of the world it now inhabits. For us, in this work, that world is modern, secular North America.

But Hans Urs von Balthasar? Deepening the Mennonite theology of peace with the reception of Roman Catholic, Hans Urs von Balthasar's Christology is not something attempted before. This might bring three questions to mind and addressing them in turn will give us a sense of what is in store. First, do *Mennonites* really need resources for a theology of peace? This project intends to offer a deeper, more dynamic doctrine of peace to a church I love. I have debated about whether to write to "Mennonites" or to "Anabaptists." "Anabaptist" has become the chosen term for the attempt to create a more portable, translatable discipleship that has shed its cultural entrapment in North Atlantic Mennonite church life. "Anabaptist" is a term that is no longer a noun so much as an adjective describing varieties of Anglicans or Catholics, or what have you, that have been shaped by Anabaptist sensibilities. Though I retain the use of "Anabaptist," I am, however, going to hold this forth as a Mennonite offering, not because I think these questions only apply to Mennonites, but because I have come to believe that Mennonites in North America can speak most authentically about their faith to others when they don't pretend their faith can exist un-encultured. As *Mennonites*, carrying all the tradition and baggage of our days in this world, we do have something to offer the faith of the one, holy, apostolic, and catholic church. I will often use the term Anabaptist to discuss the early pioneers in the sixteenth century, some of whom became Mennonites.

But what could this tradition need in the way of peace resources? They are, after all, known as "peace churches" for their 500-year rejection of violence in the name of Christ. Some have wondered whether Mennonite ethics is ever about anything *other* than nonviolence. Writing as a pacifist Mennonite pastor, however, I have seen that Mennonite ethics labors under tensions about what it means to be good people for the sake of Christ. Prior to the twentieth century, it was clear to most Mennonites that a nonresistant ethic was theological and could only be maintained within the unique worship and life of a church decisively separated from the world. Pacifism was rarely imagined as something that might work "out there" beyond the Mennonite church.

That no longer holds. In my observations as a pastor, I noted that when people came to faith, a Mennonite peace ethic was often the last thing they adopted. For new believers coming into the church from outside traditional Mennonite southern Manitoba culture, it was not at all evident that becoming a pacifist was germane to the transition. But when folks who had grown up in traditional Mennonite culture left the faith to become secular people, that Mennonite ethic was often the last thing to go. Many continued to hold to what they considered a Mennonite understanding of nonviolence, long after they had let go of any personal commitment to Jesus. What that suggested to me was the lack of an organic or natural transition between believing with the church and living the church's ethic. That transition no longer appears organic or natural to many people, not least Mennonites, in a secular age.[14]

Secularity has called into question the need for the theological underpinnings of the Mennonite pacifist ethic. Secularity has tendencies to quarantine religiously grounded ethical convictions to the church sphere, or alternatively, to orphan Christian ethical convictions out in the world with no further need of the church or theology. As several authors have noted, ethics in a secular age tends to be a sphere unto itself, seeking neither communal embodiment

---

[14]In this book, I am speaking to the situation of assimilated Mennonites. Old Colony, Amish, and Hutterite churches have a different relation to secularity and so their issues of unity in difference are unique.

nor spiritual transformation nor the involvement of God.[15] As we will discuss in Chapter 2, modern Mennonites' concern with societal peacemaking and social justice has much less need for continued reflection on doctrinal issues than the practice their older Mennonite forbears assumed.

But to point out continuities between pacifism and secularity should not be interpreted to mean that pacifism and nonviolence are the natural instincts for moderns or that shalom now comes easily for people. In a modern western society, overt violence is mostly given over to the state. This arrangement asks the nonmilitary, nonpolice citizen to rarely, if ever, act violently in an overt way. This may reduce violence overall in society (which is not a bad thing), but it also creates the abiding suspicion that secularity has not finally addressed the violent instinct in people—it has only taken away the opportunity for it to manifest.[16] For a Christian, concerned not only with people's actions but with the moral gist of their souls and the eternal direction of their desires, the reduction of violence by sequestering it in the state is not morally impressive.

I will explore this dynamic in the first two chapters. In Chapter 1, I will take a broad historical look at how pacifism has been related to the world and to Christ in early Anabaptism, and in the *Martyrs Mirror*. Here we will glimpse the deeply participationist way in which pacifism was understood in the Mennonite church. In the Chapter 2, we will look at the twentieth century specifically and at the way pacifism and secularity came to be intertwined in some problematic ways. This too will necessarily be panoramic. Here I will argue that the historic understanding of gospel pacifism as mystical union with Christ came into uncharted waters in the twentieth century with its own success. Charles Taylor will provide us with the analysis we need to understand the significant overlap in the agenda and concerns of secularity and gospel pacifism; this will give us a context within which the theological work we do later can find a home. We will also look at how leading Mennonite theologians in the twentieth century sought to re-situate the pacifist ethic in this new context of unity in difference.

---

[15]For a discussion of these problems of ethics in a modern setting see Matthew Rose, "Theology and the Limits of Ethics," *Pro Ecclesia* 23, no. 2 (May 1, 2014): 174–94.
[16]The global explosion of pornography in recent decades, much of it explicitly violent, testifies to the inability of secularity to truly cure the soul of its violent instincts.

So that then is why Mennonites may need to consider further their theology of peace. Secondly, one might ask, why does pacifism even need a *dogmatic* undercarriage? Why concern ourselves with its relation to the dogmas of Trinity, incarnation, salvation, and eternal hope? Is simple obedience to the commands in Mt. 5:38-48, Rom. 12:14-21, or 1 Pet. 2:18-25 not enough? From a secular perspective, why do Christians need ancient dogma to prevent them from committing violence? Many nonbelievers are peaceful people.

What changes when an ethic is a *theological* ethic? Most broadly, a theological ethic describes a way of living that is attuned to the highest vocation of humankind to enjoy God forever. This is wisdom for living that has a view to the great realities of God's action within us, and for the salvation of the world. Joseph L. Mangina says, "For ethics to be Christian, the theologian must think first of all in terms of what God has done, and only then proceed to consider what that implies about human beings and their choices. Rather than beginning with the question 'What should I do?', theological ethics begins by asking 'what is real?' "[17] What this already suggests is the blurring of the clean division between theology and ethics. Balthasar, in *Love Alone Is Credible*, states:

> Dogmatic theology is the articulation of the conditions of possibility of Christian action in the light of revelation. ... There is not a single proposition of dogma that Christian action can dispense with, even if the one acting does not have explicit knowledge of it or, though he knows it, does not take notice of it in relation to the existential situation of the encounter. Christian action is above all a secondary reaction to the primary action of God toward man.[18]

Note here the realism of Balthasar's vision of theology and ethics. Neither theology nor ethics is a game invented by thinkers to conjure order in things. Rather, both are descriptive activities tuned to a reality in which the truth about God and skill for living become ever more resonant. This reality is operative even for people who don't realize what sort of world they are living in. However, by learning

---

[17]Joseph L. Mangina, *Karl Barth: Theologian of Christian Witness* (Louisville, KY: Westminster John Knox, 2004), 145.
[18]Hans Urs von Balthasar, *Love Alone Is Credible* (San Francisco, CA: Ignatius, 2004), 111–12.

and reflecting on who God is and what sort of place creation is, our "secondary reaction" is better tuned to "the primary action of God toward man." This is a view of the relation between dogma and ethics that I am seeking for Mennonite pacifism. By contemplating the dogmatic reality of who God is vis-à-vis his enemies, an ethical agenda emerges that situates present human flourishing within the long arc of God's intent to bring us to his home in the Kingdom of Heaven.

Theological ethics cannot understand dogma to be merely a series of static propositions, granitized into timelessness. What the church confesses when it affirms the Apostolic, Nicaean, or Athanasian Creed, or contemplates the Chalcedonian definition of Christology is the glorious mystery of God, acting. Our convictions are like adverbs describing the action of God in his perfect love. God is revealing, moving, creating, sustaining, judging, saving; theological speech is our God-breathed attempt to keep up with God, to match with our words, in an analogous way, the drama of God in himself and in the world. Through prayer, worship, obedience, reflection, and study, our ethical teachings gain traction in the movement of God and thus gain a "dogmatic momentum." Theological ethics, in my view, has a moving, living center in the saving Lord. The church enters into these mysteries and bows before the One seen there *acting*, in love, holiness, and splendor. Participation in the mystery of God does not *become* action, it is action from the start as it moves with a God who moves, some part of which can be described by ethics. In this participation, the church is deified to live in time with divine action. This is the vision of theological ethics and it is the vision that drives this present work on pacifism.

Further, Balthasar says later in the same section, an ethic that seeks to operate apart from dogma runs into "inevitable limitations that arise from living in community." It is confined to "equalizing the interests of the I and the Thou (*suum cuique*)."[19] In other words, an

---

[19]Ibid., 112. One thinks here of Reinhold Niebuhr's argument that in the real world, love must be qualified with justice. "In the field of collective behavior the force of egoistic passion is so strong that the only harmonies possible are those which manage to neutralize this force through balances of power, through mutual defenses against its inordinate expression, and through techniques for harnessing its energy to social ends. All these possibilities represent something less than the ideal of love." *An Interpretation of Christian Ethics* (Philadelphia, PA: Westminster John Knox, 2013), 139–66. Ibid., 140.

ethic confined to only this-worldly concerns struggles to rise beyond a calculation of balancing interests. Theological ethics offers an account of why our choices matter ultimately, even eternally, beyond the balance of reciprocities in front of us. An ethic discerned within the God-revealed order of nature and grace can account for our common perception that mere reciprocity does not do justice to the vigor with which we hold forth on our moral beliefs. Pacifism, of all ethical positions, has great difficulty justifying itself, ultimately, in a context where the eternal has been foreclosed and only reciprocity and the balancing of interests remains. Though secularity has made huge strides in some areas of nonviolence, a purely this-worldly absolute refusal of violence is not only inadvisable but also almost impossible. To the extent that the Mennonite pacifist ethic is not a theological ethic, it will fail to provide a coherent wisdom for how to live in this world.

Since a theological ethic is cadenced by the divine work in the world, it will face huge dilemmas and ambiguities as it seeks to find a home in this world. To have an ethic theologically tuned to the work of God is to acknowledge that it is God's divine freedom that will make all things well, not our own strategies. There is a humble place for the Christian to act, but it is God who will finally assemble the puzzle pieces in a coherent way. This saves ethics from becoming Pelagian, desperately seeking to achieve by heroic effort what God has reserved for himself to accomplish. It also saves ethics from becoming utilitarian, trying to determine present action by peering into a dimly lit future and guessing at eventual outcomes. Theological ethics is constrained to that knowledge of the future which prophecy reveals, rather than depending on hubristic attempts to know the future through scientific prediction. Ethics becomes discipleship, following the Lord Jesus.

But we must hasten to add that ethics becoming theological is no less rational, as though participating in the mystery of God's action eliminates the need for study, debate, and experiment. Theological rationality is no less rational for being calibrated by divine revelation. It bears witness to the reality that God is moving toward the redemption, flourishing, and renewal of the world, but this calls into service all our best work. It seeks to be not only faithful to the leading of Christ, but also effective and useful in the world as a valid way to live. But this is hard. "For this I toil and struggle with all the energy that he powerfully inspires within me" (Col. 1:29). The old tension within pacifist ethics between faithfulness and effectiveness is resolved finally in the act of God's judgment, but as a vision we can claim that to be faithful is to participate in such effectiveness as God now permits the world in his infinite love.

Dogmatic ethics, of Balthasar's description, is an ethic that seeks to be conformed not only to doing the best thing in quandary cases, but also doing good as an act of worship, deep gratitude, and joyful reception of God's actions. It seeks to know not only the basic requirement to qualify as a good person but aims at "placing oneself entirely at the disposal of divine love."[20] A dogmatic ethicist begins ethical inquiry not with a moralistic calculation but with the wonder that such momentum should have been granted her at all. This does not leave behind laws, rules, norms, or virtues, which are directed to the larger horizon of participation in what God is doing.

Thus, in this work I am looking for a dogmatic momentum by which to think about and practice pacifism. Many important questions about pacifism will be left aside through this focus. This book cannot primarily be seen as an apologetic for pacifism. Indirectly, of course, a deeper connection to divine action does illuminate its attractiveness to Christians. But my audience here is those who, though they are searching for alternative solutions in conflict transformation, have failed to appreciate the need for the ethicist to participate personally in the mystery of salvation. I am also not entering into the question of whether pacifism or just-war doctrine is the appropriate Christian approach to war. I am assuming that the scriptures place a severe restriction on redemptive violence and that this restriction, if it leads to pacifism, needs to be linked up with the trajectory of God's action in the world. Likewise, I will not delve into the many important questions about how pacifism can be lived out within difficult dilemmas. I grant that the church will always struggle with how to adequately match the love of God within the structures of the world, but I will not address the nitty-gritty of how that is best done within the realities of late-modern political life. What I am assuming for the purposes of this project is that the scriptures have mandated a drastic refusal and resistance against violence for the Christian. I am trying to show that such a drastic refusal does align with the reality of who God is, as that reality has been unveiled in some of the bedrock convictions of the church across time. In the terms of the Gospel of Matthew,

---

[20]Balthasar, *Love Alone Is Credible*, 108.

if we have truly seen the perfection of the heavenly Father as this is explained to us in the incarnation, nonresistance is an appropriate imitation of that perfection (Mt. 5:48).

So much about the need for a *dogmatic* exploration of pacifism in a secular age.

Thirdly then, why should a Mennonite theological ethic of pacifism look to *Hans Urs von Balthasar* as a dogmatic resource? Balthasar is, after all, a Roman Catholic. There are many well-known disagreements between Mennonites and Catholics. This relationship has festered over time in mutual suspicion on both sides. The *Martyrs Mirror* is filled with stories of sixteenth-century Catholics who persecuted Mennonites. Why now look to one of them for counsel on peace?

However, the time is right for Mennonites and Catholics to join together in developing the church's understanding of peace. In the recent five-year official Roman Catholic and Mennonite dialogue, the theology and practice of peacemaking was identified as a key area offering substantial common ground and a site of great potential for healing the painful history between the two traditions. The title of the dialogue, *Called Together to be Peacemakers*, suggests as much.[21] As Mennonites embrace more direct cultural transformation, as Roman Catholic leadership gives stronger voice to nonviolent witness as a valid counterpart to the just-war tradition, and as both traditions now live as disestablished minority churches within a secular age, the two communions become more in need of the other's strengths.[22] As John A. Radano said of the dialogue, "Among international partners in which the Roman Catholic Church has participated, *Called Together*'s concentration on a theology of peace is the most intense, bringing into constructive

---

[21] *Called Together to Be Peacemakers: Report of the International Dialogue between the Catholic Church and Mennonite World Conference, 1998–2003* (Kitchener, ON: Pandora, 2005). See also *Sharing Peace: Mennonites and Catholics in Conversation* (Collegeville, PA: Liturgical Press, 2013).

[22] The US bishops in their pastoral letter "The Challenge of Peace" gave unprecedented weight to the pacifist tradition within the Roman church. They wrote, "the 'new moment' in which we find ourselves sees the just-war teaching and non-violence as distinct but interdependent methods of evaluating warfare. They diverge on some specific conclusions, but they share a common presumption against the use of force as a means of settling disputes." National Conference of Catholic Bishops, *The Challenge of Peace: God's Promise and Our Response* (St. Paul, MN: St. Paul Editions, 1983), para. 120.

conversation the rich experience of Mennonites ... with the vast literature and practice of Catholic social teaching."[23] This book is walking through the door opened by that dialogue.

But what about Balthasar specifically? Few words of introduction are needed.[24] Hans Urs von Balthasar (1905–1988) was an instrumental thinker in the *nouvelle théologie* movement that influenced the Catholic Church toward the renewal of the second Vatican Council. Key here was the Council's abolishing of every dichotomy between confession of faith and moral theology. Balthasar sought for his church the union of ethics, sanctity, spirituality, and theology that we are seeking for pacifism. His theology has often been referred to as a kneeling theology. His deep engagement with scripture, his interest in the early church as a resource for Christian thought, his vision for the unity of nature and grace as described by Henri de Lubac, and his knowledge of Protestant concerns through a lifelong friendship with Karl Barth, have made him an interesting bridge-builder with the Protestant church more generally.

I have struggled long and hard with the writings of Balthasar and I confess that on more occasions than I like to admit, he got the better of me. I have transitioned in one sitting from weeping at the soaring beauty of the Balthasarian cathedral emerging before my reading eyes, to pulling out my hair in frustration and despair as he dragged me down some arcane, obscure tunnel in philosophical history with nary of whisper of help or support from the author. I have discovered that the best strategy when Balthasar mystifies you is to keep reading. Like Barth in this way, he builds his argument by circling around again and again to the same ground each time with a slightly nuanced perspective for having detoured through forbidding thickets. In this way I have found Balthasar to be a guide that has profoundly enriched my personal relationship with Jesus. In reading him, I feel led by someone who has personally gazed into the fierce furnace of divine love and has come back to share some glimpses, reduced to words.

---

[23]*Sharing Peace*, ix.
[24]Many good introductions to Balthasar's thought have been published. In my opinion, the best two general introductions are Edward T. Oakes, *Pattern of Redemption: The Theology of Hans Urs von Balthasar* (New York: Bloomsbury Academic, 1997) and Mark A. McIntosh, *Christology from Within: Spirituality and the Incarnation in Hans Urs von Balthasar* (Notre Dame, IN: University of Notre Dame Press, 2000).

My engagement with Balthasar has certain limitations that need to be acknowledged. I am not claiming to uncover never-before-seen doctrinal emphases in Balthasar's work. The theology from which I am drawing is, for the most part, from the uncontroversial aspects of his thought.[25] This should not be seen as a "dialogue" between Balthasar and Mennonite theology. Mostly this will be a one-way appropriation of Balthasarian themes to Mennonite ethics. Though we need to be aware of where Balthasar is not helpful to our project, I make no attempt to suggest what Balthasar might have to learn from Mennonite theology. I take it as obvious that there are significant differences between Balthasar and North American Mennonites on issues such as the sacraments, Mariology, apostolic succession, and the role of the papacy in the church. But this was a man who wrote courageously and fiercely about the "nonresistance" he saw at the center of the gospel, and thus he needs to be heard by Mennonites who have now largely discarded that term after centuries of usage.

Balthasar brings an approach to ethics that I believe can help tether Christian pacifists in the drama of the gospel without a tactical retreat from the world. In a short synopsis of his theological pilgrimage, he remembered:

> It was clear to us from the beginning that the bastions of anxiety that the Church had contrived to protect herself from the world would have to be demolished; the Church had to be freed to become herself and open to the whole and undivided world for its mission. For the meaning of Christ's coming is to save the *world* and to open for the whole of it the way to the Father; the Church is only a means, a radiance that through preaching, example and discipleship spreads out from the God-man into every sphere.[26]

But this mission could not be accomplished except by retrieving once again a transforming vision of the acts of God. Here he stands in the train of thought developed by Karl Barth in his reaction

---

[25]So, for example, I deal directly with Christ's utter yieldedness unto deprivation and death before the Father, but I do not engage at length with Balthasar's vision of Christ's descent into hell.

[26]Hans Urs von Balthasar, *My Work: In Retrospect* (San Francisco, CA: Communio, 1993), 48.

to liberal Protestant complicity in empire and unholy culture. Ethics in modernity, according to both of these theologians, has a propensity to be "bourgeois," that is, self-authenticating, perduring without reference to God, and thus largely complicit in whatever idolatry happened to be in vogue. Too often, "ethics" names the attempt to understand the good according to "common sense" or purely "natural" norms, apart from revelation and grace. Barth's dogmatics was a mighty attempt to reject this form of ethics and to recover a way of being human rooted in God's determination to be human for and with us in Christ. This is not so much the priority of theology over ethics, but the priority of God's action and word in establishing the conditions for human action.

Balthasar was in agreement with this retrieval and, if anything, pushed this further. One concern that Balthasar had with Barth was that while Barth sought to distribute ethics throughout the dogmatic *loci,* the church, in Barth's theology, failed to retain its deep union with Christ as his body, the prolongation of the incarnation.[27] The church's sanctity remained too orphaned from the action of God in Christ. As we saw in the above quote from *My Work,* in Balthasar's view, the church was the prolongation of the incarnation, without collapsing Jesus of Nazareth into the church.[28] This disagreement is symptomatic of a larger difference between the two thinkers, and it suggests why we are looking to Balthasar for a grounding of pacifist ethics in the church's dogma. Balthasar's Christocentric view of the *analogia entis,* learned from Erich Pryzwara, was that, through the divine reconciling descent, nature could be taken up and transformed by Christ without departing from its natural qualities and ends. The qualitative difference between God and the world was figured by the union and difference of the Chalcedonian definition. No sharp dichotomy could be posited between nature and grace for those who recognized the beauty of the incarnation. What this led to was a greater expectation that the daily visible, human life of the church could be offered as an acceptable offering

---

[27]This is D. Stephen Long's argument in *Saving Karl Barth: Hans Urs von Balthasar's Preoccupation* (Minneapolis, MN: Fortress, 2014), 212–4.

[28]As noted in ibid., 219. William Cavanaugh writes that Balthasar describes the church as the incarnation's prolongation without falling into four common errors: it does not ignore the church's sins, it does not equate Christ's unique hypostatic union with the church, it does not identify the church's infallibility with its institution and fallibility with its people, and it does not conclude with a triumphalist ecclesiology.

of love to God, and that this offering was in some sense participatory in salvation. The church in all its humanness was a key sacrament through which the world is given to God. While Barth moved in Balthasar's direction on this over his life, he maintained that the church as the prolongation of the incarnation was a "blasphemy."[29]

My constructive proposal here offers three "moments" in the incarnational drama of salvation as emphasized by Balthasar: incarnation, provocation, and convocation. This is the descent of God into human conditions (Chapter 3) and the revolt that this incarnation engenders in the human and spiritual world (Chapter 4), but then also the convocation or gathering that is elicited by this divine action, all in intimate real-time union with Christ's enemy love (Chapter 5). It is my argument that as the church participates in this drama of divine descent, disturbance, and solidarity, the church inhabits the nonresistance of her Savior. It enters into the action of God as described in our bedrock dogmatic convictions. This is at once dogma, spirituality, and ethics.

Mennonites can also see a kinship in Balthasar in his keen interest in the establishment of "secular institutes" within the church. He founded such a fellowship in the Community of St. John, together with his friend Adrienne von Speyr. These institutes were for Balthasar an interesting experiment in living the counsels of perfection in a secular world. These institutes were to be "invisible" within the world, that is, those who joined these institutes would live and work in the world rather than in a typical monastic community. For Balthasar, this was an important mediating position between the more traditional monastic devotion and the life of the laity, and it was an essential witness within a secular age.[30]

---

[29]Karl Barth, *Church Dogmatics: The Doctrine of Reconciliation*, vol. IV/3.2 (New York: T&T Clark International, 2004), 729. Barth was concerned that any suggestion that the church mediated Christ would imply that Christ was absent unless the church, in its mastery over him, made him present. Cf. Long, *Saving Karl Barth*, 215–16. For Balthasar's most extended interaction with Barth's metaphysics, see *The Theology of Karl Barth*, trans. Edward T. Oakes, 3rd revised edition (San Francisco, CA: Ignatius, 1992).

[30]See "Life on the Edge: The Secular Institutes" in Hans Urs von Balthasar, *The von Balthasar Reader*, ed. Medard Kehl and Werner Loeser, trans. Robert J. Daly, and Fred Lawrence (New York: Crossroad, 1982), 300–304. Emilio Tresalti says, "The precise task of the secular Institutes is to effect the synthesis of worldliness and consecration, so that the resulting consecrated worldliness might itself become a consecrating force." http://www.theway.org.uk/Back/s033Tresalti.pdf

This was an important fruit of Balthasar's reflections on the incarnation of the gospel in the world. There was a timeliness grounded in providence for these institutes to appear in the twentieth century when secularity had destroyed the comfortable enmeshment of church and state. In fact, D. Stephen Long shows that this emphasis on the secular institutes was for Balthasar the fruit of the church freshly freed from the shackles of Constantinianism. It represented the new possibility of the church in a secular world to live by the teachings of Jesus without compromise, and with defiant resistance to the world's structures.[31]

Though we will not delve into Balthasar's theology of the secular institutes in this study, his interest alerts us, it seems to me, to a point of contact with the Mennonite tradition. Anabaptists too sought to translate the monastic counsels of perfection into the difficulties of lay, worldly life and have struggled with the tensions involved.[32] Mennonite theology has sought ways for the rigorous spirituality and discipleship of Christ taught in the Sermon on the Mount to become a reality in the streets, homes, and workplaces of the world. Baptism, the Lord's Supper, and church discipline have been important in the Mennonite tradition as the church's Christ-given ways of sponsoring the believer's "pledge" to live a holy life of peace.

Balthasar was keenly aware of the travails with which the Kingdom of God enters the world. He was both intent that Christ's teachings should be the un-surrendered ethic of the Christian, and also aware of the ambiguity and suffering that such a life entailed. His words of counsel to the institutes ring true for Mennonite church life as well:

> When hiking along the sharp ridge between the kingdom of God and the kingdom of this world, it is not just individual persons but whole institutes that can be affected by dizziness and be in danger of falling into the gulf either of one-sided spirituality or of excessive secularity. They exist and remain alive only in a daily "watching and praying," a continual discernment of spirits. Whoever is looking for a secure barn has to look elsewhere.[33]

---

[31]Long, *Saving Karl Barth*, 202–3, 213.

[32]In Roman Catholic thinking, the counsels of perfection, or the evangelical counsels, are counsels of Christ applicable for those who wish to attain perfection but are not mandated for all. These include a commitment to poverty, chastity, and obedience.

[33]Balthasar, *The von Balthasar Reader*, 303.

The Mennonite church has been no secure barn. Any criticism that this book offers must acknowledge that what these churches have sought to do, in regards to peace and nonviolence in the world, is a mighty and dizzying attempt to "hike along the sharp ridge between the kingdom of God and the kingdom of this world." The scrapes and bruises produced by such a venture are only a testimony to the height of the attempted expedition. Christ and the world are a hard union.

For Balthasar, these communities of "paradox" (in the world but not of the world) could be lived "because the whole God has involved himself in Christ for the entire world, and because the place where he does this ever anew, is the church of Christ, the 'sacrament of the world.'"[34] Because of the incarnation, both the first time in the historical ministry of Jesus, and the second time in the historical presence of the church, the Kingdom of God can verily be lived within the world—though always with suffering and weakness. Though one cannot make a straightforward translation of the secular institutes to the Mennonite believers church, there are strong continuities in the intent and the challenges, and especially in the dogmatic undercarriage, which both such outposts of the gospel in the world must assume.

But can Balthasar be called a *pacifist* and would he be interested in being used as a resource for such an ethic? This is a delicate question. My proposal does not claim that he was a pacifist, only that his theology of the incarnation can fruitfully provide a dogmatic momentum for the loving refusal of violence in the name of Christ. But it is helpful to have some sense of what he would have thought of our project. Balthasar's theology points incessantly to Christ's nonresistance and the church's union with it, and yet is very cautious about prescribing the gospel for the establishment of this-worldly political and economic structures. Thus, Balthasar frequently needs to add after an exposition of Christ's role in the world, "but this does not necessarily mean pacifism."[35] He associates "pacifism" with

---

[34]Ibid., 304.
[35]Hans Urs von Balthasar, *Theo-Drama: The Action*, vol. 4, trans. Graham Harrison (San Francisco, CA: Ignatius, 1994), 484; Hans Urs von Balthasar, *Engagement with God: The Drama of Christian Discipleship*, trans. R. John Halliburton (San Francisco, CA: Ignatius, 2008), 86; Hans Urs von Balthasar, *A Theological Anthropology* (New York: Sheed and Ward, 1967), 198; "The 'Beatitudes' and Human Rights" in Hans Urs von Balthasar, *Explorations in Theology*, vol. 5, *Man Is Created*, trans. Adrian Walker (San Francisco, CA: Ignatius, 1989), 456.

what he saw as the errors of Catholic liberation theologians who were too optimistic about the immediate translation of the Kingdom of God into earthly progress. He was nervous about the cross being used as "a 'tactical' instrument," or a "technique for the attainment of political goals."[36] Balthasar had an Augustinian instinct for the difficulty with which the gospel finds a home in the world.[37] His dismal view of the hegemonic pretensions of secularity assured him that any too-easy translation into earthly kingdoms would compromise a gospel that had only promised tears and sorrow to its disciples. Balthasar saw clearly that the old Constantinian union of state power and church sanctity was a mistake,[38] but he also saw a close relation between the new "liberation" progressivism and the old Constantinianism. Both underestimated the inherent and abiding opposition between the gospel and the world.

The atonement of Christ, for Balthasar, was accomplished through the utter nonresistance of Christ's love, and this atonement is carried forward by the church immersed in that same font. As we will see, atonement for Balthasar is a relentlessly political incursion by Christ into world affairs, an invasion that goads worldly power into a desperate revolt.[39] One would be hard-pressed to discover

---

[36]Balthasar, *Theo-Drama*, 1994, 4:484. This quote occurs in a section called "Theodramatic Dimensions of Liberation," which is his most direct engagement with the pacifism of Gandhi used in various forms of liberation theology.

[37]Balthasar, *A Theological Anthropology*, 215, describes in Augustinian terms the wretchedness of the life of the church in its earthly sojourn.

Is the cross an energy factor for the evolution of the world? The cross of Christ means to have the will of complete impotence, to the fear of the Mount of Olives, to the most extreme shame and bitterness, to being betrayed, denied, abandoned, to a death as bankruptcy. The cross signifies relinquishing all hope which one has experienced.

[38]For this argument see the good work of Stephen Waldron, "Hans Urs von Balthasar's Theological Critique of Nationalism," *Political Theology* 15, no. 5 (September 2014): 406–20.

[39]

In the Book of Revelation there is only one way to combat the trinity of hell, which is the final shape of evil: believers must bear witness in their lives and in their blood, thus fully incarnating their faith as they pit it against utter, satanic, dis-incarnation. ... This eschatological opposition between the apparent omnipotence of evil and the apparent powerlessness of believers cannot be dismissed as mere vision. It is genuine prophecy. (Balthasar, *Theo-Drama*, 1994, 4:452).

any sort of just-war doctrine in Balthasar that could offer wisdom
for how violence could itself be used in a chastened, Christ-like way.
His relentlessly rigorous understanding of Christian discipleship
as union with Christ's surrender to the Father, yielding to death,
does not lend itself easily to sanctifying these kinds of prudential
processes. Further, his strong critique of the titanism of the modern
state and its promethean arrogance, not least in its massing of
arms, offers little hope of a Christian vocation in modern military
exercises.[40] The military industrial complex, as it is sometimes
called, is positioned in demonic resistance to the mystery of the
powerlessness of Christ, according to Balthasar. Even if Balthasar
grants that monarchs can be saints, he doubts that the destructive
capacity of modern warfare can ever be accepted by a Christian.[41]

But does Balthasar have an answer for how a Christian ruler
can dispense with the sword? No. But while Balthasar disliked the
ideological stance of pacifism, he had much positive to say about
saintly nonresistance and was deeply hopeful about the fruit such
sanctity could bring to the world. This brings us to his lifelong
admiration for the German poet and novelist, Reinhold Schneider,
about whom he wrote in *The Tragedy of Grace*. Schneider was a
gospel pacifist and it was this aspect of his thought that fascinated
Balthasar. Schneider looked deeply into the question of power: "the
omnipresent drama of the encounter between two missions that are
equally original and yet stand in deadly mutual conflict: the mission
of the one who is entrusted with the task of administering the
earthly realm and the mission of the saint as the real symbol of the
kingdom of God that descends into the world."[42] This was a deadly
conflict for Schneider, but it was one that Christians nevertheless
needed to enter and suffer. It was incumbent upon Christians to
seek what power and authority the cross inherently had vis-à-vis the
world, and use it, to the extent that it was possible, for the witness to
God's original plan of creation. What made Schneider such a stark
figure for Balthasar was Schneider's commitment to maintaining
the unity in difference of the saint within a total immersion into
worldly affairs. Utterly fixed on the cross and transformed by a

---

[40]See "The Battle of the Logos" in ibid., 4:441.
[41]Balthasar, "The 'Beatitudes' and Human Rights," 456–7. Hans Urs von Balthasar,
Tragedy under Grace: Reinhold Schneider on the Experience of the West (Washington,
DC: Ignatius, 1997), 129.
[42]Balthasar, *Tragedy under Grace*, 11.

personal union with Christ to reject violence, this faith nevertheless lived in the world and suffered the travails of the "refraction" that necessarily occurred when the Kingdom of God sought to take up space in worldly reality.[43] Thus, Schneider's personal suffering of the clash between worldly power and the nonresistance of the saint had given the church a "guiding image, an image to be retained at all costs" for the secular institutes.[44] "Their fundamental aim is to combine the radicalism of the gospel with a total, active, involvement in secular work, enduring in their own selves the conflict described here."[45] *Tragedy under Grace* was dedicated to the furtherance of the secular institutes, which we have already described, suggesting that Balthasar thought they should take up Schneider's pacifism in the world. What Balthasar (following Schneider) seems to have in mind for these institutes were people molded by the love and nonresistance of Christ, quietly involved in the world, seeking to plant the seeds of a new creation. These people would be devoted to Christ and constrained by the Spirit to go and experience the tensions and conflicts that the clash between Christ and the world occasioned. Without using violence, but without withdrawing, these institutes were to be pioneers (and martyrs) in the redemption of worldly power by the church.

Secularity offered a unique opportunity for a more faithful unity in difference that gave space to nonresistance in a way the earlier more infused church–state relations had not. Balthasar believed that in the providential working of God, this kind of nonresistant involvement in the world could create mighty change. Over time the conscience of the world might develop to where a complete rejection of violence became practicable. There was today within secularity a growing "ripeness" for the claim of nonviolence. This understanding of secularity is a significant one for our thesis:

> The New Covenant is a spirit, a yeast in history ... its inner power works through all ages, and its ultimate logic will have come into force only on the Last Day. Insights that will one day break out of the womb and emerge clearly as demands develop in a mysterious maturing process, and one cannot say how much

---

[43]Ibid., 127.
[44]Ibid., 11.
[45]Ibid.

of this process is due to the natural development of humanity and how much to the gospel seed that sprouts in individuals and peoples. A few centuries ago, humanity was ripe for the insight that slavery is incompatible with human rights. Today we see the dawning of the day when responsible humanity will be ripe for the insight that bloody war contradicts its present adult state and is no longer an appropriate means to resolve questions and conflicts of the humanity that has become indivisible and takes charge of its own self; this is the day when the best men begin to be ashamed of war.[46]

And so, I might predict that in Mennonite terms, Balthasar would find the traditional Schleitheim two-kingdom theology, which withdrew the church from the world to be too immune to the travails of the world, especially in a modern secular milieu where there is a heightened consciousness about the evil of war. On the other hand, I suspect he would find current Mennonite optimism about peacemaking and social justice to be in a vulnerable place. He might worry that it could forget just how exalted the nonresistance of Jesus really was and how much of a challenge such utter self-abnegation for God's sake is to an age that takes this-worldly human flourishing as its only north star. Balthasar's message might be, open yourself daily to the Christic heart of the world, and allow yourself to be irradiated by this furnace of love at the center of the world, and then live the difficult but ultimately beautiful life that this enables. In some contexts this will be a hidden life; in others, it may be more open and welcomed.

So, I aim to show that Balthasar offers a way of uniting theology, sanctity, and spirituality that are important for Mennonites to understand and appropriate. Though he is one of the twentieth century's leading theologians, comparable in Roman Catholicism with the role Karl Barth played in Protestant theology, I have not located any attempt by Mennonite scholars to engage with him as an interlocutor.[47] I offer this work as a beginning to such an exchange.

---

[46]Ibid., 128–9.

[47]However, Harry Huebner has written a good introduction to his life and thought in *An Introduction to Christian Ethics: History, Movements, People* (Waco, TX: Baylor University Press, 2012), 277–92.

To conclude this introduction, I would like to point out three books that formed a foundation for my thought on how Balthasar's theology yields its ethical fruit. Christopher Steck's book, *The Ethical Thought of Hans Urs von Balthasar*, is a summary of Balthasar's contribution to ethics that is not likely to be surpassed, and I have benefited greatly from it in developing my root understanding of how ethics emerges in Balthasar's theology. Steck shows that the ethical in Balthasar emerges from contemplation. "Von Balthasar understands the central act of the Christian, the response of faith, not primarily in terms of an intellectual or fiduciary response, but rather as the creature's doxological response to the glory of God in Jesus Christ."[48] It is not that the glory of God *should* be acknowledged by the creature, but that the very openness and reception of the person to the glory is already in itself an ethical posture. Glory (and its earthly analog, beauty) establishes the conditions of its own perception in the one who is receptive to it.[49] Further, Steck argues that glory when it appears in the world, incites a drama, a *theo*-drama, that includes a real, earthly response. Steck shows beautifully how, for Balthasar, the theo-drama incited by the appearance of God's Christic glory in the world does not trample or overwhelm the creature, but transforms the creature to be what it was created to be. In this sense, glory has a decidedly Catholic framing in Balthasar: it includes the work of grace without leaving behind nature. But even further, Steck is helpful in his description of how ethics takes on a *bivalent* posture for the Christian, including both a vertical yielding to God and a horizontal yielding to the neighbor.[50] This was instrumental in helping me understand the Balthasarian bidirectional nonresistance I describe in Chapter 3.

A second source that has proved foundational is Melanie Susan Barrett's excellent work on Balthasar's ethics as it pertains to virtue. Barrett wants to complement the account of Steck (which argues for a modified divine command ethic in Balthasar) by offering a virtue ethic reading of Balthasar. Because ethics for Balthasar is so keyed to the contemplation of Christ as divine beauty, so keyed to the aesthetic active passivity, and so formed by the contemplation of the beauty of love, it is much more concerned with how we become

---

[48]Christopher Steck, *The Ethical Thought of Hans Urs von Balthasar* (New York: Crossroad, 2001), 150.

[49]See especially chapter 1, "Aesthetics and Human Response." Ibid., 7–33.

[50]See especially chapter 5, "Contemplation and Action." Ibid., 123–49.

certain kinds of people than it is with following commands or rules. What she demonstrates is the prevalence of love in Balthasar's theology and the ethical richness that this reality brings.[51] Love is expressed in the world in the beauty of Christ's gift of salvation on the cross. This is an educative process in which the Christian, through the encounter with this beauty, cultivates the virtues over time. What Barrett emphasizes is the strong place of desire, emotion, and ecstasy in the ethical life as seen by Balthasar. We are shaped by that beauty which presents itself before us, and which stirs us to reach for it.[52]

A third resource that has been formative is D. Stephen Long's book *Saving Barth: Hans Urs von Balthasar's Pre-occupation*. This book demonstrates the intense and often combative friendship between these two thinkers, and it shows how Balthasar welcomed so much of Barth's theological ethics while recasting it within the Catholic "and" as we have already noted. Balthasar welcomed the biblical and Christological centering that Barth's theology brought to ethics, but saw that Barth did not fully come to grips with the incarnation in the way created, human life, ordered according to the gospel, could be offered to God. Long was also helpful in helping me see the importance that nonresistance and pacifism played in Balthasar's thinking. He shows clearly how large metaphysical questions of unity in difference fund Balthasar's concern to bring the message of the gospel in all its contrariness (its ethics!) to bear on the modern world without compromising its glory. He is one of the few commentators on Balthasar who take seriously his interest in Reinhold Schneider.

So, this then is our project: to consider the travails with which Mennonite theology has struggled to bring about a genuinely world-involved, but no less Christ-centered pacifism, and then to see three moments in the Balthasarian theo-drama that form a trajectory of divine glory into the world. As believers are drawn into this divine movement, they become attuned to living peacefully, lovingly, and courageously in a world that may welcome but more likely resist their love.

[51]Cf. Melanie Susan Barrett, *Love's Beauty at the Heart of the Christian Moral Life: The Ethics of Catholic Theologian Hans Urs von Balthasar* (Lewiston, NY: Edwin Mellen, 2009), 205.
[52]Ibid., 31.

1

Mennonite Pacifism as Union with the Living Christ

There is an abiding tension within Mennonite life between pacifism as an act of participation with Christ yielding a church of disciples, and pacifism as a form of civility yielding industrious, productive citizens of modern life. The first is ecclesial, scriptural, baptismal, and spiritual. The second is instrumental, rational, and egalitarian. Both are anti-violence. In this chapter I offer glimpses of the former—pacifism in Mennonite life as the act of union with Jesus. When we have sufficiently explored this tension from both sides, we will enter the theological vision of Balthasar as a resource for living with this tension.

We cannot offer anything close to a full account of the waxing and waning of pacifist thought and practice in Mennonite history. It has become a truism to say that North American Mennonites face an identity crisis in terms of their peace position. This has been alarming to church leaders. Recently, Mennonite churches who have weakened their commitment to gospel pacifism associate it either with a legalistic past, or a liberal social-gospel mindset.[1] The ethic has struggled under these two major kinds of accusations: its irresponsibility and luxurious withdrawal from the grind of history on the one hand, and its association with liberal Protestant or

---

[1] According to the recent Global Anabaptist Profile conducted by the Mennonite World Conference, 55 percent of North American Mennonites surveyed would reject any form of military involvement. This is compared to a global rejection percentage of 62 percent. John D. Roth, Conrad Kanagy, and Elizabeth Miller, *Global Anabaptist Profile: Belief and Practice in 24 Mennonite World Conference Churches* (Goshen, Egypt: Institute for the Study of Global Anabaptism, 2017), 23–4.

secularist instincts on the other. In Willard Swartley and Cornelius Dyck's bibliography of Mennonite writings on war and peace between 1930 and 1980, 10,000 books, essays, and pamphlets are listed.[2] What this avalanche of material points to, I suggest, is not that pacifism is secure and established within Mennonite life, but that it is questioned, shifting, and in need of much assistance.[3]

Early Anabaptist Views on Christ and Nonresistance

What was the original sixteenth-century vision of the Anabaptist churches around violence and love? Recent historical work has shown that nonresistance was not the original default conviction of all Anabaptists but rather the conviction arrived at after debate, catastrophe, and the elimination by persecution of those who held certain positions.[4] Anabaptism was first a spiritual awakening of the laity within Swiss and South German regions that united around a rejection of priestly mediation of the sacraments, the renewal of a personal devotion by the laity, and the rejection of infant baptism.[5] The twin poles of anticlericalism and the direct engagement with scriptures by obedient disciples formed its first and uniting impulse. In the first years after the initial believer's baptism in Zurich in January of 1525, it was not always easy to distinguish between Anabaptist and peasant unions more generally. After the Peasant Revolt of 1525 was viciously stamped out, many disaffected peasants found the new emerging Anabaptist conventicles in the

---

[2]Willard M. Swartley and Cornelius J. Dyck, eds., *Annotated Bibliography of Mennonite Writings on War and Peace, 1930–1980* (Scottdale, PA: Herald, 1987).

[3]Instability is not necessarily a sign of trouble. Chris K. Huebner has argued in *A Precarious Peace* that there always needs to be a certain "crisis of certainty" about an ethic like Mennonite peace theology. What most needs to be feared is Mennonite attempts to secure and lash it down as a denominational possession. Chris K. Huebner, *A Precarious Peace: Yoderian Explorations on Theology, Knowledge, and Identity* (Scottdale, PA: Herald, 2006).

[4]James M. Stayer, *Anabaptists and the Sword* (Lawrence, KS: Coronado, 1972) has convinced a recent generation of scholarship that pacifism was not one of the uniting convictions of the first generation of Anabaptists.

[5]This a distillation of John D. Rempel's assessment in *The Lord's Supper in Anabaptism: A Study in the Christology of Balthasar Hubmaier, Pilgram Marpeck, and Dirk Philips* (Scottdale, PA: Herald, 1993), 32–9.

Swiss cantons to be the most appropriate continuation of their instincts. The failure of the Peasant Revolt led many to embrace the nonresistance being advocated by leaders such as Conrad Grebel, Felix Mantz, and Michael Sattler.[6]

At the time the Schleitheim Confession was written by the Swiss Brethren led by Michael Sattler in February 1527, the question of "the sword" was not yet settled. However, within ten years the rather stark separatist position taken in the Confession came to represent much of Swiss, South German/Austrian, and Dutch Anabaptism, even though the Confession itself never had the status of an authoritative creed across the movement's groupings.[7]

The Confession can form an entry way to seeing how pacifism was positioned and argued for at this early stage. Specifically, we can observe the way scripture is used to make the argument on the sword in the Confession. Rather than appealing to Jesus's commands against revenge found in the Sermon on the Mount, Sattler refers to the manner of the incarnate Christ in relation to the world around him. Should Christians be involved in using violence to protect the good out of love for neighbor? Sattler answers:

> Christ teaches and commands us to learn from Him, for He is meek and lowly of heart and thus we shall find rest for our souls (Mt. 11:29). Now Christ says to the woman who was taken in adultery, not that she should be stoned according to the law of His Father ... but with mercy and forgiveness and the warning to sin no more, says: "Go, sin no more." Exactly thus should we also proceed, according to the rule of the ban.[8]

---

[6]In September 1524, Conrad Grebel, a future Anabaptist, wrote Thomas Müntzer, a leader in the Peasant Revolt, and said, "The gospel and its adherents are not to be protected by the sword, nor [should] they [protect] themselves, which as we have heard through our brother is what you believe and maintain. True believing Christians are sheep among wolves, sheep for the slaughter." Leland Harder, *The Sources of Swiss Anabaptism: The Grebel Letters and Related Documents* (Scottdale, PA: Herald, 1985), 290.

[7]Howard John Loewen notes that it is only alongside the "Anabaptist Vision" statement of Harold Bender in 1944 that Schleitheim finally comes to an authoritative status within Mennonite life. *One Lord, One Church, One Hope, and One God: Mennonite Confessions of Faith in North America: An Introduction* (Elkhart: Institute of Mennonite Studies, 1985), 28.

[8]John Howard Yoder, ed., *The Legacy of Michael Sattler* (Scottdale, PA: Herald, 1973), 39–40.

Should Christians be magistrates? "Christ did not wish to decide or pass judgement between brother and brother concerning inheritance, but refused to do so (Lk. 12:13). So should we also do."[9] Should Christians take up political office?

> Christ was to be made King, but He fled and did not discern [therein] the ordinance of His Father. Thus we should also do as He did and follow after Him. ... Peter also says: "Christ has suffered (not ruled) and has left us an example, that you should follow after in his steps" (1 Pet. 2:21).[10]

In each of these appeals to scripture, it is observing Christ's manner of life and observing his manner of submitting to the Father that determine the believer's posture. Sattler assumes a union between the believer and Christ, which determines the believer's place in a world of evil power and violence. "In sum: as Christ our Head is minded, so also must be minded the members of the body of Christ through Him, so that there be no division in the body, through which it would be destroyed."[11] It is a pacifism rooted in *Nachfolge Christi*, the imitation, participation, and solidarity of the body of Christ with the meek, incarnate Christ. To use an anachronistic expression, nonresistance in the Confession demands a *contemplative* posture vis-à-vis Christ, that is, a posture of attention and imitation through spiritual union to the Lord portrayed in the scripture.

C. Arnold Snyder has argued that Anabaptism in the hands of Sattler, the author of the Confession, is an extension and translation of Benedictine monastic values. The Confession's emphases of the denial of the self, the battle between spirit and flesh, and meek, humble suffering in union with Christ are traced by Snyder back to the Bursfeld Benedictine renewal led by Johannes Trithemius of which Sattler had been a part. Regarding the rejection of the sword, for the Bursfelds, "the point is not simply a renunciation of killing. More fundamental than the command not to take life is the following of Christ which lies at the heart of monasticism."[12] Snyder also states, "Michael Sattler understood the incarnate Christ to have

---

[9] Ibid., 40.
[10] Ibid.
[11] Ibid., 41.
[12] C. Arnold Snyder, "The Monastic Origins of Swiss Anabaptist Sectarianism," *Mennonite Quarterly Review* 57, no. 1 (1983): 17.

been, above all, meek and lowly, the rejected, persecuted, suffering Christ who yielded up his will and, trusting wholly in God, walked the way of earthly trial through the cross on to death."[13] According to Snyder, it was union with this suffering Christ that formed the separatism apparent in the Schleitheim Confession, rather than the failure of the Anabaptists to achieve political ends. "On the issue of the Christian's involvement in political or temporal affairs, Sattler agrees with the Benedictines that a following of Christ precludes any such involvement."[14] In Anabaptism, the way of Christ became the disciplined pattern of the whole church, for every baptized member, set against the kingdom of the world.

This personal identification of the meek Christian with the lowly Christ became the spiritual center of the Anabaptist peace conviction. Pilgram Marpeck, one of Anabaptism's first-generation theologians is instructive here. Though untrained as a theologian, Marpeck wielded the traditional Chalcedonian Christology of the church in some of Anabaptism's most creative and original ways to refute spiritualists such as Caspar Schwenkfeld. He emphasized the incarnational pattern of divinity, God speaking, and acting through the lowly humanity of Christ.[15] This pattern is formative for the church that integrates the inner and the outer in the same way. External actions of the church are a witness that points to the earthly Christ who lived an "unglorified countenance on earth."[16] In "Pilgram Marpeck's *Response* to Caspar Schwenkfeld's *Judgement*" he writes,

> If Schwenkfeld recognized Christ truly, not only by his glorified reigning countenance, but how he lived and worked on earth before his glorification and works today through his unglorified body on earth, he might understand our language better and be

---

[13]Ibid., 12, 17.

[14]Ibid., 17.

[15]Marpeck is sometimes clumsy in how he refers to the divinity of Christ. Often he seems to conflate the divine nature of the Word with the Holy Spirit. Or he talks about "the Father, through the power of the Spirit," acting in Christ, in addition to more traditional language. See Neal Blough, *Christ in Our Midst: Incarnation, Church and Discipleship in the Theology of Pilgram Marpeck* (Kitchener, ON: Pandora, 2007), 147 for a discussion.

[16]Pilgram Marpeck, *Later Writings by Pilgram Marpeck and His Circle*, trans. John D. Rempel, Walter Klaassen, and Werner O. Packull (Kitchener, ON: Pandora, 1999), 84.

able to judge how we speak about Christ. Because Schwenkfeld's eye is always on the degree of transfiguration, as it is pictured above, he doesn't take seriously what the unglorified face of Christ did on earth, together with the internal working of the Father and the simultaneous co-operation of the invisible Word. Even today he works through his unglorified body (which is the church). It is the very temple of God—at work outwardly because God is at work inwardly.[17]

Note the profound union between God's indwelling of human flesh and the indwelling of Christ in his "unglorified body," the church. The Lord's "untransfigured body (understand, his church) ... is his outward work: teaching, baptism, Lord's Supper, admonition (ermanen), ban, discipline, evidence of love and service for the common good, a handclasp, improving and retaining Christ's commands and teachings." This outward work "is brought about in and through the church by the reigning, glorified Christ with his and the Father's Holy Spirit."[18] In another writing against Schwenkfeld, Marpeck talks about the unity of the physical voice of Christ with his "Spirit and life," which taught and performed miracles. "The physical voice of Christ never simply came from Christ without Spirit and life."[19] And as the divinity of Christ did not coercively demand acknowledgment of those who heard his physical voice, so the church must work gently on those coming to believe in Christ.

This union between Christ and the churched believer is salvific; it effects both the justification and sanctification of the believer, which for Marpeck are joined inseparably as they were for most Anabaptists. To be justified is to be given the free gift of the power of the Spirit of Christ for sanctification. It is this incarnational pattern that yields the meek, gentle, forbearing love of the church for each other and for enemies.

This extends further than a general ethic of love. It results in the Spirit-empowered imitation of the manner of Christ in matters of force, precluding the use of arms for the benefit of the churches. The question of the Schmalcadic league of 1530, which the Lutheran churches of Strasbourg and Augsburg participated in against

---

[17]Ibid.
[18]Ibid., 85.
[19]William Klassen and Walter Klaassen, eds., *The Writings of Pilgram Marpeck* (Kitchener, ON: Herald, 1978), 378.

Emperor Charles V, galled Marpeck for decades.[20] Near the end of his life, as the league was days away from defeat, Marpeck wrote a kind of "told-you-so" letter called "The Deep Humility of Christ" to small clusters of Anabaptist churches in Grisons, Appenzell, St. Gall, and Alsace. To point out again how opposed this violent evangelical defense of the faith was to the spirit of Christ, Marpeck described how Christ descended into hell, "and dwelt with the condemned and those imprisoned in perdition, and with those held in death."[21] The descent into hell was not triumphant as some wrongly proclaimed.[22] Rather,

> the Son conquered the sin of many precisely by this descent into the depths, this greatest humility with which he humbled himself before the Father and by which the Father afflicted and humbled the Son. All the saints of God must learn the depths of Christ, these same depths of humility and damnation, into which the leaven of our sin brought Christ.[23]

To "learn the depths of Christ" in this way is what it would mean for the church to be the physical, defenseless body of Christ.

As Neal Blough points out concerning the soteriology implicit in this use of the *descensus ad infernos*, Marpeck understands the salvation wrought by Christ in his death historically, narratively, and concretely. *Both* by the events carried out in the death, descent, resurrection, and ascension of Christ, and by the manner of humility and patience with which Christ embarked on this

---

[20]His most famous writing on pacifism, "The Uncovering of the Babylonian Whore," was written early in 1532 in reaction to Strasbourg's decision to enter the league. Neal Blough, "The Uncovering of the Babylonian Whore: Confessionalization and Politics Seen from the Underside," *Mennonite Quarterly Review* 75, no. 1 (2001): 39. Walter Klaassen calls this "the most penetrating treatment of the subject of Christ and the sword that the sixteenth-century Anabaptists produced." Walter Klaassen, "Investigation into the Authorship and the Historical Background of the Anabaptist Tract Aufdeckung Der Babylonischen Hurn," *Mennonite Quarterly Review* 61, no. 3 (1987): 261.

[21]Klassen and Klaassen, *The Writings of Pilgram Marpeck*, 432. In a gloss written in the margins of this letter, Marpeck writes, "that is the way it was in the Schmalcald War and in Switzerland with Zwingli."

[22]This is an interesting parallel to Balthasar, whose theology of the descent into hell also resisted the triumphant proclamation of the traditional harrowing of hell.

[23]Klassen and Klaassen, *The Writings of Pilgram Marpeck*, 434.

journey, "redemption is indeed accomplished in time and history."[24] Salvation is the divine imprinting of a like pattern and posture in the believer.

One final witness to Anabaptist Christology as it relates to nonresistance comes from Menno Simons. He is instructive because aspects of his Christology could have led him in the direction of a stark separation between a heavenly Christ and the earthly church. Menno is known for his quasi-heretical "heavenly flesh" Christology, which posited that Christ's human flesh did not originate from Mary but was implanted in her from heaven.[25] Several other Anabaptists at the time rejected this for diminishing Christ's embrace of the human condition.[26] And it is certainly the case that more than any other Anabaptist, the pure perfection of Christ, and thus of his church is emphasized throughout Menno's work.[27]

However, whether or not his theology of the incarnation was docetic, Menno's understanding of the relationship between Christ and the saint's daily moral life is one of the closest possible union. The nuptial metaphors used repeatedly throughout Menno's work convey this: a lush, immediate, and transformative encounter between Christ and the church. The church is "the lovely bride of Jesus Christ, flesh of his flesh, and bone of his bone ... which he placed in His chamber, and kissed with the mouth of His eternal peace."[28] It is this mystical participation of the church in Christ

---

[24]Blough, *Christ in Our Midst*, 200. Thus it is obvious that for Marpeck as for other Anabaptists, the necessity of Christ's death could be joined with a *christus victor* understanding of the atonement. It was necessary that by means of his nonviolent surrender to the powers, Christ would take death down into hell.

[25]This heavenly flesh Christology has been well studied by scholars; however, no one has proven that Menno's understanding of Jesus lacked an adequate humanity. In other words, the Christ that was born through this heavenly implantation of flesh was every bit the human.

[26]Peter Riedemann rejects this explicitly in 1543. *Peter Riedemann's Hutterite Confession of Faith*, trans. John J. Friesen (Scottdale, PA: Herald, 1999), 68. Pilgram Marpeck engaged with Caspar Schwenkfeld on this matter.

[27]This, according to some interpreters, resulted in the severe and imbalanced practice of church discipline in the Dutch Mennonite church. See C. Arnold. Snyder, *Anabaptist History and Theology: An Introduction* (Kitchener, ON: Pandora, 1995), 381.

[28]Menno Simons, *The Complete Writings of Menno Simons: c. 1496–1561*, trans. Leonard Verduin (Scottdale, PA: Herald, 1966), 274. See also 59, 94, 148, 191, 221–4, 232, 234, 300. For a discussion of this theme see Beth Kreitzer, "Menno Simons and the Bride of Christ," *Mennonite Quarterly Review* 70, no. 3 (1996): 299–318.

that is the source of the church's holy life.[29] In another passage he describes the "burning love" with which the church is loved by Christ, who "in love taught and preached unto you the eternal kingdom of God; in love performed miracles; in love prayed, suffered tribulation, anxiety ... in love was beaten, mocked ... in love was raised up, has ascended to heaven." This stream of "burning love" elicits, in this same passage, Menno's oft-quoted statement on true evangelical faith, which will not lie dormant but will clothe the naked, feed the hungry, and return good for evil.[30] Menno wields every Scriptural metaphor he can to show that the church's holy life comes through her intimate communion with Christ in heaven. Through the church's in-grafting to Christ, the church takes on Christ's means of fighting his enemies with the sword of his mouth.[31] As co-reigning with Christ, the servants of the Lord bear no sword of iron or steel but the Sword of the Spirit for "eternal welfare and peace."[32] Menno's statements on the peaceful life of the church are thus steeped in a potent experience of a lavish love union between Christ and the church.[33]

This glance at a trio of Anabaptist writers has seen that in its Swiss, South German, and Dutch manifestations, Anabaptism's original vision of nonviolence emerged from a theology of spiritual union with Christ by all believers in the church. Rather than simply relying on a curt recital of Christ's commands not to revenge oneself, Anabaptist pacifism (at least in these three influential expressions) sought a living, daily experience of the living Christ that just was a life attentive and imitative of his manner, through the Spirit. It sought a meek and humble life for all believers within a mystical participation with the Master. It reached at times for the most erotic

[29]"For they are born with Him of one Father, they are the new Eve, the pure, chaste, bride. They are flesh of Christ's flesh and bone of His bone ... They are the children of peace who have beaten their swords into plowshares and their spears into pruning hooks, and know war no more." Simons, *The Complete Writings of Menno Simons*, 94.
[30]Ibid., 306–7.
[31]Ibid., 44.
[32]Ibid., 217, 223.
[33]Speaking against those who use violence in and against the church he writes, "If they were the bride of Christ they would not be hateful, cruel, and bloodthirsty, but meek, gentle, and merciful, minded as is the good and faithful bridegroom, Christ Jesus." Ibid., 232.

of metaphors to glimpse the relation between Christ and the church that yielded the fruit of nonresistance.

This utter union with Christ seemed to demand, either initially or with time, a separation from the mechanisms of the state, though these were still seen to be ordained by God for the suppression of evil. Anabaptists were unable, by and large, to articulate a vision for involvement in society that remained coherent with their core conviction of the believer's union with the meek and peaceful Christ. Even Marpeck, who in fact sought to live such involvement, did not offer an explicit description of how such involvement could be justified and delimited. He saw the dangers and complexities but did not articulate a political theology to guide the discernment needed. All they could assert was the incompatibility of their experience of union with Jesus with the sword. Their extension of this mode of life to the whole congregation put them at odds with sixteenth-century assumptions about how public order was maintained. Both persecution and the inability of Anabaptists to articulate a theology of involvement apart from the Christendom model of their world resulted in their withdrawal.

Martyrs Mirror and the Translation of Anabaptism into Daily Gelassenheit

Europe was not ready for this Anabaptist claim about discipleship and persecution extended in some areas for centuries. But early on, Mennonites and Hutterites began negotiating truces with the powers around them, agreeing that if they were left to live quietly without persecution, they would set up productive, orderly settlements in Holland, Switzerland, Prussia, and later in Russia and America. A second-generation Anabaptism emerged that integrated pacifism within a theology of mundane suffering and a willingness to follow Christ in life. Colonies and villages developed as self-sufficient church-led communities in which worship, piety, and rural family life wove together with a spirituality of nonresistance.[34] Here we

---

[34]Recent scholarship has awakened to this second-generation spirituality as a source for modern devotion. An early essay of significance for this recovery was Ethelbert Stauffer and Robert Friedmann, "The Anabaptist Theology of Martyrdom,"

begin to note how the Mennonite tradition began to feel the pull between union with Christ and good civil behavior. However, though Mennonites' "apologetic" before rulers often pointed to their contributions to civility, one major devotional work sought to translate the older spiritual union into lives that had begun to be shaped more and more by the new civility.

To demonstrate the way second-generation Mennonites translated the nonresistance of the martyrs into more mundane lives, it is helpful to see how the Dutch Mennonite pastor Thieleman J. van Braght positioned the martyr tradition vis-à-vis his readers. These readers had become comfortable seventeenth-century Dutch Mennonites. *Martyrs Mirror* was written during the "Golden Age" of Dutch Mennonite life when Mennonites were becoming heartily involved citizens of the new Dutch Republic and when uncertainty prevailed about the continuity of the original Anabaptist vision. More than any other work, *The Bloody Theater, Or, Martyrs Mirror of the Defenceless Christians* published in 1660, has tempered and sustained a particular Mennonite spirituality as a nonresistant church.[35] This work was not written for strict separatists. His work recast the spirituality of first-generation Anabaptism as an enduring piety for subsequent Mennonites much more at home in their society. Here I want to focus on the devotional commentary that van Braght provided in the introductory material to mediate the martyr stories.

Mennonite Quarterly Review 19, no. 3 (1945): 179–214, which showed how hymnody, devotional writings and especially the *Martyrs Mirror* were instrumental in transporting a martyr spirituality into a non-persecuted context. Robert Friedmann (1891–1970) was a scholar who worked to recover spirituality as a focus for research in Anabaptist studies. More recently, see Walter Klaassen, "'Gelassenheit' and Creation," *Conrad Grebel Review* 9, no. 1 (1991): 23–5.

[35]Thieleman J. van Braght, *The Bloody Theater or Martyrs Mirror of the Defenceless Christians: Who Baptized Only upon Confession of Faith, and Who Suffered and Died for the Testimony of Jesus, Their Saviour, from the Time of Christ to the Year A.D. 1600*, trans. Joseph F. Sohm (Scottdale, PA: Mennonite Publishing House, 1951). The *Ausbund*, a hymnal, which has been used among Mennonites and Amish since the sixteenth century, should also be noted here. It contains numerous hymns that recite the torment and death of the martyrs. However, the *Ausbund* has not had the breadth of exposure across the Mennonite community that the *Mirror* has. The *Martyrs Mirror* has been through twenty English editions alone, still sells several thousand copies a year, and has been used broadly in both the Russian and Swiss traditions. Cf. *Ausbund* (Lancaster, 1815), http://hdl.handle.net/2027/hvd.ah69g6.

At the time of writing, van Braght was a pastor in his thirties who was often sick. He died shortly after completing the book. In the "Author's Invocation," he describes how, during the course of this work, this fellowship with the martyrs strengthened him: "snares of death had compassed me, keeping me bound nearly six months during last fall, winter, and spring, so that I often thought I could not survive. ... Nevertheless Thy power strengthened me ... for the zeal and love of Thy saints had taken complete possession of me."[36] This "offering ... was accompanied with many tears caused partly by my distress." In his own experience of pain, van Braght felt his own life to be mingled with that of the martyrs:

> Yet that which more than all else caused my tears to flow was the remembrance of the suffering and death of Thy martyrs. ... Ah! how often did I wish to have been a partaker with them; my soul went with them, so to speak, into prison. ... It seemed to me as though I accompanied them to the place of execution, scaffold or stake, saying to them in their extremity, Fight valiantly dear brethren and sisters; the crown of life awaits you. I almost fancied that I had died with them; so inseparably was my love bound up with them; for Thy holy names sake.[37]

What van Braght describes here seems to be a drama of mystical unity between the reading Christian, the martyrs, and Christ. Van Braght describes the writing of this book (and thus also its reading) as a tortuous and ascetic spiritual pilgrimage. At the half-way point of the book, arriving in the story at the end of the fifteenth century, he pauses and says,

> We long to take our leave from this century, since we cannot longer behold this misery. However, we have only reached the summit of the mountain of martyrdom. In our ascent we have met scarcely anything but skulls, thigh-bones and charred skeletons. In our descent deep pits ... threaten us. ... But the merciful Lord, who has led us by the hand, and thus far aided us, will lead and help us still further ... for when the bands of death were around

---

[36]Ibid., 5.
[37]Ibid.

me, by reason of a half year's severe sickness, which attacked me in the midst of this work, His gracious hand restored me.[38]

Besides suggesting the early influences of pietism on the Dutch Mennonites, these descriptions suggest that for van Braght the function of the martyr story is to mediate an experience of suffering and a surrender to God in the reader. As the reader prayerfully lingers over these accounts, she will be lifted up into the realm of Christ and there be found faithful to him. The holiness of the martyr becomes the reader's sanctity through reading: "Read it again and again, and with the same attention and emotion with which we have written and re-written it."[39] This communion leading to sanctity belongs not to the "blind worldly-minded" but to the "heavenly-minded who, as spiritual eagles, contemplate with the eyes of the soul the mysteries of God ... and find their delight in His saints and well-beloved who sacrificed their lives for His holy truth."[40]

What facilitates this sanctifying encounter with the martyrs is the framework of apostolic succession within the book. The entire arrangement of the book is structured to immerse the reader in a personal succession of saints who have confessed their faith in bodily witness—blood. After an account of Scriptural figures who faced martyrdom—"Yea the whole volume of holy Scriptures seems to be nothing else than a book of martyrs, replete with numerous, according to the flesh, sorrowful, but according to the spirit, happy, examples of the holy and steadfast martyrs"[41]—van Braght describes the crucifixion of Christ: "To Jesus Christ, the Son of God, we have accorded the first place among the martyrs of the new covenant; not in the order of time ... but on account of worthiness of the person, because He is the head of all the holy martyrs, through whom they all must be saved."[42] He then works meticulously forward through each century in Christian history devoting a section to the practice

---

[38] Ibid., 352.

[39] Ibid., 8.

[40] Ibid., 7. This contemplating with the eyes received new meaning in the second edition of the *Mirror*, printed after van Braght's death, which included 104 copper engravings by Jan Luyken depicting martyr events. See Sarah Covington, "Jan Luyken, the Martyrs Mirror, and the Iconography of Suffering," *Mennonite Quarterly Review* 85, no. 3 (2011): 441–76.

[41] Van Braght, *The Bloody Theater,* 12.

[42] Ibid., 67.

of baptism and nonresistance, which that century evinced, and a section to the martyrs of that century. This creates an unbroken chain from Abel to Antwerp of "Anabaptist"[43] succession.[44]

This succession is both personal and doctrinal, consisting of a train of right teachers and also right teaching. The doctrinal succession of the church is "a sign and evidence" of the personal, so that the personal cannot exist without the doctrinal. Where there is an obvious succession of doctrine, the succession of the personal "need not be looked for so carefully. But where both are found in truth and verity, it is not to be doubted that there is also the true and genuine church of God, in which God will dwell."[45]

The succession, both of the personal and the doctrinal, is carried forward through each century by the mediation of believer's baptism, suggesting that through the readers' baptisms they too will be inducted into this procession.[46] Baptized into this ecclesial solidarity across time, the reader will be imprinted with the martyr's image of holiness.

To show doctrinal succession, he includes in the introduction the full text of the Apostle's Creed[47] and three Dutch confessions

---

[43]Van Braght insists that these all be called Anabaptists, though he understands that the term does not properly apply to Christians before the sixteenth century. However, the opponents of the Anabaptists in the sixteenth century derisively gave those who practice believer's baptism this ancient title and so he will let them have their day. Ibid., 16.

[44]I would hold up *Martyrs Mirror* and the tradition of its use as at least a partial challenge to Dennis D. Martin's accusation that Mennonites have "split the institutional from the spiritual" sense of tradition and have rejected any continuity with the past. He writes, "One necessary prerequisite for the modern worldview is common to all Mennonites. This prerequisite is the rejection of continuity in history, a rejection of tradition. It is a revolutionary approach that shoves off against the immediate past in order to pursue a present or future utopia." We may find the *Mirror's* polemical rejection of the old catholic church ill considered (as Martin does), but it cannot be explained as a spiritual versus institutional dichotomy. Van Braght goes to considerable pains to show that the "Anabaptist" church has existed continuously in the writings, lives, and visible churches of each of the past sixteen centuries. The question for van Braght was not whether the church was spiritual versus institutional, but what sort of institutional continuity there existed between Christ and his church. Dennis D. Martin, "Nothing New under the Sun: Mennonites and History," *Conrad Grebel Review* 5, no. 1 (1987): 4.

[45]Van Braght, *The Bloody Theater*, 26.

[46]Ibid., 8.

[47]"This is the most ancient and simple creed, which it appears, was confessed already in or about the time of the apostles; and for which many, yea the greater part of the first Christian believers, have sacrificed their lives." Ibid., 27.

written between 1627 and 1632, which van Braght says were meant to more fully interpret and explain the Apostle's Creed in light of problems that have arisen in the church. In my calculation these official confessions, together with other official church confessions sprinkled throughout the *Mirror*, take up approximately 57,000 words.[48] This was the confessional era of the Mennonite church when the distinctive convictions of the early Anabaptists, asserted on the run, were being solidified and located within the broader beliefs of the church.[49]

For van Braght the spiritual transformation of reading is a mingling of several elements. By reading of believer's baptism, nonresistant martyrdom, and true dogmatic confession as it proceeds through the centuries, the reader will be mystically joined in this company with Christ and will thus live as they did, though under different conditions. The confessions of faith illuminate martyrdom for van Braght. In the second confession that van Braght includes, the October 7, 1630, confession of Amsterdam, Christ is presented as prophet, priest, and king. Under kingship we read,

> But since His kingdom was not of this world, He did not take possession of it by carnal weapons of iron and steel, but through suffering and fighting in the flesh; to which end he prepared Himself for temptation, tribulation and suffering, and took upon Him the cursed death on the cross, under Pontius Pilate; we confess moreover that this same Lord Jesus Christ, who was crucified at Jerusalem, and tasted death on mount Calvary, with exclamation of his groaning Spirit, and amidst the convulsions of heaven and earth, was the only and own Son of God, and that we are reconciled unto God by the blood and death of His Son, who by Himself purged our sins.[50]

Then further we read on the "Office of the Secular Authority" that this office is ordained of God "but we do not find that ... Christ taught His disciples such a thing, or called them to it; but, on the

---

[48]In addition to the confessions included as introductory material, there is an extended confession on ibid., 373.

[49]Karl Koop includes the writing of martyrologies themselves as an aspect of the confessionalization of churches. *Anabaptist-Mennonite Confessions of Faith: The Development of a Tradition* (Kitchener, ON: Pandora, 2004), 32.

[50]Van Braght, *The Bloody Theater,* 35.

contrary, that he enjoined them to follow Him in his defenseless life
and cross-bearing footsteps, prohibiting all revenge."[51]

In addition to these formal confessions, *Martyrs Mirror* is full
of personal confessions of faith given by various martyrs in their
interrogations, some of them mirroring and expanding on the
Apostle's Creed.[52] Countless letters, diaries, last testaments, written
prayers, hymns, and interrogation transcripts were included, which
repeat endlessly the faith convictions and beliefs of the martyrs.[53]
According to van Braght, the witness of the martyrs was much
more than a moral protest against the violence of the oppressor—it
was the confession with the ancient church, worshiping the Christ
revealed in scriptures.

Van Braght envisioned that all his compiling and mediating work
would induct his readers into the drama of union with Christ. As
readers linger on these martyrs situated now within the church of
Jesus spread across time and place, their own sufferings would come
to be suffered in faithfulness. I would argue that this is van Braght's
translation of the Anabaptist *Nachfolge Christi* that we noted above
in relation to Sattler, Marpeck, and Menno: the believer shares in
the sufferings of Christ as she is baptized and assumes his manner
of gentle response to evil and mistreatment exemplified in the
saints.[54] The mediation between Christ and the present-day saint is

---

[51]Ibid., 36.

[52]Van Braght's first goal in this book is to show that true baptism has always been
preceded by confession of the church's faith. In addition to his voluminous use of the
patristics to this end, see the confessions of the Waldenses, ibid., 284, those submitted
by Hendrick Terwoort and Jan Pieterss, ibid., 1017, and the extensive transcripts of
interrogations he includes, such as the one by Claes De Praet, ibid., 554–60.

[53]This contrasts with the *Hutterian Chronicle,* which, while it lists 2,173 martyrs,
contains little more than a short account of the place and means of death for each.

[54]Here the words of Anna of Rotterdam in a last testament to her son Isaiah express
a common view within the compilation:

> Behold, I go the way of the prophets, apostles and martyrs. ... I go, I say, the way
> which Christ Jesus, the eternal Word of the Father, full of grace and truth, the
> Shepherd of the sheep, who is the Life, Himself went. ... Having passed through,
> He calls His sheep and His sheep hear His voice and follow Him. ... This way
> was trodden by the dead under the altar. ... In this way walked also those who
> were marked by the Lord, and have received the *Thau* upon their foreheads
> (Ezek. 9:6).

Van Braght, *The Bloody Theater,* 453.

the succession of martyrs and the witness of baptism, apprehended through spiritual reading.

David L. Weaver-Zercher, in his recent book on the social history of the *Martyrs Mirror*, has alerted me to the ornamental title page included in the original 1660 version, a feature missing in many English copies.[55] This frontispiece is a collage of images summing up van Braght's spiritual vision for his book. Around the side are scenes of martyrdom taken from the Bible and history, the largest of which is the stoning of Stephen. Near the top is the figure of Christ bearing the stigmata of his death, holding his empty cross and looking heavenward. At the very top we see a scene in heaven with the ascended Saviour standing in the multitude of Rev. 7:7-17. In the center is a banner held aloft by two cherubs bearing the title of the work. In this mosaic of images, we have in one presentation the spiritual and theological vision of van Braght. Christ as the proto-Martyr leads and points his apostolic succession of defenseless Christians to their heavenly home. It is an artistic "icon" intended to draw the reader into this company of pilgrims destined for the culmination of glory with Christ in heaven, if they will yield themselves now to follow the Crucified.

Which leads us to ask about how nonresistance fits into van Braght's vision of a Christocentric communion of the saints in a succession of suffering *Nachfolge Christi*. At first glance it is most obviously believer's baptism that qualifies members to consider their pain as participating in this succession. However, it is also clear that van Braght considers nonresistance to be an integral part of what constitutes a true martyr.[56] This is, after all, the mirror of the *defenseless* Christians. Throughout the book, these martyrs are depicted as nonresistant and gentle lambs who testify with their blood against the violent regimes that torture them.[57] As Mennonite

---

[55]David Weaver-Zercher, *Martyrs Mirror: A Social History* (Baltimore, MD: Johns Hopkins University Press, 2016).

[56]In his discussion of martyrdom in the fourth century, he notes that now "many errors began to arise among some of those who were called Christians ... who went so far as to resort to carnal weapons ... through which the defenseless and meek lambs of Christ suffered not a little distress, fear and sorrow." However, he has done his utmost diligence so that none of the martyrs reported on can be "shown to have been guilty of gross errors, much less of the shedding of blood." Ibid., 174.

[57]See especially the accounts of Hendrick Alewijns (754), Wouter Capelle (1096), Jacques Dosie (498), John Schut (655), Adriaen Brael et al. (655).

historian John Roth, a commentator on the Mennonite martyr tradition, has written:

> From beginning to end, the entire structure of the book offers a testimony to the Christocentric worldview of the Anabaptists: Christ's life, his death, and the Christian's victory— through Christ—over the powers of death are the subtext of the martyr stories. In van Braght's eyes, it is God's expression of love incarnated through Christ in the world, Christ's violent death at the hands of the world, and his triumphant resurrection over the principalities and powers of the world which sustained the Anabaptists' own witness of nonviolent suffering love.[58]

Further, for van Braght, the martyrs themselves are warriors. "Through earthly wars countries and their inhabitants are destroyed, the innocent killed, the fugitive robbed of their property, and much weeping and mourning caused among those who remain."[59] But through the warfare of the martyrs, "the prosperity of the countries and their inhabitants was promoted because of the fervent prayers offered up by the martyrs to God for those who did them harm and for the common welfare of the inhabitants." Real, tangible changes occurred in the lives of people on account of the martyr's "medicine" for the world: "The estates of men generally, both according to the soul and the body, they improved and multiplied, causing them to increase thirty, sixty, and even a hundred fold, by their uprightness, fidelity, benevolence, compassion, and incomparable mercifulness toward their fellow men."[60] Here the blood of the martyrs is not only the seed of the church, but of mundane society as well. This too was a communion of the saints whereby the martyr's witness worked beyond her life to effect real change in the history of the world. This was the martyr returning good for evil.

And yet, for the modern reader tuned to hear arguments for and against participating in war, there is very little in the *Martyrs Mirror*. The unwillingness of Anabaptists to serve as magistrates is mentioned by numerous interrogators, but the refusal to kill or participate in the state's arms is not a large issue in the *Martyrs*

---

[58] John D Roth, "The Significance of the Martyr Story for Contemporary Anabaptists," *Brethren Life and Thought* 37, no. 2 (1992): 104.
[59] Van Braght, *The Bloody Theater*, 14.
[60] Ibid.

Mirror. Mennonites were denied entrance to the army of the Dutch Republic in any case, and so there was little to be gained here. What nonresistance has become, is the gentle lamb-like meekness of the martyr willing to share the suffering of Christ and through this weakness overcome the enemy, be that enemy human or spiritual. I would argue that van Braght has spiritualized the "enemy" from the literal assailant of the sixteenth century to seventeenth-century entities such as "numerous large, expensive and ornamented houses ... which are seen on every hand." It is the image of the martyr's defenseless suffering that will lead the believer to remain steadfast. To resist this enemy one must yield to Christ and witness the devotion of the martyrs even to death. It is this participant with Christ that deserves the title "defenseless."[61]

A full reception history of the *Martyrs Mirror* through four centuries cannot detain us here.[62] Our interest here is in the way this book itself mediated a theology of peace from first-generation Anabaptism and translated it into discipleship for less austere times. Defenselessness, seen vividly in the portrayals of Christian martyrdom, became the meekness, gentleness, love, and forbearance of Christ that these saints inspired in those who lingered over their stories and looked at their pictures. Readers would receive the strength to accept their own sufferings, like van Braght's own approaching death, as coming from the hand of God. The way in which the Mennonite and Amish churches revived their interest in the *Martyrs Mirror* in subsequent centuries, especially during those

---

[61]"The Christian reader may here perceive and firmly conclude that the cross is also the ensign of those who serve and follow Jesus Christ, the Captain of the faith; and that, on the contrary, those who afflict others, with crosses and sufferings, do not belong to this Captain, but are under another leader." It is the willingness to suffer persecution rather than inflict it that is emphasized as the root of the nonviolent example of Christ to be followed. Ibid., 357.

[62]Is it the case, as Julia Kasdorf somewhat cynically suggests, that this is a big book with much influence but no readers? Julia Kasdorf, "Mightier than the Sword: Martyrs Mirror in the New World," *Conrad Grebel Review* 31, no. 1 (2013): 44–70. However see Gerald C. Studer, "A History of the Martyr's Mirror," *Mennonite Quarterly Review* 22, no. 3 (1948): 163–79; John D. Roth, "The Complex Legacy of the Martyrs Mirror among Mennonites in North America," *Mennonite Quarterly Review* 87, no. 3 (2013): 277–316; Roth, "The Significance of the Martyr Story for Contemporary Anabaptists."; Rodney James Sawatsky, *History and Ideology: American Mennonite Identity Definition through History* (Kitchener, ON: Pandora, 2005), 9–38. The definitive description will now be Weaver-Zercher, *Martyrs Mirror.*

times when looming war threatened to dissuade young men from nonresistant practice, points to the way this kind of suffering was understood to be part and parcel with pacifism.[63]

But here again, as with the sixteenth-century Anabaptists that we reviewed, nonviolence is not so much a principle or self-standing ethic as it is a way of speaking about the Christ in whose company believers have walked through the course of the world's days.

So this is the union of Christ by which significant shapers of the Anabaptist tradition prior to the twentieth century understood the refusal of violence. Many of these themes were carried through and maintained in the twentieth century, though, as we shall see, other concerns emerged as well. Mennonite pacifism prior to the twentieth century sought to be orthodox in its affirmation of the divinity and humanity of Christ and understood the church to be a continuation, in some sense, of what God was doing in Christ. This participation of the believer in Christ was a salvific, Spirit-empowered likeness to Christ from which flowed the obedience of the disciple. It was particularly attentive to defining Christ-likeness by examining his manner, or posture vis-à-vis the authority structures in the world about him. It understood this participation with Christ as embedded in an "apostolic succession" of suffering disciples who had confessed through baptism their willingness to be "defenseless Christians" across the centuries. It was closely connected with believer's baptism, the voluntary surrender of the saint to participation with Christ as Christ moved through the world. Though it was focused intensely on Christ and his willingness to suffer, it was not entirely deaf to the ways a defenseless life yielded benefits to the societies Mennonites lived in.

We are treading here at the level of churchly ideals and grant that the practice of nonresistance for individuals was fraught with difficulty. We are not claiming that everyone *lived* like van Braght's martyrs, only that this was the vision many Mennonites placed before themselves. The foundation and development of pacifism as it moved through these centuries revolved around a vision of Christ and of the way Christians come to participate in his life in the world.

---

[63]See Studer, "A History of the Martyr's Mirror," 174. See Sawatsky, *History and Ideology*, 9–38, for a description of how in the nineteenth century the martyr tradition moved from being a symbol of the alien church in America to being an artifact of Mennonite denominational history.

2

The Troubled Defense
of Defenselessness in the
Twentieth Century

Pressures from within and without

Chapter breaks create a tidier picture than is warranted by the reality of history. It cannot be said that before the twentieth century pacifism was only about union with Christ and that this then changed to secular concerns going forward. There was plenty of awareness of the practical apologetic for pacifism in Mennonite circles before 1900, and there has been much thought about its spiritual and theological rhetoric in the 1900s. But a basic distinction needs to be seen as we think theologically about the history of pacifism in the life of the Mennonite church. It also needs to be remembered as we go forward that secularity does not banish the religious, it only casts it as one option among many, and thus changes its location in life.

The evolution of Mennonite pacifism in the twentieth century has been detailed elsewhere and here we will paint in broad strokes.[1] I am interested in the changing context of the Mennonite apologetic of pacifism. In general terms, prior to the twentieth century, Mennonite pacifism had "gone down into the bones" as

---

[1] A general history for North America has been written by Leo Driedger and Donald B. Kraybill, *Mennonite Peacemaking: From Quietism to Activism* (Scottdale, PA: Herald, 1994). See also Ervin R. Stutzman, *From Nonresistance to Justice: The Transformation of Mennonite Church Peace Rhetoric, 1908–2008* (Scottdale, PA: Herald, 2011), and Perry Bush, *Two Kingdoms, Two Loyalties: Mennonite Pacifism in Modern America* (Baltimore, MD: Johns Hopkins University Press, 1998).

a spirituality of *Gelassenheit*. Its main external manifestation had been the regular need to negotiate and renegotiate *privelegia* with the reigning monarchs to allow the church to live in peace with its war refusal, and the consequent attempts by church members to forgo violence in their dealings with their neighbors. As we saw in Chapter 1, defenselessness also became another word for the Christian's willingness to receive the trials of life in submission to Christ's lordship.

But at the dawn of the twentieth century, this was increasingly seen as inadequate by Mennonites. It failed to measure up to the mission of the church for the world. In the gradual awakening of interest in international missions and relief work at the end of the nineteenth century, Mennonites increasingly took on the optimistic, can-do, assertive religion of their Protestant cohorts.[2] Christianity now became something to be promoted and extended. How could *Gelassenheit* cohere with this more confident promotion of the Christian faith? Withdrawal into enclosed communities no longer seemed an adequate expression of faithfulness.

In addition to the question of how pacifism could fit into the mission of the outreaching church, there were external events that pushed nonresistance into a precarious position needing shoring up. World War I brought suffering to American Mennonites in the form of imprisonment and death sentences for conscientious objection.[3] Churches exerted great effort to clarify their position in the face of a cultural wave of patriotic furor in favour of the war effort. In spite of this great effort though, many Mennonite boys enlisted, fought,

---

[2]Theron F. Schlabach, "Reveille for Die Stillen Im Lande: A Stir among Mennonites in the Late Nineteenth Century: Awakening or Quickening, Revival or Acculturation?" *Mennonite Quarterly Review* 51, no. 3 (1977): 220–6.

[3]Due to lack of clarity in the legislation, it was left to the US military to deal with objectors. Mennonites were drafted and placed at the mercy of generals who had little sympathy. One hundred and thirty-eight Mennonite men were imprisoned, many were mistreated in army camps by misinformed generals, and several were put to death. Governments during World War II were more humane for Mennonite war resistors, though Jehovah's Witness with their more absolute resistance to government cooperation saw 6,000 imprisoned. See Guy F. Hershberger, Albert N. Keim, and Hanspeter Jecker, "Conscientious Objection," accessed August 7, 2014, http://gameo.org/index.php?title=Conscientious_Objection&oldid=103534 and Charles C. Moskos and John Whiteclay Chambers, *The New Conscientious Objection: From Sacred to Secular Resistance* (Toronto: Oxford University Press, 1993), 12–13.

and returned wondering if they would be received in their churches. Further, 26,000 Russian Mennonites immigrated to North America in the mid-1920s. In the anarchy of the Russian Revolution, some of these Mennonites had formed their own militias to defend their colonies. This was a decision that haunted memory and raised dark questions for some about the efficacy of nonresistance but for others inspired a firm resolve never to go down that path again.[4]

During World War II, many Mennonite men in North America enlisted to fight. Almost 40 percent of the eligible Mennonite men drafted in Canada and the United States entered combative roles rather than alternative service.[5] This created a sense that pacifism truly was a beleaguered ethic that needed fierce reinforcement from churches trying to fend off worldliness. And yet, as Perry Bush argues, the adoption of "total war" in the world wars made it increasingly difficult for Mennonites to withdraw from the "industrial-military complex."[6] Merely refusing to enlist in direct combat did not seem sufficient when the whole of society had now become an instrument of war. Mennonites began to realize that being nonviolent was becoming more complicated than it had seemed in the past.

But it was not only opposition that created stresses. Western governments in the twentieth century became increasingly humane in their willingness to tolerate conscientious objection. For centuries Mennonite leaders had worked to secure these exemptions where ever they lived. But now that they had secured this tolerance, what remained of the prophetic witness which such war-refusal should involve? Perry Bush shows that this was, in fact, the explicit intent of the US Selective Service in its adoption of alternative service opportunities for conscientious objectors. If war-refusers were

---

[4]Of interest here is the assertion by John B. Toews's account of the *selbschutz* in Russian Mennonite life, that prior to the October Revolution, "for more than a century the Mennonites in Russia, except for splendid isolated examples, did not expand their views of nonresistance to include a martyr-theology and the doctrine of the suffering church." "Origins and Activities of the Mennonite Selbstschutz in the Ukraine, 1918–1919," *Mennonite Quarterly Review* 46, no. 1 (1972): 10.
[5]Driedger and Kraybill, *Mennonite Peacemaking*, 73; Regehr, *Mennonites in Canada, 1939–1970*, 58; Bush, *Two Kingdoms, Two Loyalties*, 97–8.
[6]"Was it still sufficient, for example, to imagine oneself as uninvolved in the sin of war when the government urged people, as it did in the First World War, to 'Win the War with Wheat,' or when it proclaimed 'Every Garden a Munitions Plant'?" Bush, *Two Kingdoms, Two Loyalties*, 16.

sequestered in alternative work in a mental hospital, they would not create additional trouble for the mobilizing of war effort.[7]

By the second half of the century, refusing to serve in the military took much less courage. It had also become a much less distinctively religious action as the Vietnam War especially elicited much secular anti-war action.[8] Furthermore, as warfare evolved after World War II, governments relied less on massive numbers of recruits and, in the United States, conscription ended in 1973.[9] So what is left of a prophetic Christian pacifist witness if governments generously respect conscientious objection, many nonbelievers also refuse to fight, and the army doesn't even need you that badly?

Alongside this increased tolerance, there was interest in pacifism from war-weary Protestant churches who looked to Mennonites as exemplars. Mennonites, who were already deeply involved in their own fundamentalist/modernist controversy, could not help noticing that those most interested in pacifism were liberals— not the companions fundamentalists wished to embrace. In this bitter controversy, could a fundamentalist Mennonite still hold to pacifism?[10] It was a certain kind of pacifism that was lauded by liberal Protestants, an activist attempt to end war. This role as the "paradigmatic peace churches" in the eyes of liberal Protestant churches has been a significant factor in the shifting self-understanding of Mennonites. Pacifism was becoming part of a political program and this was something new to Mennonites who had assumed their nonresistance disqualified them from political engagement.[11] This has been an external pressure shifting assimilated Mennonite pacifism to the left on the political spectrum.

---

[7]Ibid., 269.

[8]Moskos and Chambers, The New Conscientious Objection, describes the secularization of conscientious objection in detail across the West.

[9]This will only develop further as militaries turn to drone and cyber warfare.

[10]Goshen College, one of the earliest Mennonite postsecondary schools in North America, was closed for the 1923–4 school year over the controversy. The church sought to reestablish control of its school by purging it of liberal elements. Harold Bender, author of "The Anabaptist Vision," was hired when it reopened. The association of pacifism with liberal theology still lingers in those parts of the Mennonite community most affected by Evangelicalism.

[11]See Guy F. Hershberger, "Biblical Nonresistance and Modern Pacifism," The Mennonite Quarterly Review 17, no. 3 (July 1943): 115–35 as but one example of the great effort exerted to distinguish Mennonite nonresistance from liberal pacifism in the first half of the twentieth century.

But the possibilities for nonviolent government involvement were also evolving. The increased interest from "liberals" must be seen in tandem with the rise of the welfare state after 1960. Governments in the West became increasingly involved in providing social insurance against the ills of life and greatly expanded the percentage of GDP committed to these ends. Social programs began to be developed to help the poor, disabled, and the victims of all manner of oppressions. This not only enlarged the sphere of opportunities for a Mennonite wishing to be involved in societal change in a nonviolent way, but it also made possible the argument that the greater a role the state played in *these* ways, the less violence a society would experience.[12]

In the civil rights movement of the 1950s and 1960s Mennonites recognized an ally in the thinking of Martin Luther King Jr., and he was invited to speak at Goshen College in 1960. His language of *agape, community*, and *love* resonated with the emerging language of involved discipleship. King was especially condemning of those who stood by and merely prayed for change in the long run. What King offered Mennonites was a picture of Christian pacifism strategized to change society for the better. However, his willingness to break unjust laws raised questions.[13]

So these, in broad strokes, were some of the winds swirling about in the twentieth century that changed the context within which pacifism was held by the Mennonite church. In all kinds of ways, the correlation between pacifism and good civil citizenship was being accentuated and its specifically spiritual foundation was becoming ambiguous. These new dynamics called into question the need and the sufficiency of "union with Christ" as the core center for nonviolent witness. Secular opportunities beckoned in which peace could be achieved not only through spirituality but through hard work, social engagement, and political organization.

What this resulted in, by the end of the century, was a situation in which it could be said that assimilated North American Mennonites already knew what the Lord required before they went to church.

---

[12]Alternative service work in mental health hospitals gave Mennonites in the United States and Canada helpful exposure to the possibilities of this kind of service to society in the name of war resistance.

[13]For a discussion of the tensions the civil rights movement elicited among Mennonites in North America, cf. Tobin Miller Shearer, "A Prophet Pushed Out: Vincent Harding and the Mennonites," *Mennonite Life* 69 (2015). https://mla.bethelks.edu/ml-archive/2015/a-prophet-pushed-out-vincent-harding-and-the-menno.php

If rank-and-file Mennonites in the pews often struggled to hold to any form of pacifism, denominational leaders and academics had largely come to believe that nonviolence, social justice, and peacemaking were an obvious, even common-sense translation of Anabaptist pacifism in a secular age. This was so not only for those in the social science aspects of conflict transformation but also to a degree in biblical studies and theology. There was little debate or questioning, or any real sheepishness about not being able to live the ethic. Nonviolence had become Mennonites' good news for the modern world and they could live it. Bigger, more ironic questions emerged: could our understanding of God be made to cohere with what we already know is the right thing to do?[14]

But that is probably to assert more than to argue. What is needed is a closer comparison of the trajectory of secularity and Mennonite pacifism. To that we now turn.

The Relation of Anabaptism and Secularity

The internal and external challenges described above thrust Mennonite pacifism into uncharted territory and triggered the avalanche of writing noted earlier in the Swartley bibliography. However, to get a fuller sense of why Mennonite nonresistance exists now in a state of ambivalence vis-à-vis its earlier understanding of union with Christ, it's helpful to see it against the backdrop of the history of secularization. A secularizing trend presents both opportunities and challenges for a pacifist church.[15] Traditionally

---

[14]Thus, a key debate for Mennonites in the twenty-first century has not been about whether we can be nonviolent but whether God can be. How are we to understand the violent images we see of God in the scriptures? See J. Denny Weaver, *The Nonviolent Atonement* (Grand Rapids, MI: Eerdmans, 2011) and *The Nonviolent God* (Grand Rapids, MI: Eerdmans, 2013).

[15]I recognize that the meaning of the term "secular" has shifted. In the Middle Ages, "secular" referred to temporal existence between Christ's ascension and second coming. "Secular" named a time, not a space. In late modernity, "secular" rather became the autonomous sphere of rule, now opposed to "religious." Secularity names a set of conditions pervasive in twentieth-century Western societies in which a high value is placed on order and civility; the role of religion vis-à-vis society has become smaller, various, and pluralist; religion has become more attentive to individual

Constantinianism, the vision for a society ruled by church and state together, has been the perceived opponent of Mennonite peace theology. But how is secularity related to Constantinianism? Constantinianism and secularity are not mutually exclusive ways of understanding Western society but rather two different maps by which the same geography can be measured.[16] The growth of secularity can look like the receding of Constantinianism because here the sphere of religion becomes separated from the spheres of the state, education, media, and trade. The bishop is ejected from the royal court and from many other courts as well. But in the West, churches have shown the ability to retain forms of power and responsibility within society in spite of, or even through disestablishment. These mutations have been troubling to Mennonite theologians.[17] However, the culmination of secularity has been much more difficult for the churches to adapt to then the demise of Constantinianism. The relation of Mennonite pacifism to secularity has not been studied in depth.[18]

The aspect of secularity that I am interested in here is the end point in a trajectory in which it comes to be assumed that specific religious convictions are possible but no longer inherent in human flourishing. Belief in God becomes one option among many and is not required to be a member-in-good-standing within

---

personal engagement and authenticity; the church and the state have separated into distinct spheres, and therewith, the methods for achieving the commonweal have become distinctly instrumental, rationalist, and bureaucratic.

[16]I partake of the growing agreement that *secularism* as an ideology is only one possible aspect of *secularity*. *Secularism* has an agenda for the future that applauds the withering of religion with the rise of science, rationalism, and humanism. It is what Charles Taylor calls the subtraction thesis of secularization theory, which says that for every advance toward secularity, religion must thereby retreat. *Secularity* as I use it is what Taylor describes as the modern possibility of living as though God does not exist. In 1500 this was impossible. Today it is possible, and for many people, almost inevitable. *A Secular Age*, 1st ed. (Cambridge, MA: Belknap Press of Harvard University Press, 2007), 26–7.

[17]See John H. Yoder, "Constantinian Sources of Western Social Ethics," in *The Priestly Kingdom: Social Ethics as Gospel* (Notre Dame, IN: University of Notre Dame Press, 1984), 141–4.

[18]Earl Zimmerman begins to do some of this work in "Beyond Secular and Sacred: An Anabaptist Model for Christian Social Ethics," *Conrad Grebel Review* 25, no. 2 (2007): 50–67. His account is tuned to what Anabaptist theology can offer a society seeking to be rid of the secular/sacred divide. It does not address ways in which secularity and Anabaptism are part of the same set of early modern impulses.

society. Pacifism as a gospel-based ethic is suspicious from both a Constantinian and a secularity viewpoint. The Constantinian welcomes the bishop in the court, as long as he leaves his pacifism at the door. The secular welcomes the bishop in the court as long as he leaves his religion at the door and enters with only the intent to reduce societal violence by instrumental means. Through these means, secularity eventually creates large sectors within society where no one, religious or not, is expected to engage in overt violence. As twentieth-century assimilation occurred, Mennonites became exposed to the persuasiveness of this secularity in new and potent ways.

To see how this has affected Mennonite theological ethics, it is helpful to understand Anabaptism in a dialectical relation to the secularizing trajectory over centuries. This complicates our original presentation of pacifism as union with Christ prior to the twentieth century by showing that there always was a certain pressure toward civility that Mennonite pacifism labored under, but which became much more overt and sometimes invincible in the twentieth century.

Charles Taylor is a commentator on the secular trajectory who is particularly sensitive to the close affinity that religious impulses toward reform had with what eventually became the "exclusive humanism" we now know as the secular age.[19] One aspect of Taylor's argument that needs to be kept in mind is that none of the "stages" on the road leading to secularity predetermine the end point to be a life lived without reference to God. Each of the steps could have always gone in another direction. This is important to keep in mind in subsequent chapters when we seek to reimmerse pacifism in the event of Christ's incarnation.

In *A Secular Age*, Taylor tells the long and zigzag story of how secularity had its original impetus in late medieval attempts to finally Christianize Europe all the way down to the bottom of society.[20] What this often looked like was the abolishing of various

---

[19]One of the major arguments of his work is that secularity began not with the loss of faith but with its intensification and expansion. In understanding Taylor's work I have benefited from James K. A. Smith, *How (Not) to Be Secular: Reading Charles Taylor* (Grand Rapids, MI: Eerdmans, 2014).

[20]Taylor, *Secular Age*, chapter 2, "The Rise of a Disciplinary Society" is a central section for us. Kenneth Davis shows how Anabaptism partook of the growing conviction by the sixteenth century that reform leading to a real change in lay piety would need to be a cataclysmic replanting of the church, rather than an increased adherence to

forms of barbarity. A disgust with the vulgar brutality of premodern society was a key impetus for this reform from both the church and the state's perspective. This began among the elites but was eventually pushed across society. This reform eventually led to the suppression and monopolization of violence by the state, the rejection of religious warfare, the gradual regulation of warfare, and a general repression of the violent inner frenzy that was earlier believed to be innate and needed to be unleashed, say, at Carnival.[21] Commoners needed to be tamed and ordered. A quote from Jan Laski, the sixteenth-century Polish reformer who debated Menno Simons, distills this societal vision of order, decency, virtue, and piety, which propelled the making over of the masses:

> Princes and magistrates would be more peaceful; wars would cease among the nobility; the ambition of prelates would be punished; and all would do their duty in their calling. Children would be instructed from a young age in holy discipline; doctrine would be purely preached; the sacraments properly administered; the populace held in check; virtue would be prized; vices corrected; true penance restored and excommunication pronounced on the obstinate and the rebellious; God's honour would be advanced together with the proper invocation of his holy name; the most honourable estate of marriage would be restored to its original form; brothels would be abolished; the poor would be cared for and all begging eliminated; the sick would be visited and consoled; and the dead honoured with an honest burial devoid of superstition.[22]

A key impulse against random and chaotic societal violence, according to Taylor, was the rising Renaissance notion of "civility,"

---

laws already in place and only needing to be obeyed. He affirms Albrecht Ritschl's assertion that "the first [Anabaptist] leaders were primarily motivated by ascetic ideals which still permeated much of early sixteenth-century society owing to the vitality of late medieval ascetic reform movements." Kenneth R. Davis, *Anabaptism and Asceticism: A Study in Intellectual Origins* (Scottdale, PA: Herald, 1974), 127.
[21]Taylor, *Secular Age*, 47–50, 119–20, 121. "Barbarism" was a concept that was sharply debated over reports that the inhabitants of the new world were cannibals. For a discussion of how this concept emerged in early modern Europe, see Lee Palmer Wandel, *The Reformation: Towards a New History* (Cambridge: Cambridge University Press, 2011), 58–62.
[22]As quoted in Taylor, *Secular Age*, 105–6.

a refined ideal of human interaction that was defined over against
the "savages" that were coming to the attention of Europeans now
exploring the world. "It is what we have, and those others don't, who
lack the excellences, the refinements, the important achievements
which we value in our way of life."[23] To leave behind the savage
existence "one needed to be governed in orderly fashion, under a
code of law." Civility required a civil government that "badgered,
bullied, pushed, preached at, drilled and organized [commoners] to
abandon their lax and disordered folkways and conform to one
or another feature of civil behaviour." This government would not
"consort with rowdiness, random and unauthorized violence, or
public brawls, either in young aristocratic bloods, or among the
people."[24]

Several broad mindset changes were important in the rise of
civility. Key was a new awareness of the malleability of the human
person and community, that everyone could really and truly change
to live a different life. Another mindset was the religious realization
that all vocations and stations of life came under the blessing
and providence of God's graces. This became the affirmation or
ordinary human life that secularity has centered around.[25] Another
mindset change involved the subsiding of the whole "enchanted"
understanding of space and time in which humans lived at the mercy
of spirits and other forces.[26] What became the modern "buffered
self" is a person who has the freedom and power to make her own
choices about how to live and is not in thrall to greater powers
round about. In all these ways, early-modern society moved toward
being a society that could suppress unruly violence. Each of these
changes of mindset eventually became part and parcel of the secular
mind.[27]

In the sixteenth and seventeenth centuries, there was a seamless
connection between the religious reforms that sought a sanctified
church and the social reforms that sought an ordered, less brutal
society.

---

[23]Ibid., 100.
[24]Ibid.
[25]Ibid., 104.
[26]Ibid., 131.
[27]As Taylor shows, none of this anti-barbarism was necessarily anti-religious. In fact
it often grew out of a more intense religious fervor.

Religious Reform ... was inhabited by a demand, felt with increasing power during the late Middle Ages and the early modern period, that not just the élite, but as far as possible all the faithful live up to the demands of the gospel. ... Everyone was called on to live their faith to the full. And this meant that the lives and practices of ordinary people couldn't just be left as they were. They had to be exhorted, commanded, and sometimes forced and bullied into giving up [impious practices].[28]

Taylor shows that time and again, when reform originated in the church with spiritual renewal, it would soon become evident that once achieved, the new "civility" could stand on its own.

There's a long story here; but shortly put, we can see that this new understanding of world and time, originally arising within a Christian outlook ... gradually slips over more and more in a secular direction. ... Among other things, modern versions of this latter [social order] are much less tolerant of violence and social disorder than earlier variants. The sixteenth century sees the taming of the unruly military aristocracy, and its domestication in court service, court attendance, or estate management. The eighteenth century begins to see the taming of the general population. Riots, peasant rebellions, social disorders begin to become rarer in Northwest Europe. Until we reach the rather high standards of nonviolence which most Atlantic societies expect in their domestic life.[29]

Because a key part of the move to civilize the masses was the elevation of the "natural" aspects of life (marriage, work, and so on), it was not a far step to see the natural value of the life apart from its relation to God.[30] Faith is most susceptive to secularization at the point where the rubber meets the road, in daily ordinary living. A good action is a good action whether done out of obedience to God or out of a desire to be rational. In summary, Taylor shows that in the early modern period there was a growing symbiosis between religious revival, the imposition of decency and civility on all levels of society, and anti-violence.

---

[28]Taylor, *Secular Age*, 104.
[29]Ibid., 124–5.
[30]Ibid., 143.

In this description we can glimpse some of the larger currents swirling in Europe at the same time Anabaptists were gaining their footing. It is not difficult for someone familiar with Anabaptist ideals to see that in some key features, they were not living against the spirit of the age when they began their churches. Anabaptist discipleship was based on the belief that lay people could live holy lives and that through strong community discipline all could attain the love of Christ. Anabaptists yielded to no one in their belief in the malleability of the person. Conrad Grebel's pre-Anabaptist letter to Thomas Müntzer shows the connection between the reform of all people, the malleability of all, the discipline needed for this, and its connection to nonviolence:

> There is more than enough wisdom and counsel in the Scriptures on how to teach, govern, direct, and make devout all classes and all men. Anyone who will not reform or believe and strives against the Word and acts of God and persists therein, after Christ and his Word and rule have been preached to him, and he has been admonished with the three witnesses before the church, such a man we say on the basis of God's Word shall not be put to death but regarded as a heathen and publican and left alone.[31]

In its focus on the suffering lowly Christ, Anabaptism found a way to connect Christ and his commands to the disenfranchised commoners that swelled its ranks.[32] Kenneth Davis in his classic work, *Anabaptism and Asceticism*, showed that one cannot understand Anabaptism except against the background of late medieval lay vitalization movements such as the *Devotio Moderna*, which manifested a concern "that the church, visibly and practically, should manifest moral righteousness and holiness of conduct and life, patterned on the imitation of Christ motif, guided by the 'Rule of Christ' and explicitly obedient to the law of Christ in the New Testament."[33]

---

[31] Harder, *Sources of Swiss Anabaptism*, 290.

[32] Taylor shows that a growing awareness of the human accessibility of the Christ, seen especially in paintings, was a key devotional plank in this laicization of the faith in the early modern period. Taylor, *Secular Age*, 93–4.

[33] Davis, *Anabaptism and Asceticism*, 296. Mediating this into the Anabaptist churches can be explained through its close connection to the humanism of the time, especially to Erasmus. Anabaptism was also deeply apocalyptic in places, and manifested many

The rejection of public order cornerstones such as infant baptism and penance was entailed by the Anabaptist quest to bring discipleship "down" from the monastery and the high church to a band of common souls who could answer to their Lord without recourse to the hierarchy of priestly mediation. Adult baptism, a plain Lord's Supper and the ban were answers to the question of how each person, in no matter what station in life, could take responsibility and live a godly, orderly life.[34] Anabaptism's theology of the unity of the believer with the pattern of Christ's life was the way this could transpire in concrete practices of daily life. In all this, Anabaptism can be seen as a vanguard movement in the quest for "civility," which Taylor describes as the trajectory of secularity. Again, this is not to suggest that early Anabaptists were somehow "secularizing" the gospel. But attempts like theirs to bring the gospel to bear on common, lay life placed the gospel in a secularizable sphere.

Pacifism followed this. Anabaptist writings abound with condemnations of the brutal barbarity of peasant life and the constant warfare of aristocrats jockeying for honor and land.[35] Loud denunciations of religious violence were common.

---

of the expectations, developed in the tradition of Joachim of Fiore, that a *third age* was breaking upon the world, an age of the Spirit when hierarchies would crumble and all would be priests. Apocalypticism, developed by Anabaptists such as Hans Hut and Melchior Hoffmann, was deeply utopian and anti-hierarchical. I discuss this in my book, Layton Boyd Friesen, *"Seditions, Confusion and Tumult": Why Reformation Europe Thought Anabaptism Would Destroy Society* (Evangelical Mennonite Conference, 2019). See also Jarold K. Zeman, "Anabaptism: A Replay of Medieval Themes or a Prelude to the Modern Age?" *Mennonite Quarterly Review* 50, no. 4 (1976): 259–71.

[34] It is this application of ethics to everyone which has occasioned the claim heard frequently in the "Anabaptist Vision" tradition of Harold Bender that Anabaptism was the culmination of the reformation. Harold S. Bender, "The Anabaptist Vision," *Mennonite Quarterly Review* 18, no. 2 (1944): 74.

[35] Menno Simons provides a sample:

Man, o Man, look at the irrational savage creatures and learn wisdom. Roaring lions, fierce bears, and rending wolves keep the peace among their kind. But you, weak and wretched worms, you are created after God's own image and are called rational beings, born without tusks, claws, and horns and with a frail and feeble nature, born without rationality, speech and power; yea, unable to walk or stand up, and dependent entirely upon a mother's help—all of which ought to teach you to be peaceable and not contentious. But when you attain to understanding and manhood, you are so turbulent, tyrannical, and cruel, so bloodthirsty and

But in even larger terms, Anabaptism contributed to the rejection of a whole understanding of society that determined when violence was permissible by one's station in the world. In this older medieval concept, the counsels of perfection, which included the nonresistant commands of Christ, applied to clergy and monks but hardly to commoners. Traditional clerical exemption from war, such as Thomas Aquinas prescribed, was built upon a multifaceted approach to the gospel and culture in which some members of society (the clergy) gave witness to salvation through nonresistance, while other members served as soldiers and were not expected to be Christian in the nonresistant way.[36] This was how medievals solved the vexing and age-long problem of how the square peg of the Kingdom of God could fit the round hole that was daily life in the world.

But in the Anabaptist priesthood of believers, a new form of uniformity was expected, and this expectation of moral consistency across the board, throughout the year, is a trademark of the secularizing trajectory that Taylor describes.[37] Now, one's station in society or the church, or the day of the church calendar, did not determine the licitness of deeds. In Anabaptism clerical abstention from war was extended to the laity, and was impressed upon them

unmerciful, that it is inconceivable and indescribable (Simons, *Complete Writings of Menno Simons*, 190).

A similarity with Erasmus is obvious here. Compare his "A Complaint of Peace" Erika Rummel, ed., *The Erasmus Reader* (Toronto: University of Toronto Press, 2015), 292.

[36]Aquinas said clergy are forbidden to kill because

all the clerical Orders are directed to the ministry of the altar, on which the Passion of Christ is represented sacramentally, according to 1 Cor. 11:26. ... Wherefore it is unbecoming for them to slay or shed blood, it is more fitting that they should be ready to shed their own blood for Christ, so as to imitate in deed what they portray in their ministry.

Also, clergy "should imitate their master" who "when He was struck did not strike." *Summa Theologica*, trans. the Fathers of the English Dominican Province, Benziger Bros. edition, 1947, II–II, 40.2, 64.4. The widespread understanding that soldiers were barred from the Mass until they had done penance, even after a licit war, further testifies to a nuanced understanding of how sin affected all, but affected each differently, depending on the role they played in society.

[37]See his excellent discussion of the worldview behind medieval Carnival, those times of misrule and societal chaos when hierarchies and moralities could be flipped upside down. Mutually contradictory moralities could be in play depending on the day of the year. Taylor, *Secular Age*, 45–54.

for reasons not unlike Aquinas' reason for clerics to abstain from killing: all Christians are those who mingle with Christ in his crucified response to evil and should thus sooner be killed rather than kill.

Anabaptists, like many who called the church to order, were repulsed by what they perceived as the corruption and decadence of the church hierarchy, and Anabaptist application of heretofore clerical counsels of perfection to the ploughboy was part of their revolt against those who had failed to uphold it in their given station.[38] It is also significant that key Anabaptist statements on the sword such as the Schleitheim Confession, and the records of the Bern Disputation in 1538, placed the sword not in the hands of the nonbelieving layperson, but in the hands of the state. In this way they participated in the governmentalization of violence.[39]

In these key areas, Anabaptists fit into the trajectory of overcoming barbarity and elevating the ethics of the commoner that Taylor describes. This laicization of Christ's commands yielded results. As fragmented as Mennonite commitment to pacifism has been, the broader life that this ethic entailed, and the way such believers needed to prove themselves useful to society in spite of refusing to fight, resulted in cities set on hills.

Going forward from Anabaptist beginnings, the "Mennonite apologetic" through the centuries, by which they secured their *privilegia*, relied heavily on their claims to offer productive, peaceful, and orderly service to their hosts.[40] This was most obvious in Russia during the nineteenth century when impeccably disciplined, peaceful Mennonite colonies endeared themselves to Czarist governments and offered themselves as exemplars and instructors of the civilized society Russian governments sought. Through the well-documented leadership of Johann Cornies (1789–1848), the industrious and zealous promulgator of new forms of agriculture as well as higher education and cultural reform, Mennonites proved to "out-modernize" their neighbors and demonstrate that nonresistant

---

[38]Snyder, *History and Theology*, 27–9.
[39]See Harold Stauffer Bender, "The Pacifism of the Sixteenth Century Anabaptists," *Mennonite Quarterly Review* 30, no. 1 (1956): 122–3; John Christian Wenger, "The Schleitheim Confession of Faith," *Mennonite Quarterly Review* 19, no. 4 (1945): 250.
[40]For a description of this exchange of economic and political benefit to the state for privilege in return see James Urry, *Mennonites, Politics, and Peoplehood: 1525 to 1980* (Winnipeg: University of Manitoba Press, 2011), 43–8.

Christians produced a peaceful, harmonious society that could
further the economic prospects of its host.[41] As Natila Venger, a
Ukrainian scholar of Russian Mennonite history, concludes in
her study of Mennonite industrialization, "in objective terms the
Mennonite settlements played the role of an experimental field for
Russian modernization. ... [Mennonites] were the architects of the
[modernization] process."[42] Though other Mennonite migrations did
not offer the same autonomy to establish self-sufficient pacifist life,
similar stories could be told wherever Mennonites had settled: they
justified their refusal to bear arms by the peaceful, harmonious, and
productive communities this pacifism resulted in.[43]

The Russian "experiment" with Mennonite colonies also shows
that though the path began with both religious and secular concerns
working in unison, when this order was in fact achieved it soon
became evident that the order pursued could be maintained just
as well without specifically Christian foundations.[44] E. K. Francis
wrote, in his sociological description of Russian Mennonite life,

> Amidst all this rapid progress and worldly success the role of
> religion, once the raison d'être of the group, almost recedes
> into the background. It seems that at the moment when a
> Mennonite utopia, the community of the saints and saved, lay
> within reach of realization, it became secularized and void of its
> spiritual content, a commonwealth of ordinary people with the
> ambitions and motivations of sinners and the fallen nature of

---

[41]John R. Staples, "'On Civilizing the Nogais': Mennonite-Nogai Economic Relations,
1825–1860," *Mennonite Quarterly Review* 74, no. 2 (April 2000): 229–56, shows
how Johann Cornies sought to modernize the nomadic Nogai people in Molotshna
by constructing a model agricultural village for them, among other things.
[42]Quoted in John R. Staples, "Johann Cornies, Money-Lending, and Modernization
in the Molochna Mennonite Settlement, 1820s–1840s," *Journal of Mennonite
Studies* 27 (2009): 122.
[43]This is not to say that pacifism alone resulted in these productive Mennonite
exemplars, but rather pacifism as part of a larger commitment to be a useful, benefit
in society. For example, during World War I when Canadian Mennonites from the
prairies presented their case for exemption in person to Prime Minister Borden, they
reminded him of what Lord Dufferin had told them back in 1877 as they first came
to Canada: "the battle to which we invite you [the Mennonites] is the battle against
the wilderness. ... You will not be required to shed human blood." Epp, *Mennonites
in Canada, 1786–1920*, 370.
[44]Taylor describes this aspect in the section "The Turning Point." *Secular Age*, 221–98.

man. Religious convictions and interests now were one aspect of everyday life, perhaps still a central but by no means the only aspect. Many concessions had to be made to other conflicting interests which frequently dominated and determined action. Religion, at one time a spiritual power permeating all personal hopes and desires, was institutionalized, and religious institutions were but one factor among many other institutions, often more in the foreground of attention.[45]

Francis perhaps understates the role that still remained for faith in Russian Mennonite life, but one can see how religion and the rule of the colony had not become Constantinian so much as secularized. The role of religion had shifted and while still "central" had become partially dispensable for the well-being of the colony. Other more instrumental processes assumed vital roles within the well-being of this church-based group. And all this time Mennonite ministers continued to read Menno Simons and the *Martyrs Mirror*. Mennonite pacifist ethics could be established and maintained as a union with Christ, but could also entail a civility, a good and decent way of living in harmony that fit well with religion but was not utterly dependent on it. The two could coexist in ways that did not always feel like tension.

The twentieth-century shift, documented thoroughly by Leo Driedger and Donald B. Kraybill in *Mennonite Peacemaking: from Quietism to Activism* and by Perry Bush in *Two Kingdoms, Two Loyalties*, is in keeping with this historic kinship between secularity and the Mennonite peace position. Both activist peacemaking and the now increasing secular conscientious objection stem from the belief that ordinary people can be reformed, made over into civilized, cooperating agents in community. Both flower with new urgency as "lay" individuals are constantly enjoined to "do their part" for the creation of just societies.[46] Restorative justice, conflict mediation, poverty reduction, and many other elements of the new peacemaking are at home in a society that seeks civility—the

---

[45]E. K. Francis, "The Mennonite Commonwealth in Russia, 1789–1914: A Sociological Interpretation," *Mennonite Quarterly Review* 25, no. 3 (1951): 178–9.
[46]Anecdotally, "We Day" festivities in Canada gather tens of thousands of children into arenas and stadiums to hear high-octane exhortations to work for social justice and peace from celebrity activists like the Kielburger brothers.

orderly, egalitarian, disciplined, society of authentic individuals that Taylor describes.

Prior to the twentieth century, because Mennonites had been recused from much direct involvement in society, the pressure toward this civil understanding of ethics was not as directly felt, though it was present nonetheless. It was also the case that pre–World War I societies had not ripened to embrace instrumental peacemaking as a broad goal. Mennonite social action discovered in the 1900s that there is in fact a genuine cooperation possible between those who question violence from a dogmatic background, and those who have no religious foundation at all.

But are the values and beliefs of the secular mind conducive to peace in the long run? Can a secular society seeking civility be enduringly peaceful without God? Here it is helpful to hear to voice of Steven Pinker, a cognitive scientist and psychologist, who has argued that *because* of secularity humans are living in the most peaceful era in human history. Using a wide array of data, he makes the claim that war, crime, abuse, and all forms of killing are at a historical low and are decreasing.[47] This is not obvious to everyone and there are those who think his optimism is illusory, but clearly *something* significant has happened in the last few centuries.[48] What is important for us is his interpretation of the cause of the decline, which to most people in a secular age will seem to be common sense. Pinker is correct in asserting that today, even devout religious believers do not look first to the church or another religious institution to solve the problem of violence.[49] We may still give lip service to violence as a spiritual problem but when we set about to do something about it, we use instrumental means.[50] For individuals who are inclined to be violent,

---

[47]Steven Pinker, *The Better Angels of Our Nature: Why Violence Has Declined* (New York: Penguin, 2011).

[48]See for example David Peterson and Edward S. Herman, "Steven Pinker on the Alleged Decline of Violence," accessed September 2, 2014, http://zcomm.org/znetarticle/steven-pinker-on-the-alleged-decline-of-violence-by-edward-s-herman-and-david-peterson/. Also see John Gray, "Steven Pinker Is Wrong about Violence and War," accessed May 29, 2017, https://www.theguardian.com/books/2015/mar/13/john-gray-steven-pinker-wrong-violence-war-declining.

[49]Pinker, *Better Angels*, 17; David Bentley Hart, "The Precious Steven Pinker," *First Things*, accessed October 29, 2015, http://www.firstthings.com/article/2012/01/the-precious-steven-pinker.

[50]Pinker, *Better Angels*. Though Pinker deals with declines that began much earlier, his chief "angel" in reducing violence is the Enlightenment with its rationalization

psychotherapy, education, and employment are the solution, rather than penance, virtue formation, or church discipline. He also argues that nonreligious factors have made a vast difference in how we view violence. For example, he argues that the modern novel has created an unprecedented ability for empathy toward one's fellow humans in modern life. We are now able to feel what another person is feeling in a way that was inconceivable to premoderns. This rise of mutual empathy is a key reason we no longer tolerate the brutal practices of our forebears.[51] Whether or not secularity ultimately is as successful as Pinker claims it is, our approach to solving violence in our communities shows that we do assume that something like his description is correct.

And this creates temptations for a Mennonite nonresistance that has traditionally rooted the answer to human violence in the believer's unity with the manner of Christ through believer's baptism, and the creation of separated church communities. Not only does a theological undercarriage for nonviolence seem unnecessary, it seems beside the point. In Pinker's world, it is the state and its monopoly on violence, as well as its resourcing and control of a panoply of social educational programs, that now, and over time, reduce violence.[52]

What this secular concern for order has done is change the manner in which pacifism has come to be practiced. As secularization became more explicitly persuasive through Mennonite assimilation in the twentieth century, it became more possible for Mennonite pacifists to get involved in advocacy, legislation, international mediation, and restorative justice because these practices go with the grain of a developing secularity to begin with. These are characteristic ways in which people in the West get things done. These practices are made possible by constitutionally guided democratic governments presiding over societies in which, at least in theory but partially in practice, victims are granted the individual human rights necessary for justice, and individuals are permitted to advocate before

---

of human society. Charles Taylor describes the secular trajectory as one in which an instrumentalist view of the world becomes axiomatic; the good life comes not through conforming to the *telos* or nature of a thing, but by using things with effective techniques and strategies extrinsic to the thing in itself. Taylor, *Secular Age*, 97–9.

[51]Pinker, *Better Angels*, 175–7.

[52]One could also point out that traditional Mennonite nonresistance was not about "reducing violence." It simply rejected it for the church member.

governments. Secularity provides at least the illusion of achievability for those interested in reducing violence as a human problem. This is not to say that individuals or churches don't get involved in these causes for Christian reasons. It is to say that these reasons are not felt to be of essence by either the church or society.

This is a tremendous source of dissonance in the Mennonite witness. At this point in our argument, we have now viewed several solutions for how the lofty and severe life of Christ could possibly "fit" into a fallen world. For medievals, this "fit" came by stratifying society into those capable of living the counsels of perfection, and the rest. The "religious" would live the higher life that "secular" commoners were not capable of. In secularity, this "fit" between Christ and the world is achieved by jettisoning the specifically doctrinal and ecclesial undercarriage of Christ's ethic and using instrumental, rational means to suppress, redirect, and discipline violence. Mennonites, to use the language of Balthasar in our introduction, have sought to walk a high and dizzy ridge that maintains a doctrinal, ecclesial commitment to Christ, indeed envisions a personal union with Christ, but also expects this to be lived by *all* the church. Mennonites traditionally tried to have the best of both the medieval and the secular worlds, both a Christ-centred ethic, *and* an ethic for all. However, the only way Mennonites could make this "fit" work prior to 1900 was by creating a separated church that bore little responsibility for the wider society. But in the twentieth century, Mennonites struggled to really have it all—an ethic linked spiritually to Christ, achievable by the whole church *plus* now taking responsibility for society, involved in secular institutions such as the state for the flourishing of ordinary life beyond the faithful. This is why unity in difference questions have come to a bursting point.

But going further, not only is there affinity between a civilized order and gospel nonviolence, but sometimes the tables turn. The quest for human flourishing has turned the criticism of violence back against the very churches that raised the banner against violence in the first place. A secular age, even if originally schooled for peace by the church, may not thank the church when society takes up the affirmation of ordinary life that is its outcome. In fact, some of the very founts of nonviolence within the church's witness, such as Christ giving himself utterly in self-abnegation to the point of crucifixion, come to be seen by a secular age as dangerous and unhealthy. Charles Taylor describes this vividly:

And hence what was for a long time and remains for many the heart of Christian piety and devotion: love and gratitude at the suffering and sacrifice of Christ, seems incomprehensible, or even repellent and frightening to many. To celebrate such a terrible act of violence as a crucifixion, to make this the centre of your religion, you have to be sick; you have to be perversely attached to self-mutilation, because it assuages your self-hatred, or calms your fears of healthy self-affirmation. You are elevating self-punishment, which liberating humanism wants to banish as a pathology, to the rank of the numinous. This you frequently hear today.[53]

A central motif behind the move toward the secular age which Taylor demonstrates is the drive toward *exclusive humanism*,[54] that is, an abiding quest for the flourishing of ordinary people in this life, without asking people to sacrifice their well-being for the next life, or for a transcendent God. This finds new emphasis in the cult of personal authenticity articulated with greater cultural consensus since the 1960s. What has come under withering attack in the secular trajectory is the way Christian calls for suffering, self-giving, and commitment have compromised the ability of people to experience the kind of wellness in life that is presumed to be the duty of all to pursue.

Mennonites, with their martyr's tradition, have not been excepted from this response from the wider world. At first, *Gelassenheit* was criticized by Mennonites because it ran counter to the healthy self-image one needed to be evangelistic and mission-minded. In his description of the American Mennonite awakening to mission work, which first stirred in the last decades of the nineteenth century, Theron Schlabach says,

The activist mood ran contrary to earlier, self-effacing American Mennonitism. But was it nevertheless a revival of the evangelistic spirit of sixteenth-century Anabaptists? Probably not. Rather than that, it seemed akin to the culturally self-confident, sometimes almost cocky, "Onward Christian Soldiers" mood of

---

[53]Taylor, *Secular Age*, 650. See also Martin, *Breaking of the Image*, 63–4.
[54]Taylor defines a secular age as "one in which the eclipse of all goals beyond human flourishing becomes conceivable; or better, it falls within the range of an imaginable life for millions of people." Taylor, *Secular Age*, 19–20.

the modern Protestant missionary movement that had become so strong in the nineteenth century. And that was apparently quite different from the *Gelassenheit* and *Nachfolge* (yieldedness and discipleship) of which sixteenth-century Anabaptists spoke so often. Borrowing from the modern missionary movement enabled aggressive Mennonites to be religious and still not want to be "nobody," still want to "make something of oneself."[55]

With time, Mennonites have become more sensitized to the way this tradition of *Gelassenheit* was implicated in a sinister form of violence against women and others who did not have the power to assert their voices. As Mennonite theologian Ted Koontz writes,

> our commitment to and understanding of nonresistance has permitted other evils to thrive as well—evils connected more to the piety or spirit or personality of nonresistance than to its social ethics. For example, teaching on nonresistance can easily perpetuate a "doormat" view of the self and create feelings of being unvalued, uncared for. It can lead people, particularly women who are socialized to "give of themselves," to accept being devalued or abused in ways which are not "gospel" or "good news."[56]

Thus, the nonresistant tradition of suffering, humility, and self-abnegation, which began in the sixteenth century as an opportunity for the commoner to get on the path toward holiness and access to God, began to be suspected in the twentieth century as a tool for elite, white males to exercise control over the church and imprison the weak in their victimhood, as Taylor shows this too is in keeping with secularity's long quest to affirm ordinary human life.

And so, secularity challenges the possibility and location of nonresistance for Mennonites. It separates the sphere of church and state, calling into question the vocation of the church to be the place where the sword is removed from human affairs. It sets aside religious sanctification and claims to reduce violence dramatically through human instrumental means. And it criticizes the humility

---

[55]"Reveille for Die Stillen Im Lande," 221.
[56]Ted Koontz, "Grace to You and Peace: Nonresistance as Piety," *Mennonite Quarterly Review* 69, no. 3 (1995): 356.

and yieldedness to suffering earlier demanded by a mindset that located ultimate human meaning in the crucifixion. In these conditions, it is hard to be a gospel pacifist. Unity in difference becomes a fraught relation.

Responses to the Unity in Diversity of Mennonites in Secularity

Questions of unity in difference have always been important existential and theological questions for Mennonites. What does it mean to be "worldly" and is the appropriate difference from the world still being maintained by this or that practice? The awakening to mission within the twentieth century goaded these questions to new intensity. Difference from the world was no longer adequate. Now separation was to be combined with a responsibility to the world. Assimilated Mennonite churches still tried to maintain the language of being an "alternative story" to the world; the challenge was now to achieve a difference without the outer, geographical, linguistic, and sartorial distinctions that had earlier made uniqueness clear. But having rid itself of traditional markers of non-worldliness, and then finding even its nonviolence welcomed and included in influential parts of society, Mennonites had a lot of work to do to establish their identity.

Much twentieth-century Mennonite theology written on the theme of peace and nonviolence is seeking to secure a place for this ethic within the affinities and resistances of secularity that we have just outlined. Was pacifism to be an item of perpetual *difference* from the world, the reason for a withdrawal from efforts at human flourishing, the prophetic *critique* of society, and the reason why Christians could *not* become involved? Or was it to be the church's very "selling point" and gift to those who otherwise rejected the church's dogma? Was this perhaps the confident contribution Mennonites could offer a world grown weary of the orgies of violence the world descended to in the twentieth century? Could pacifism be directly "effective" in resolving national and global conflict or was it a form of "faithfulness" that could only be effective indirectly as martyrdom, or at best, as a sectarian church presence? Because the pacifist stance was now "in the world" in a way it had not been before, the necessity of broader articulation in a theological voice became evident if ethics was to be included in the new missional urgency to incarnate this gospel to unbelievers and non-Mennonites.[57]

Mennonite Peace Theology: A Panorama of Types, a work edited by John Richard Burkholder and Barbara Nelson Gingerich, is an important publication that took an inventory of ten distinct varieties of pacifism advocated by Mennonites in contemporary North America.[58] For our purposes here of indicating basic approaches to unity in difference over against the world of secularity, I have chosen three of these types: historic nonresistance, messianic-community pacifism, and progressive realist pacifism. My purpose is not to make a critique but only to offer a glimpse of how recent Mennonite theology has sought to navigate these issues of pacifism within secularity.

Historic nonresistance is represented by Harold Bender and Guy Hershberger.[59] Burkholder describes this position as the "baseline" North American Mennonite peace position. It includes an emphasis on the literal obedience to Matthew 5, is expressed in conscientious objection from military service, seeks alternatives to violence in other areas of life and largely assumes the church's withdrawal from statecraft, though not from society otherwise.[60] Bender and

---

[57]It can also be said that the possibility of a peace *theology* became evident at this point in history. Dogmatics such as Karl Barth's and exegesis such as Oscar Cullman's made it possible for Mennonites to imagine their earlier more implicit and in-house maintenance of the doctrine speaking within a larger, more respectable field.

[58]John Richard Burkholder and Barbara Nelson Gingerich, eds., *Mennonite Peace Theology: A Panorama of Types* (Akron: Mennonite Central Committee Peace Office, 1991). These are (1) historic nonresistance (Bender, Hershberger, Wenger), (2) culturally engaged pacifism (Dutch-Russian Mennonites), (3) social responsibility (Lawrence Burkholder), (4) apolitical nonresistance (*The Sword and Trumpet*), (5) Messianic community pacifism (Yoder), (6) radical pacifism (Ronald Sider), (7) realist pacifism (Duane Friesen), (8) Canadian pacifism (John H. Redekop), (9) liberation pacifism (Arnold Snyder), and (10) neo-sectarian pacifism (Ted Koontz).

[59]Bender, "Anabaptist Vision"; Guy F. Hershberger, *War, Peace, and Nonresistance* (Scottdale, PA: Herald, 2009); J. C. Wenger, *Introduction to Theology* (Scottdale, PA: Herald, 1954) are exponents of this early stage of Mennonite theological reflection on pacifism.

[60]Burkholder and Gingerich, *Mennonite Peace Theology*, 6. While these are theologians at work, a full theological basis for pacifism is still in the future. Bender and Hershberger make appeals to scriptures but make relatively little attempt to think through doctrines of ecclesiology, pneumatology, soteriology, and the doctrine of God proper in their articulation of pacifism.

his colleagues devoted themselves tirelessly to building the visible structures and institutions of the Mennonite church in accordance with their vision of Anabaptism.

What set this mid-century articulation apart from earlier Mennonite writing was its new claim to establish an *historical* link between early Anabaptism and normative Mennonite faith for the twentieth century.[61] While Thieleman von Bragt was also in his way doing historical work in *The Martyrs Mirror*, there is a significant distance between von Bragt and Bender. Von Bragt's work is hagiographic and iconic. It was a historical portrait that offered itself as a site of communion and prayer. Bender sought an academically responsible scientific reconstruction of history that would give his church a story to stand on. It was this historical argument that was to help calibrate Mennonite unity in difference. In fact, no explication of Mennonite pacifism before or since has made itself so dependent upon a specific historical portrait of early Anabaptism.

Rejecting centuries of negative dismissal by Lutheran and Calvinist historians, this generation sought to show that the Anabaptists were the "culmination of the Reformation."[62] Bender and his colleagues believed that in this way an identity for Mennonites could be created over against modernity and over against the whole modernist/fundamentalist polarity, a Mennonite identity that was nevertheless not dependent on separatism. According to biographer Albert Keim, Bender's epoch-making essay, "The Anabaptist Vision," gave assimilating Mennonites a "useable past."[63]

Though Bender was concerned about the history of Anabaptism in a distinctly modern way, his aim was not to encourage modern Mennonites to sit comfortably within secular North America, believing their ancestors had been the very progenitors of modern freedom and democracy. Bender resisted the temptation to legitimize Anabaptists by making their chief contribution the gift of modern freedom and democracy. In "The Anabaptist Vision," Bender happily grants Rufus M. Jones his claim that Anabaptism

---

[61]Sawatsky, *History and Ideology*, is the foundational text that examines Mennonites' use of history within the twentieth century to shape their identity.

[62]Bender, "Anabaptist Vision," 74.

[63]Albert N. Keim, *Harold S. Bender, 1897–1962* (Scottdale, PA: Herald, 1998), 327.

is the first plain announcement in modern history of a programme for a new type of Christian society which the modern world, especially in America and England, has been slowly realizing—an absolutely free and independent religious society, and a State in which every man counts as a man, and has his share in shaping both Church and State.[64]

Because of this sentence, writers such as Hans-Jürgen Goertz have overemphasized Bender's identification with these Anglo-American ideals. Goertz says that Bender's "description exercised a pacifying, relaxing effect upon the Mennonites of North America and Europe," which alleviated their prophetic dissonance with modernity. Bender, according to Goertz, thought "Anabaptists must be restricted to figures presentable to the contemporary Western world."[65] However, Bender's larger concern in this essay is to prevent any relegation of Anabaptism to the status of primal modernists.[66] "Great as is the Anabaptist contribution to the development of religious liberty, this concept not only does not exhaust but actually fails to define the true essence of Anabaptism." The true essence of Anabaptism was "a new conception of the essence of Christianity as discipleship, second, a new conception of the church as a brotherhood; and third, a new ethic of love and nonresistance."[67] He proceeded to demonstrate the intense commitment of the Anabaptists to order the holy life in communities separated from the world and patterned after the early church.

Bender's "Anabaptist Vision," in my view, established as normative, via a selective reading of Anabaptist history, a Mennonitism that distilled gritty "discipleship" as the motif enabling them to live

---

[64]Bender, "Anabaptist Vision," 67.
[65]Hans-Jürgen Goertz, "The Confessional Heritage in Its New Mold: What Is Mennonite Self-Understanding Today?" in *Mennonite Identity: Historical and Contemporary Perspectives*, ed. Calvin Wall Redekop and Samuel J. Steiner (Lanham, MD: University Press of America, 1988), 6–8.
[66]He was consciously resisting Roland Bainton's contemporary interpretation asserting that Anabaptists were the "left-wing" of the Reformation. Bainton had concluded that the regulative principle of the Anabaptists was their separation of church and state. This led to an interpretation of Anabaptism as proto-individualism. Bainton's explicit motive in writing his essay was to demonstrate the cleavage (in 1941) between Germany and the "West": Germany had rejected the liberal ideals of the Anabaptists while England and America had accepted them. The outcome in Nazi barbarity was the fruit of this rejection. Roland H. Bainton, "The Left Wing of the Reformation," *Journal of Religion* 21, no. 2 (1941): 124–34.
[67]Bender, "Anabaptist Vision," 78.

against the world.[68] This was a bracing moral agenda that distilled and ramped up the ideal of Christ-centered obedience as a bulwark against the world in order to restore the World War II–era Mennonite church to a position of being over-against its militaristic nation. Christians who followed the Anabaptists "must consequently withdraw from the worldly system and create a Christian social order within the fellowship of the church brotherhood."[69] Surely, Bender seemed to reason this was more than could be expected of Protestant fundamentalists or liberals.

Another key aspect of *historic nonresistance* was its acceptance of Robert Friedmann's critical distinction between the spirit of Anabaptism and Pietism. Pietism, according to Friedmann was fixated on the sweet, inner well-being of the saint and lacked the gritty obedience by which the disciples provoked suffering.[70] Some have seen within this Bender-school rejection of Pietism the unwitting diminishment of the spiritual tradition of Anabaptism, a tradition which had made it amenable to Pietism, rather than contrasted from it.[71] This inadvertently resulted in a twentieth-century pacifism not only loosened from the spiritual resources of its tradition but also sitting loose from a personal experience of salvation in Jesus.[72]

Nonresistance, Bender claimed, "was thoroughly believed and resolutely practiced by all the original Anabaptist Brethren and their

[68]It must be asked how the "Vision" changed in the translation of "*Nachfolge Christi*" as "discipleship." In this writer's judgment there is an abstracting that occurs in that translation, a loss of the relational aspect of earlier Anabaptist ethics.
[69]Bender, "Anabaptist Vision," 88.
[70]"The pietist ceased to lay the emphasis upon the outer life which was in any case unsatisfactory, but rather upon the pure inner perfecting of holiness, on the possession of Christ in prayer, song, sacrament, and fellowship." Robert Friedmann, "Anabaptism and Pietism I," *Mennonite Quarterly Review* 14, no. 2 (1940): 97.
[71]See, for example, the essay by John D Roth, "Pietism and the Anabaptist Soul," in *The Dilemma of Anabaptist Piety: Strengthening Or Straining the Bonds of Community?*, ed. Stephen L. Longenecker and Ronald C. Arnett (Bridgewater: Forum for Religious Studies, Bridgewater College, 1997). Roth argues that Friedmann has seriously underplayed key historical, theological, and spiritual continuities between the traditions.
[72]This is surely an unintended consequence of Bender's approach to Anabaptism. In seeking to articulate something distinct about Anabaptism, Bender assumed many things that later could not be assumed. This reality is explored in Stephen F. Dintaman, "The Spiritual Poverty of the Anabaptist Vision," *Conrad Grebel Review* 10, no. 2 (1992): 205–8.

descendants throughout Europe from the beginning until the last century."[73] They held this view before Quakers emerged and in a time when "both Catholic and Protestant churches not only endorsed war as an instrument of state policy, but employed it in religious conflicts." While Bender acknowledges a certain continuity between the Anabaptist free-church concept and modern secular notions of liberty and individualism, he sees no continuity there for pacifism.[74]

And yet, viewed now with the trajectory of secularity we have seen as a backdrop, it can be pointed out that the "Anabaptist Vision" prioritized that stream of Anabaptism that best fit with emerging sixteenth-century notions of order and civility. It left behind the holy war Anabaptism of Bernard Rothman, the apocalyptic pacifism of Hans Hut, and the spiritualistic pacifism of Hans Denk, Leonard Schiemer, and Hans Schlaffer. It focused on the sober dualistic pacifism of the Swiss Anabaptists and the Hutterites as well as the moderate dualistic pacifism of Marpeck and Menno Simons. Bender's Anabaptist pacifists were those who held to a strict separation of church and state and exercised due discipline to maintain *ordnung* in the fellowship.

Though the Bender generation could be seen as distilling a "naked" historic Anabaptism that was useable in modern North America, they nevertheless "clothed" this Anabaptism through a heroic generation of institution building. By developing Mennonite colleges, publishing houses, academic journals, and mission agencies this generation sought to preserve an Anabaptism that was both Christ-centred, unstained by the world, and responsible to and for the world in its own limited way.

Historic nonresistance sought therefore to establish, using modern historical-critical tools, a form of modern discipleship that would stand against the world without complete withdrawal. It also underplayed the spiritual, mystical aspects of the tradition, focusing more on obedience. This was a key way in which Mennonites sought to live their unity in difference in the twentieth century.

Messianic-community pacifism is represented by John Howard Yoder.[75] In many ways there is a seamless development between Bender and Yoder. Yoder continued the emphasis on discipleship

---

[73]Bender, "Anabaptist Vision," 86–7.
[74]This is the argument of Bender, "Pacifism of the Sixteenth Century Anabaptists."
[75]Yoder's legacy has been grievously complicated by his history of abuse toward women. This present work can be seen as an attempt to move beyond Yoderian categories in Mennonite theology. However, his continuing influence cannot be denied.

and retained a strong instinct to direct the church against the world. He was deeply concerned about the way Mennonites had "sold out" and he critiqued the earlier Bender–Hershberger school for being too confined to the denominationalism of Mennonites in North America.[76] To be different from the world for Yoder was not about creating distinctive Mennonite church institutions.

Yoder cast his vision in the second half of the century when the cultural noninvolvement of Mennonites in society was being severely criticized, and new words such as social justice, nonviolent resistance, and peacemaking were naming a positive ambition to influence the direction of society toward peaceableness. Yoder extended Mennonite exposure to the broader ecumenical community where he was challenged to frame his pacifism vis-à-vis Protestant and Roman Catholic theological and ethical categories.

The literature by and about Yoder is vast, and his legacy is now hopelessly complicated by his own sexual violence that has come to light.[77] Here we will lay out the tension between two poles that Yoder sought to keep taut in his argument for unity in difference throughout his life.[78] At the one pole, in his description of Jesus and the church, Yoder engages in a lifelong drive to the historical, socio-ethical, human reality of God's nonviolent, loving action in time. Yoder picks up on both the Anabaptist emphasis on *Nachfolge Christi* as attentiveness to the human choices and actions of Christ and Bender's location of gritty discipleship as the central motif of Anabaptism. He wields this concern for the concrete as an unrelenting insistence that God is to be understood and followed as the One acting in history to direct its flow. This emphasis on the historical, concrete actions of God in Christ is the hermeneutical key by which Yoder determines what is a genuine faith and church. He seeks to get rid of all individualist, pietistic, spiritualist, or metaphysical moves that abstract or insulate the church from

---

[76]John Howard Yoder, "Anabaptist Vision and Mennonite Reality," *John Howard Yoder Digital Library*, accessed October 16, 2015, http://replica.palni.edu/cdm/ref/collection/p15705coll18/id/3618.

[77]On Yoder's actions that the Mennonite Church's response, see especially Rachel Waltner Goosen, "'Defanging the Beast': Mennonite Responses to John Howard Yoder's Sexual Abuse," *Mennonite Quarterly Review* 89, no. 1 (2015): 7–80.

[78]Yoder wrote relatively little devoted solely to arguing for pacifism. His argument for pacifism is almost always part of a larger argument for the kind of church he thought Jesus had in mind, and for the way such a church would interact with the world.

becoming the social *polis* that Jesus called together over against the powers of his time and ours. For Yoder, pacifism is the name for a set of ecclesial but always-human practices lived out in the to and fro of history. He resists Reinhold Niebuhr's assertion that pacifism such as Mennonites practiced was an irrelevant symbol that had no answer to the challenges of history. Pacifism is part of the new social dynamic actually created by the church's embodiment of the eschatological breaking in of the Kingdom of God into the grind of history. As such, Yoder's definition of Christian faithfulness is described in relentlessly ethical categories.[79] And also as such, this definition of discipleship is decidedly *achievable* in this present life. There is little need to allow for ambiguity and patience in so far as one is waiting to live the life of Jesus on earth.

And yet, and here is the second pole, the contours of this concrete, historically embedded, achievable social reality can never be determined by what he calls "the theology of the natural."[80] All forms of "the theology of the natural" seek "guidance from common sense and the nature of things" and erroneously believe that "it is by studying the realities around us, not by hearing a proclamation from God that we discern the right." Yoder was not necessarily opposed to all formulations of natural law or of the created orders; what he was opposed to was any expectation that these entities could arrive at the church already formed and demanding the church recognize their epistemological sovereignty.[81] The political community of Jesus must be rebuilt from the ground up in defiance of customary practice through a hearing of the scriptures. Here is Yoder's campaign against "natural" notions of effectiveness, such as he felt Reinhold Niebuhr taught.

---

[79]Yoder consistently advocated his claim "that the Christian life is defined most basically in ethical terms. While forgiveness, membership in a social order, participation on worship, or receiving a revelation may all be very relevant factors, they do not rob *obedience in ethics (Nachfolge)* of primary rank." John Howard Yoder, "The Anabaptist Dissent: The Logic of the Place of the Disciple in Society," *Concern* 1 (June 1954): 45. Emphasis original.

[80]John Howard Yoder, *The Politics of Jesus*, 2nd ed. (Grand Rapids, MI: Eerdmans, 1994), 20. Here Yoder gives several examples of how this "theology of the natural" is seen; the Reformation's ethic of "vocation" or "station"; the "currently popular form of the "ethic of the situation" or in older catholic forms of natural law.

[81]Paul Martens, "With the Grain of the Universe: Reexamining the Alleged Nonviolent Rejection of Natural Law," *Journal of the Society of Christian Ethics* 32, no. 2 (2012): 113–31.

For Yoder then, the gospel was concrete, this-worldly, and historical but rooted in the lordly voice of Jesus as mediated by the scriptures, resisting reduction to "common sense." In the tension between these poles Yoder was envisioning the church as a deeply human reality living its life within the world on the plain of time and space, but nevertheless not established by common human realities. Pietism, spiritualism, and Constantinianism were all in their various ways the slackening of the tension between these two poles.[82]

Yoder's mighty attempt to maintain the tension between these two poles led Mennonites (and many others) to "historicalize" traditional nonresistance into "secular" practices such as conflict mediation, restorative justice, community development, and nonviolent protest.[83] No longer was the pacifist's exemption from the draft the main concern, but a new interest arose in the nonviolence of the church's witness in a host of society-influencing practices. This can be seen as the outcome of the first pole. The fruit of the second concern is not as obvious, but Yoder has provoked a whole generation of ethicists to be more careful and attentive to whether their proposals are in fact *Christian* and scriptural in any determinative way.[84] We cannot allow worldly agendas to compromise our ethics if they are to truly be Christian.

---

[82]There have been strong voices questioning whether Yoder's ideal of the church was finally as dependent on the scriptures as he claimed. His description of the historical concreteness of the gospel community seemed, to some, rather modern and secular, and not actually needing Jesus in the end. A. James Reimer held forth this critique in much of his writing. See for example, "Mennonites, Christ and Culture: The Yoder Legacy," in *Mennonites and Classical Theology* (Kitchener, ON: Pandora, 2001), 288–99. See also Paul Martens, *The Heterodox Yoder* (Eugene, OR: Wipf and Stock, 2012).

[83]The most extensive exploration of "effective" nonviolent action in Yoder's writings may be the section called "Effective Peacemaking Practices: The Case for Proactive Alternatives to Violence" in the book published posthumously as John Howard Yoder, *The War of the Lamb: The Ethics of Nonviolence and Peacemaking* (Grand Rapids, MI: Brazos, 2009), 123–98.

[84]Stanley Hauerwas's extolling of Yoder is key in mediating this influence. Richard Mouw speaks for many when he says, "My own wrestlings with [*The Politics of Jesus*] ... have forever shaped the ways in which I think about questions of violence and the normativity of Jesus' redemptive ministry for the patterns of our social-political witness." As quoted in Mark Thiessen Nation, *John Howard Yoder: Mennonite Patience, Evangelical Witness, Catholic Convictions* (Grand Rapids, MI: Eerdmans, 2006), 126.

But here again, as Bender's pacifism was distanced from the spiritual heritage of Anabaptism by its allergy to Pietism, Yoder's Jesus was not primarily accessed through prayer and the disciplines of *Gelassenheit* that earlier Mennonite devotion seemed to assume. Historical critical exegesis rather than an experience of spiritual union was central. It would be difficult to write a book exploring the role of prayer in Yoder's theology, since these practices play only a minor role.[85] He advocated for a communal-centric approach to discerning the scriptures that was open to historical-critical discoveries. Yoder also had little patience for the way Mennonite churches had carefully worked out a *Gelassenheit* in their relation with the world over centuries of Mennonite life. Mennonite life was more a compromise of the politics of Jesus than an example. This too speaks to a secularizing aspect within his thought, an impatience with the ambiguous nature of the church's faithfulness across generations. It was not an inner spiritual union with Christ worked toward with much failure and weakness over time that fueled his vision, but the courage to obey Jesus in achieving sociopolitical outposts of the Kingdom of God.

A key question regarding Yoder is the extent to which he influences today's peace and justice studies in Mennonite academics. His own sexual violence has made this a charged issue. But even beyond this dilemma, Stephen Dintaman's point needs to be heard:

> Yoder's *Politics of Jesus* became the bible of a new activism that took the concrete economic patterns of Jubilee and Jesus' commitment to absolute nonviolence and made them a kind of canon within the canon for Anabaptist social activism. But having traveled across the bridge and moved from sectarian separatism to world engaging activism, it also became possible to burn the bridge. A strange reality of the current generation of Mennonite social thinkers and peace activists is that while Yoder's significance is recognized and usually praised, his work, or at least his work beyond *The Politics of Jesus*, is not widely read and discussed. Current social thinking in Mennonite colleges and social service

---

[85]Yoder occasionally gives lip service to the earlier spirituality of *Gelassenheit* but personal spirituality cannot be said to be a decisive component of his theological ethics. Craig Carter states this in an otherwise sympathetic engagement. *The Politics of the Cross: The Theology and Social Ethics of John Howard Yoder* (Grand Rapids, MI: Brazos, 2001), 237. Cf. Yoder, *The Politics of Jesus*, 17–18.

programs is focused primarily on social analysis, a commitment to working at social justice, and highly developed, pioneering programs for teaching and practicing "conflict transformation." ... Nonviolent action directed to increasing peace and justice has become a kind of self-authenticating program that hardly needs theological rationales beyond "that's what Jesus called us to do."[86]

This echoes my earlier, rather brash statement that at this juncture assimilated Mennonites already know what does the Lord require of them before they come to church.

Historic nonresistance and Messianic-community pacifism could be described as pacifisms of difference, as they generally sought to resist the straightforward continuities between traditional nonresistance and this-worldly nonviolence. Our third type, *progressive realist pacifism*, has sought to demonstrate similarity and compatibility rather than difference. Often associated with Dutch/Russian Mennonites as opposed to the Swiss Mennonites of the Bender/Yoder variety, these theologians draw on a tradition going back to nineteenth-century Russian Mennonite engagement with culture that was much more at home in statecraft and other societal involvement.[87] As a broad generalization this form of pacifism has been more at home in the Canadian context.[88]

An early exemplar of this direction is H. P. Krehbiel, a Mennonite leader who, in 1909, served in the Kansas legislature. His book, *War, Peace, and Amity*, published in 1937, appeared while Mennonites were grappling with their dismal experience during World War I on the one hand, and the proliferation of "peace committees" across the Protestant churches calling for an end to war on the other.[89] Krehbiel took the side of embracing the new ecumenical optimism in condemning war. His theological basis for this was a conviction

---

[86]Stephen F. Dintaman, "On Flushing the Confessional Rabbit out of the Socio-Ecclesial Brushpile," *Conrad Grebel Review* 24, no. 2 (2006): 33–49.
[87]See Lauren Friesen's essay, "Culturally Engaged Pacifism," in Burkholder and Gingerich, *Mennonite Peace Theology*, 15–25.
[88]John H. Redekop describes Canadian pacifism as having a more positive view of the state, being more comfortable in joint ventures with the state, and having a deeper history of political involvement than its more Swiss-dominated American counterpart. Ibid., 60–1.
[89]Paul Toews, "The Long Weekend or the Short Week: Mennonite Peace Theology, 1925–1944," *Mennonite Quarterly Review* 60, no. 1 (1986): 38–57.

that "the cause of Christ cannot be defeated" and that Jesus will
eventually disturb and teach the world to reject its warfare over
time.[90] He called for a decisive separation of the church and state,
with the church attending to spiritual and ethical matters, and the
state looking after the body in secular affairs. The state, however,
depended on the church to develop peace-loving "amitists." In this
way, Krehbiel expected the church to have a great impact on the
future of the nation. He did not accept that the church itself needed
a political agenda, but what we see in Krehbiel is an ambitious,
positive anticipation that a church committed to the nonviolent
love of Christ will eventually produce those kinds of citizens who,
when they become involved in government, will gradually move the
nation to the illegalization of war and private arms.

> Christianity is a New Way of life, which revolutionizes the
> religious, spiritual, moral, social, economic and political life,
> not only that of the individual, but in spreading, also that of the
> community, and ultimately it is destined to transform all religious,
> ethical, social, political and governmental institutions, bringing
> them ever nearer the standards of Jesus Christ the Lord.[91]

In Krehbiel we see a Mennonite theology of culture that believes
that its message of peace will be welcomed in society and that this
can make real differences in how nations conduct their affairs.[92]

Duane Friesen is a more recent writer who picked up this impulse
and has argued that the church is a

> people who are called by God to embody an alternative cultural
> vision to the dominant culture of North America, and at the
> same time, a people whose purpose is not to withdraw into safe
> sectarian enclaves but rather to be a "presence" in the dominant
> culture by "seeking the shalom of the city" wherever the church
> exists.[93]

[90]H. P. Krehbiel, *War, Peace, Amity* (Self-published, 1937), 191.
[91]Ibid.
[92]Toews, "Long Weekend or the Short Week," 51.
[93]Duane K. Friesen, "Toward a Theology of Culture: A Dialogue with John H Yoder
and Gordon Kaufman," *Conrad Grebel Review* 16, no. 2 (1998): 39. Friesen's most
extensive work on a theology of culture is *Artists, Citizens, Philosophers: Seeking the
Peace of the City: An Anabaptist Theology of Culture* (Scottdale, PA: Herald, 2000).

In Friesen we can see the anti-Niebuhrian reaction of Mennonites at its strongest. Friesen insists that the *agape* love of Jesus can and will work over time within groups and is not a merely personal principle.[94] Following Gordon Kaufman (another Mennonite in this tradition), he considers theological ethics as the task of constructing God as a "symbol" that orients the world toward a creative and fruitful future of shalom.[95]

His suggestions have a pragmatic dimension that expect to be tested on the street and effect real change in the most desperate contexts. Following Sally McFague[96] to suggest that "process" is the fundamental reality we work with, whether in describing God or ourselves within culture, Friesen sets out to describe a theology of culture that is both attuned to the alternative values and ideals which he sees embodied in Jesus, and the realities of life in the modern world. To this end his pacifism is at once decidedly mainstream Mennonite, sounding quite like Yoder at places, but also much more positive about the possibility of nonviolent witness actually cohering with the construction of a real society.

Writers in this *progressive realist* school do not accept culture uncritically. However, this is a distinct path taken by some Anabaptist theologians to grant more weight to the values and goals of culture to shape the church's language and discourse about God. The church must seek to embody the deep agenda of the world as society struggles with its existence, and craft a theology that will move the world in the direction of peace. Of the three types we have surveyed here, this impulse would be the most at home in secularity, and the most optimistic that the way of Jesus can be embodied by secular people, even if only unconsciously.

These then are three kinds of argument by Mennonite theologians to help their churches grapple with what it means to be gospel pacifists in a secular age that, while still violent, is providing more

---

[94]He accuses J. Lawrence Burkholder of succumbing to Nieburian despair in his grim assessment of the compromises for which peacemakers need to be prepared in the "real world." J. Lawrence. Burkholder, *The Limits of Perfection: Conversations with J. Lawrence Burkholder*, ed. Rodney Sawatsky and Scott Holland (Waterloo: Institute of Anabaptist-Mennonite Studies, 1993), 130–1.

[95]Friesen, though adapting Kaufman's starting point in crafting such a theology that yields creative nonviolence, nevertheless retains a stronger sense of the church as an alternative society which stands against prevailing norms. *Artists, Citizens, Philosophers*, 69–71.

[96]Friesen, "Toward a Theology of Culture," 61.

latitude for nonviolent methods to effect cultural change. Against the shifting context of conscientious objection, the new possibilities held out by the civil rights movement, and the rise of the welfare state, among many factors, it became possible to dream that one could have it all: one could remain devoted to Jesus, belong to a church that is decidedly different than the world, and yet offer the Christian ethic as something achievable, to varying extents, beyond Christian commitment.

What is noteworthy for our project is that in all three, the personal experience of mingling with the suffering presence of Christ in the world as we saw in early Anabaptism and the *Martyrs Mirror* is no longer the dominant motif.[97] *Gelassenheit* does not fit. It is my own observation that with the nigh impossible dilemma of unity in difference that Mennonites sought to solve in the twentieth century, it was this aspect that needed to be left in the background, or so it was felt. To say it differently, twentieth-century Mennonites were no longer willing to wait until a soul-deep, almost mystical union with Christ had achieved its results, either in personal, ecclesial, or societal transformation.

Conclusion

We come now to the conclusion of our attempts to grasp the place that pacifist ethics have played in Mennonite life in the preceding five centuries. We have been grappling with an abiding tension in the life of the Mennonite church. On the one had we have glimpsed a nonviolence rooted in a personal union with Christ, and entered into in ways best described as mystical. As it developed in the sixteenth century and as it was transposed into a spiritual participation in a communion of saints by the *Martyrs Mirror*, nonresistance was the result of a determination to be drawn up into the very actions and postures of the Incarnate Christ. Through this mystical, personal union, the attitude of Christ toward his enemies and the power structures of his day became the Christian's. Via believer's baptism,

---

[97]Which is not to say that any of these three groups would be inherently opposed to "spirituality" as an aspect of social ethics; quite the opposite. But in none of them is a real-time spiritual experience of union with the suffering Christ, as described in the *Martyrs Mirror*, the crucial issue.

a Christian came to share in the communion of the defenseless Christians at which Jesus stood as head.

But the very success of this vision of intense union with Christ then resulted in a personal and communal life that was just what modernizing societies were looking for. In a world seeking to overcome the brutal barbarity of late-medieval life, in a world weary of futile religious wars, and in a world glimpsing for the first time the possibilities of unlimited economic expansion, Mennonite pacifistic life was attractive. Even if Mennonite pacifism was primally grounded in a personal union with Christ, what society rewarded was civility, a fruitful, attractive life that epitomized the goal of the secularizing trajectory to create ordered peaceful and prosperous societies, disciplined all the way down to every commoner, and affirming of ordinary human life. Leaving pacifism only at the level of union with Christ seemed to leave it withdrawn from society. At that level it struggled to account for the missional aspect of the church, which also came to the fore with the advance of an instrumental, can-do approach to the world that modernity encouraged.

Pacifism strictly at the level of personal union with Christ could also be vulnerable to secularity's long critique of *Gelassenheit* as anti-humanist. Was this spirituality even good for people? Did it solve any of our problems? Did it help us live happier, fuller, more satisfying lives, or was it only a form of sin suppression? Was it evangelistic, drawing people to the joy and strength of renewal in Christ? Could it offer assurance of salvation?

And so, in the twentieth century, questions of faithfulness versus effectiveness became acute. If what we have is such a fresh alternative to what the world is growing weary of, could we not find ways to offer it that don't demand the personal union with Christ, and don't have *Gelassenheit*'s troubling anti-humanism? Strange allies appeared on the horizon, not all confessing faith in Christ.

But in light of the need for greater clarity on the unity in difference between nonresistance in the Mennonite tradition and similar but not identical concerns in general society, North American Mennonites have neither turned to a recovery of the earlier spirituality of mystical union with the human and divine Christ, nor to a rediscovery of the function of believer's baptism in inducting the believer into a communion of defenseless Christians. Rather, in the three broad patterns we have surveyed, attempts have been made to redress the situation through the creation of a historical normative Anabaptism, through the creation of "discipleship" as the translation of this normative Anabaptism, and through the theological and exegetical work of demonstrating the political, socio-ethical relevance of a Messianic community. They have also turned to a more pragmatic confidence in immersing oneself in the culture and applying the lessons of the alternative community of Jesus to the problems at hand and gradually influencing directions. Our project here should not be seen as rejecting the abundantly scriptural instincts that each of these three paths have shown us in their own ways. However, it is the argument of this book that work needs to be done at a dogmatic level, and at a spiritual level, that draws up but ultimately goes beyond the categories that have so far been explored for unity in difference.

By the end of the twentieth century, not all were satisfied with these options.[98] Stephen F. Dintaman's 1992 essay, "The Spiritual Poverty of the Anabaptist Vision," described the way Bender's "Anabaptist Vision," as it had been taken up by Yoder, Friesen, and company, ended up securing a peace ethic at the cost of losing the transformative aspects of grace.[99] Bender assumed larger doctrines about the nature of Christ, the Trinity, and the Spirit's work of sanctification but did not state them, leaving an arid description of ethics. It also left the church without spiritual power and depth, a strangely Pelagian community that was unable to address the failures in its own midst. The church cannot live by ethics alone, Dintaman said. The thunderous response to Dintaman from the Mennonite community, much of it positive, suggests that Mennonite academic

---

[98]There is a small but growing literature diagnosing the irrelevance of theology for modern Mennonite ethics. See the work of Paul Martens in "How Mennonite Theology Became Superfluous in Three Easy Steps: Bender, Yoder, Weaver," *Journal of Mennonite Studies* 33 (2015): 149–66, and *The Heterodox Yoder* (Eugene, OR: Wipf and Stock, 2012). See also Thomas N. Finger, "Did Yoder Reduce Theology to Ethics," in *A Mind Patient and Untamed: Assessing John Howard Yoder's Contributions to Theology, Ethics, and Peacemaking*, ed. Ben C. Ollenburger and Gayle Gerber Koontz (Telford, PA: Cascadia, 2004), 318–39. Dallas E Wiebe's startling essay "Can a Mennonite Be an Atheist," *The Conrad Grebel Review* 16, no. 3 (1998): 122–32 argues that the best of Mennonite ethics is available to atheists as well as believers. The wide-ranging discussion about Anabaptism and the creeds could also be entered as an exhibit in this deliberation. Alain Epp Weaver, "Missionary Christology: John Howard Yoder and the Creeds," *Mennonite Quarterly Review* 74, no. 3 (2000): 423–39 is a place to enter this conversation.
[99]Stephen F. Dintaman, "The Spiritual Poverty of the Anabaptist Vision," *Conrad Grebel Review* 10, no. 2 (1992): 205–8.

attempts to transfer Mennonite pacifism into the secular age had now left many unsure how it was still a Christian ethic.[100]

The large question that forms a hinge between the two sections of this book asks: Could a personal, mystical union with the Christ who entered this world and engaged with evil in an utterly loving, self-less gift of himself for the world's reconciliation with God, pace our steps as we walk in this secularized world? Could such a *Gelassenheit* actually link us to the very mission of God in which the human person, though losing herself, nevertheless paradoxically finds an infinite fulfillment at last?

---

[100]The current schisms in the Mennonite churches over sexuality are still too close for objective historical analysis, but this may also be exposing a deep ambivalence over how, exactly, modern civility is related to Scriptural union with Christ.

3

Incarnation: Bidirectional Nonresistance

Back to Nonresistance

We now turn to the constructive work of exploring Hans Urs von Balthasar's Christology for wisdom in living with the dilemma between union with Christ and civility that gospel pacifism labors under. This may seem like an abrupt turn, but my hope is that the dilemma we observed in the last section will stay in mind as we look at Balthasar's Christology. In order to "hike along the sharp ridge between the kingdom of God and the kingdom of this world" that Balthasar described in our introduction, we need our eyes fixed on Jesus, and this is what dogma is for.

In the next three chapters I want to describe a divine descent that Balthasar articulated in his theology that can be captured by three words: incarnation, provocation, and convocation. God enters human history in Christ provoking two responses, either the violence of post-Christian revolt or the fraternal love of ecclesial adoration. It is this trajectory that I hold to be the divine action faith contemplates and unifies with as a dogmatic momentum in ethics. This dogmatic momentum acts as a gyroscope keeping us in step with Jesus as we seek to live the life of Christ in ways that risk but does not succumb to the secularizing tendency. In this chapter, we begin in incarnation.

I am claiming that the traditional practice and spirituality of nonresistance (*Wehrlosigkeit*) as it has been practiced by pacifist communities like the Mennonites should assume its theological form and chart its spiritual path as participation in Christ's *bidirectional* nonresistance, at once a nonresistance to his Father and an

openness to the beauty and wretchedness of the human condition.
This bidirectional nonresistance I aim to show is a Chalcedonian
theological ethic.[1] The definition of the Chalcedon council witnesses
to a path of union with God in which the Christian comes to
participate in Christ's defenselessness before the Father and his
defenselessness before the world. Union in Christ's bidirectional
defenselessness or nonresistance exposes the confessing church to
the ethical momentum of Jesus depicted in his specific, concrete
actions in the gospels. It does this without permitting the church's
ethics to fade into a reductive, this-worldly moralism; rather the
very actions and life choices of Christ are seen here to induct the
church into inner-trinitarian love. To mingle in the incarnation of
Christ in this way is to realize, in new creation life, the paradoxical
fulfillment of human life, both now and in the age to come. It is to
become a *person*, living the beauty of created life as God intended.
But this does not preclude suffering and self-sacrifice.

In order to validate this claim, I will describe the way Balthasar
builds his Christology on the achievements of Maximus the Confessor
(c. 580–662 AD). Here is a Chalcedonian way of understanding
the relation of God to the world that is open both to the infinite
transcendence of God and to the concrete reality of the world.
I want to show here that nonresistance can be the theologically
thick, ethically evocative posture of a disciple, in the world but not
of it, fixed on that north star, which is Jesus, Son of God, and human
for us. As such, this ethic is grounded in a confession of faith from
which to contemplate the texture of Christ's life in the gospels and
there to experience the power of the Holy Spirit for a life of peace.

Balthasar's Christology was always deeply Chalcedonian. As
Mark McIntosh says,

> On the one side, he is unvarying in describing the personal
> identity of Christ as the eternal Son of God; for Balthasar, that is
> *who* Jesus of Nazareth is. On the other side, he takes Chalcedon's
> assertion that Christ is recognized "in two natures" as far more
> than a simple negation of the Eutychian extreme opposed at the
> council. This means that the existence of the Person of the Word,

---

[1]Chalcedon was the council in 451 that addressed "*how* the confession of the '*one
Christ*' may be reconciled with belief in the '*true God and true man*,' '*perfect in
Godhead, perfect in manhood*.'" Alois Grillmeier, *Christ in Christian Tradition*, vol.
1 (New York: Sheed and Ward, 1965), 482.

is a definitively complete *human* existence whose every human characteristic, including a human mind and will, is actually preserved and perfected, not circumvented or supplanted, by coming into existence in the eternal Person of the Son.[2]

As will hopefully become evident, in Balthasar's Christology, there is no zero-sum competition between divinity and humanity in Christ. It is precisely the Logos in the power of his divinity who establishes and makes vivid the true and full humanity of Jesus. It is the glory of the divine that enables the human to be finally what the first Adam was destined to be.

But let's back up a step. A Chalcedonian font for nonresistance, as I will describe it, may challenge gospel pacifism as it has developed, at least in Mennonite thought, in three ways. First, as the late A. James Reimer often lamented, Mennonite theologians have not found the creedal era to be morally interesting, and the Chalcedonian definition has offered even less hope for biblical ethics than the Nicene Creed.[3] Perhaps they have followed Adolf Harnack's assessment that at Chalcedon the church "was robbed of its faith" and was calcified into Hellenic philosophical categories.[4] John Howard Yoder concludes about Chalcedon's aftermath:

---

[2]McIntosh, *Christology from Within*, 4–5. See Hans Urs von Balthasar, *Theo-Logic: Truth of God*, trans. Adrian J. Walker, vol. 2 (San Francisco, CA: Ignatius, 2004), 281; *The Glory of the Lord: The New Covenant*, ed. John Riches, trans. Brian McNeil, vol. 7 (San Francisco, CA: Ignatius, 1989), 401; *The Glory of the Lord: Seeing the Form*, ed. Joseph Fessio and John Riches, trans. Erasmo Leiva-Merikakis, vol. 1 (San Francisco, CA: Ignatius, 1982), 432.

[3]It is difficult to find serious Mennonite engagement with Chalcedonian Christology in any length. But see Thomas N. Finger, "Post-Chalcedonian Christology: Some Reflections on Oriental Orthodox Christology from a Mennonite Perspective," in *Christ in East and West* (Macon, GA: Mercer University Press, 1987), 155–69, as well as Thomas N. Finger, "The Way to Nicea: Some Reflections from a Mennonite Perspective," *Journal of Ecumenical Studies*, March 1, 1987. See also Darrin Snyder-Belousek, "God and Nonviolence: Creedal Theology and Christian Ethics," *MQR* 88, no. 2 (April 2014): 233–69. Recovering creedal faith is a theme throughout Reimer's writings. See his essay "Confessions, Doctrines and Creeds: Symbols and Metaphors of Ultimacy," in A. James Reimer, *Mennonites and Classical Theology* (Kitchener: Pandora Press, 2001), 355–72.

[4]*Dogmengeschicte* 2, Tübingen 1931, 395–6, as quoted in Alois Grillmeier, *Christ in Christian Tradition* (New York: Sheed and Ward, 1965), 483n.

Hosts of technical terms were developed in order to safeguard the things which the council had compromised, but the life of the popular church went on being Monophysitic, that is, affirming such a swallowing up of humanity in deity that it did not really matter what kind of man Jesus was.[5]

One can already see the serious difference between Balthasar's understanding of what divinity is and does in Chalcedonian theology, and what Yoder sees. For Yoder here, divinity and humanity operate on a zero-sum basis at Chalcedon.

But our project also demands a certain understanding of what dogma is. What we need to show is that in Balthasar's hands, Chalcedon exposes the confessing church to the choreography of the divine economy and moves it into gospel-driven action. Dogma, in my view, cannot be reduced to some ancient rules for theological language, or even worse, timeless propositions in granite that merely establish the parameters of what is orthodox. Dogma does define what a true Christian church believes, but it does so by giving the church a key by which she is able to unlock the mystery of divine salvation in the pages of scripture and participate in its movements. Through the creedal tradition of the church, the eyes of the saints are trained to see Jesus in scriptural truth and to know the power and beauty of the work of God in the days of the world's life. To live like Jesus demands that we see Christ as the church has discerned him.

But second, the term "nonresistance" has been all but discarded in ethical discourse and replaced with terms like pacifism, nonviolent direct action, or peacemaking. The disdain for "nonresistance" associates the word with a merely passive, "doormat" approach to evil that is too reminiscent of Mennonites recused in villages blissfully allowing others to create such justice as the world is satisfied with.[6] It lacks any regard for the missional nature of the faith. We trust that it will become

---

[5]John Howard Yoder, *Preface to Theology: Christology and Theological Method* (Grand Rapids, MI: Brazos, 2002), 218. Yet, he claimed that his reading of Jesus was a more "Chalcedonian" reading than others because he took seriously the claim that in Christ's teachings of an alternative human community, Jesus spoke with full divine authority. Yoder, *The Politics of Jesus*, 102.

[6]In short, that Mennonites are who Reinhold Niebuhr said they were; useful symbols of an unachievable and impracticable ethic.

obvious that our incarnational use of the term envisions an active service to God involved in the world. But we must also show that simple "activity" or involvement is not the answer. There is both an activity and a passivity included in Chalcedonian nonresistance, a making happen and a "letting be." Nonresistance in the way we are trying to rehabilitate the word is the active, assertive, personal affirmation of the work of God unfolding before us. It is a deep, inner posture of "letting be" the manner by which God is now involved in the world, of giving assent in one's spirit and then in one's life to God's providential work. It is an involvement in the world directly "nonresistant" to Christ, and through this nonresistant to the condition of the world in all its beauty and wretchedness. This is no principle that can be detached from contemplation in a secular way, but is rather an inner watchfulness and daily following of the Saviour.

As we have seen, traditional Christian and Mennonite *Gelassenheit* has been accused of giving aid to an oppressive church. Heeding this warning, we will need to ask whether a Chalcedonian bidirectional nonresistance offers a challenge to these abuses. Is a pacifism whose actions are calibrated by Christ's nonresistant response to evil necessarily bad news for oppressed people? However, a lingering hunch behind my argument is that the present disdain for "nonresistance," though understandable at one level, has contributed to the loss of the Mennonite spirituality surrounding this peace ethic. When "nonresistance" becomes "pacifism" or "peacemaking," it tends to leave behind a posture before God, which opens the person to the mystery of God's involvement in daily life. The term nonresistance carries with it more of an awareness of the providence of God within which one is working. This is one of the reasons why I am going back to this abandoned word and asking Balthasar to redescribe it for us.

Third, "nonresistance" in the Mennonite tradition has almost exclusively been used to refer to the Christian's response to evil or harm: "resist not evil (Mt. 5:39 KJV). I am not intending to turn from that usage but to broaden it to show that this response to evil is encompassed within a broader trinitarian and incarnational "nonresistance" into which the believer is initiated through salvation. In Balthasar's terms, it refers to an encompassing "letting be" that forms the soul of sanctity. With this larger drama in view, it will become evident that gospel pacifism is not only a form of politics but a form of spirituality, prayer, and adoration.

Balthasar and Maximus the Confessor

Our resources in this chapter are complex. As Mark L. Yenson and Mark A. McIntosh have argued, to talk about Balthasar's Christology is to describe the inheritance he received and reworked from Maximus the Confessor.[7] Our task therefore is to understand Maximus through the eyes of Balthasar in that which pertains to our argument. Balthasar's book on Maximus the Confessor, *Cosmic Liturgy*, originally published in 1941, spearheaded the twentieth-century revival of interest in this seventh-century theologian and martyr. At the time, according to Balthasar, "it had the stage to itself."[8] To enter the thickets of Balthasarian theology and seventh-century Christology at the same time requires some courage. However, we do need to venture into these ancient visions, foreign as they may seem, to try to glimpse the theological ethic presented there. I believe the payoff is considerable: the discovery of a spiritual nonresistance for a secular setting. In Balthasar's hands the incarnation is seen again as a transforming, dramatizing act of God in which the saints mingle and become "defenseless," with exactly that paradoxical power by which God overcomes the world's enmity.

Balthasar took the achievement of Maximus and accented its personal, spiritual, and missional fruit. Balthasar was able to approach what looked like a decidedly formal patristic Christology and see within it the furnace of the Son of God's loving atonement for the world. Balthasar was able to see within this Christology a

---

[7]Hans Urs von Balthasar, *Theo-Drama: Dramatis Personae—Man in God*, trans. Graham Harrison, vol. 2 (San Francisco, CA: Ignatius, 1993), 199–203. See McIntosh, *Christology from Within*, 39–42; Mark L. Yenson, *Existence as Prayer: The Consciousness of Christ in the Theology of Hans Urs von Balthasar* (Bern: Peter Lang, 2014), 7–10. David Yeago says, "Von Balthasar is perhaps the twentieth-century theologian most indebted to Maximus, [and] I believe that a careful examination would show that the inner structure, especially of his *Theodramatik* is deeply Maximian. "Jesus of Nazareth and Cosmic Redemption: The Relevance of St Maximus the Confessor," *Modern Theology* (April 1996): 191, n. 40.

[8]Hans Urs von Balthasar, *Cosmic Liturgy: The Universe According to Maximus the Confessor*, trans. Brian E. Daley (San Francisco, CA: Ignatius, 2003), 23. Though a pioneer, Balthasar's treatment of Maximus has not been without its critics. See the essay by Brian Daley, "Balthasar's Reading of the Church Fathers," in *The Cambridge Companion to Hans Urs von Balthasar*, ed. Edward T. Oakes and David Moss (New York: Cambridge University Press, 2004), 187–206, for a discussion.

vocation for the Christian to participate with Christ in his embrace of the world while remaining fixed on the Father.

We cannot even begin to do justice to Balthasar's work as a whole on this saint, but we do aim to glean insights from it to shape a christological form of nonresistance. What we are interested in here is the way in which Maximus provided Balthasar with a *neo-Chalcedonian* Christology that moved beyond the patristic use of Greek philosophical concerns with fixed essences and natures to a vision for the historical, missional, and dramatic occurrence of the Incarnation. Through Maximus, the church was able to finally pay its philosophical debt to the Greek tradition and return to the action of the gospels, without leaving behind what had been gained through philosophy in terms of precision and clarity. It is this entrapment in Greek, static, philosophical categories that some pacifist theologians have pointed to as the failure of patristic Christology believed to neglect the humanity of Christ and obscure the call to discipleship in the life of Jesus.[9] We want to demonstrate that this need not be the case and that a dramatic Chalcedonian spirituality is possible.

This missional, dramatic element in Christology comes into view by ascending from the lower peak of Chalcedon to the summit of patristic Christology in Maximus two centuries later. It is now increasingly recognized that the council of Chalcedon in 451 was not the final climax of patristic christological development.[10] As

---

[9]C. Norman Kraus, *God Our Savior: Theology in a Christological Mode* (Eugene, OR: Wipf and Stock, 2006), 27–8. Kraus holds that the tendency of Chalcedon "in spite of its precision" has made it "virtually impossible to formulate a logically consistent theological definition of the unity of Jesus' self-consciousness and activity." Thus the missional aspect of Christ's life is lost. C. Norman Kraus, *Jesus Christ Our Lord: Christology from a Disciple's Perspective* (Eugene, OR: Wipf and Stock, 2004), 48. Kraus maintains that because of its inability to describe the unity of Christ a "docetic tendency had been almost universally present in orthodoxy theologies, and one cannot but suspect that it is in some major part inherent in the metaphysical conceptualization itself, based upon an analogy of a physical being." Ibid. Kraus's concerns about Christ's unity betray a misunderstanding of the relation between divinity and humanity in patristic theology, where they were not seen as zero-sum realities. These are also the kinds of statements that in my view fail to reckon with the way the Christology of the Church culminated at the third counsel of Constantinople in 680–1 when Maximus the Confessor was vindicated posthumously.

[10]Sarah Coakley, "What Does Chalcedon Solve and What Does It Not? Some Reflections on the Status and Meaning of the Chalcedonian 'Definition,'" in *The Incarnation: An Interdisciplinary Symposium on the Incarnation of the Son of God,* ed. Stephen T. Davis, Daniel Kendall, and Gerald O'Collins (New York: Oxford

interpreted by Maximus two centuries after the council, Balthasar perceived that Chalcedon opened new vistas in the engagement of theology with the manner of life unveiled in Jesus.

Neo-Chalcedonians, of whom Maximus emerged as the great champion, redirected the christological problem from one in which inquiring minds asked how two natures, infinitely different, could be united, to one asking who this *Person* was, Christ the Son of God, who so eagerly assumed the human condition and elicited from this nature such beautiful human and divine love. How did Christ do this without doing violence to human nature, trampling or commandeering the humanity he assumed? And on the other hand, how did the Son of God "let be" the dignity of his humanity without creating such division between the two that human nature remained un-salved by grace? Neo-Chalcedonianism moved from the simple assertion of two natures unconfused, unchanged, undivided, inseparable to a deeper understanding of how in the event of the incarnation those two natures came to be united *hypostatically* in the Person of the Son. Neo-Chalcedonian Christology regained the drama of the descent of the one Logos. It was this turn to the order of *hypostasis*, to the real-life existence of the Logos in time, that enabled the church to regain its dogmatic footing in the details of the gospel events.[11] This understanding of a missional, dramatic incarnation provides the inner momentum for the gospel nonresistance I am envisioning.[12]

University Press, 2004), 143–63. See also Yenson, *Existence as Prayer: The Consciousness of Christ in the Theology of Hans Urs von Balthasar*, 30–45; International Theological Commission, "Select Questions on Christology," http://www.vatican.va/roman_curia/congregations/cfaith/cti_documents/rc_cti_1979_cristologia_en.html.

[11]For a good description of the evolution of Chalcedonianism to neo-Chalcedonianism, see Yeago, "Jesus of Nazareth and Cosmic Redemption," 166–8. These two are not opposed. Neo-Chalcedonianism is the completion of some aspects opened at Chalcedon but not fully resolved. As by *Nicene* we normally mean the Niceno-Constantinopolitan completion of Nicaea, so by Chalcedonian we should understand that Christology which was finally endorsed in the third Council of Constantinople in 680–1.

[12]Mark McIntosh argues that the Balthasarian development of Maximus in more missional intensity is properly seen as an Ignatian fulfillment of the neo-Chalcedonian Christology. McIntosh, *Christology from Within*, 7, 42–4.

The Unguessable Improvisation on
a Nature

Maximus received the Greek philosophic tradition of thinking about *essence* and its relation to *existence* and reordered it to the soteriological concerns of the church. Here is how John Meyendorff explains Maximus's emphasis:

> Maximus formally opposes the concept of essence as it exists "with the philosophers", where it is "a reality in itself necessitating nothing else in order to exist" ... to that of the Fathers who recognize in it "a natural entity" ... proper to numerous and different hypostases. This conception of hypostasis as the concrete source of existence is not a simple return to Aristotelianism, nor even less a reduction of the notion to a simple relationship, as in Leontius; the context shows clearly that Maximus has a *personalistic* concept of the hypostasis: "the hypostasis" he writes, "is, according to the philosophers, an essence with characteristics; for the Fathers, it is each man in particular as distinct from other men."[13]

For Maximus, the hypostasis emerges as "the center of every concrete reality that determines and qualifies the 'mode of existence' ... or 'movement' of the nature."[14] A shift is occurring from an interest in nature as such, to an interest in the specific way nature is exercised by *this* hypostasis. In other words, a shift to an interest in the way this nature takes up occurrence here, in this concrete substantiation of the nature. As Balthasar explains, within Maximian Christology, the term hypostasis can mean an essence's "being-for-itself," that which distinguishes a concrete being from others of the same genus. As such, hypostasis answered the question "Who?" "It is the indicator and affirmation of a subject, an 'I.'"[15] But going further, hypostasis came to add the idea of *possession*, or perhaps better self-possession. "Here ... the concentration is tied

---

[13]John Meyendorff, *Christ in Eastern Christian Thought* (Washington, DC: Corpus, 1975), 110. Emphasis added.
[14]Ibid., 111.
[15]Balthasar, *Cosmic Liturgy*, 223. As Balthasar warns though, we should not attribute consciousness to hypostasis. A rock or a tree is also a hypostasis. Ibid.

to a 'having', to a way of *being the possessor* of essential being."[16] Though this may seem formal, seeing hypostasis in the register of *possessor* of essential being, gives Maximus the tool he needs to return Christology to a concern for the events of the gospel, to the way in which the *Person* of the Son of God *possesses* his human nature, to the actions of the Son of God creating flesh for himself and living human existence as God. In this we can see that Maximus is seeking to retain the essential Cyrilline character of Chalcedon, the emphasis on the fact that the subject of the Incarnation is always the one Logos, who never changes but who in his lordly descent takes to himself human nature and possesses it for his own purpose.[17] We will see in the next section how Maximus preserved this single-subject Christology without compromising the humanity of Christ as had been the hazard of Alexandrian thinkers.

Greek philosophy had been most concerned about the general, the essential, the natural. It focused more on *humanness* than upon the specific person, Paul, or Peter, in his existence. It did not focus on the particular, on that which distinguishes a hypostasis from others of the same nature. As long as theologians remained at the essential level, Christology remained an insoluble dilemma.

Maximus insisted that the reconciliation between God and the world could not be understood viewed at the level of essence. He thought this much should have already been seen as the fruit of Nicaea: if the Incarnation was an essential union between God and humanity, Jesus could not be of one substance with the Father since a divine/human mixture at the level of essence could not be either fully divine or fully human. Besides, an essential union between two natures would need to be violent. One nature would subsume the other.

In the christological debates, it was this rock that stumbled both the Eutychians who posited a "natural union" or mixture of the

---

[16]Balthasar, *Cosmic Liturgy*, 223.
[17]The case for Chalcedon being an essentially Cyrilline victory has been made with eloquence by John Anthony McGuckin, *St. Cyril of Alexandria: The Christological Controversy: Its History, Theology, and Texts* (Yonkers: St. Vladimir's Seminary Press, 2004), 233–40. Cyril of Alexandria in the years prior to the council of Chalcedon struggled to resist the Nestorian heresy which he felt separated Christ into two entities, and destroyed the unity of the Lord. This victory however still did not fully imagine how the One Lord could sustain a genuine humanity, and this was Maximus the Confessor's contribution, among others.

natures, and the Nestorians who posited an "accidental, extrinsic, moral union of an intellectual relationship, σξεσισ, between the natures."[18] It was not that the Eutychians united the natures of Christ too much and the Nestorians too little, but that they both imagined union at the level of nature or essence.[19] It was only under the stern eye of the Chalcedonian four adverbs (unconfusedly, unchangeably, indivisibly, inseparably), combined with Cyril of Alexandria's victory on the Logos as the single subject of the Incarnation, that a new ground in historical, evangelical existence became possible by ruling out an essential union and discovering the possibility of union at the level of hypostasis.

The reconciliation of God and world happened thus not in the realm of essences or natures, but in the realm of existence, in history, in the event of this Person's appearance within earthly time, in his lordly possession of human nature, and in the unpredictable ways he gave concrete existence to his divine and human natures. It happened through what Balthasar would call theo-dramatic mission—the Son descending into the world and making his own those characteristics of humanity in such a way as to become *this* person, making *these* choices, in *this* time and place. In Maximus this emphasis on the hypostatic union becomes a *diachronic* understanding of Chalcedon, an account tuned to see the Incarnation as a particular, an event, a mission, and a narrative in the life of God.[20]

Here the incarnation becomes unguessable and unpredictable because it is hypostatic, that is, determined by the free and lordly "I" that inhabits and possesses this human and divine nature in a way not contradicting the natures, but also not fatalistically determined by the natures. This "unguessable" quality to the incarnation is a huge aspect of our project here to retrieve a dramatic, dogmatic gospel pacifism. There can be no extractable principle of divine and human relations, no principle of unity and difference, that can be separated from this event and applied in a "secular" way. Christology with this hypostatic center can no longer be grasped simply by thinking philosophical thoughts about essences, nor by reducing it to a norm like "hospitality" or "nonviolence." It can only be understood contemplatively, by attending to the free, lordly

---

[18]Balthasar, *Cosmic Liturgy*, 212.
[19]Ibid.
[20]Yenson, *Existence as Prayer*, 49–51.

way in which the Logos, in fact, takes humanity to himself and makes choices and lives his life in the gospels. The very manner of his actions, the hypostatic doing *this* and not *that*, in this and not that unique manner, is the expression of God in human flesh.

We have turned here from a theology that begins by thinking to a theology that begins by contemplating, seeing what is actually happening, and which then subsequently thinks about what it has witnessed.[21] As Brian Daly says, Christology was now "primarily to be defined not by nouns and verbs, but by adverbs."[22] Its weight fell not in describing essences (nouns) or uniquely divine actions (verbs) but in describing the divine manner in which Christ lived his human life. Christian theological ethics finds its fount in this realization of Christology as hypostatic intentionality and choice. God is here living among us an unguessable, unpredictable, uncalculable life. Here in the incarnation, divine life, godly life becomes something to be imitated in human living.

We may perhaps be allowed to indulge in some comments about our larger theme of gospel pacifism from what we have already seen here. Gospel pacifism attends to the specific actions whereby the Son of God entered the world and confronted his enemy beset with sin. It is not looking to extract a portable principle of nonviolence, but to rather enter into a union with the Person who possessed his nature in the way Christ did. In the Schleitheim Confession, we noted the way Sattler and company based their ethic of peace on a contemplation of the manner in which Christ lived his life. Without claiming that Sattler was consciously applying Chalcedonian theology, he was certainly involved in a renewal of the faith in which *imitatio Christi* was the leading motif. This is a faith steeped in exactly this instinct nurtured in the church's christological debates, that the glory and beauty of the union of humanity and divinity in Christ is seen and imitated, rather than predicted, and extracted as a portable principle. This is a Christology that has taken the *hypostasis* as it center of union. Secularity, of course, claims it can dispense with imitation in any personal sense and extracts principles of nonviolence from

---

[21]Balthasar's trilogy begins with theological aesthetics, the seeing of the glory of God, moves to theo-dramatics, the actions of God seen in history, and finally to theo-logic, thinking that springs from the actions of God witnessed in history.

[22]Stephen T. Davis, Daniel Kendall, and Gerald O'Collins, *The Incarnation: An Interdisciplinary Symposium on the Incarnation of the Son of God* (New York: Oxford University Press, 2004), 165.

the Christian faith that no longer need to depend for their life on contemplation.

A Christology that retains this unpredictable hypostatic center will not be content with a "principle" to establish its ethics. While never violating nature, as we will see in the next section, the Person cannot be deduced from the natures. Alternatively, we could say that its only "principle" will be the free missional choices of the Person assuming human nature. Christology must retain its contemplative gaze on the events of the incarnate life of Christ.

Balthasar is attracted to this neo-Chalcedonian redirection of Greek philosophical achievements because this retrieval gives new depth for a modern Christology turned to the subject and the missional engagement of infinite freedom with finite freedom. This is also a Christology that begins to open the door to understanding how Christ's brothers and sisters come to participate in his hypostatic existence. In the Eutychian error, Christ was a divine–human hybrid that did not share human nature with us and so was not imitable. It also depicted what amounted to a violation of the human nature, subsumed into the divine. On the other hand, the Nestorian view ended up with a Savior who left human nature untouched and unaided in its ascent to union with God. In its effort to safeguard the proper divinity and the proper humanity of Christ, it left humanity to itself. This humanity was of course imitable, but it was not the imitation of God.

We can look at these two heresies from another angle. For our project we could say that a Eutychian theology would in fact be guilty of a divine ethic that overran frail humanity. Here, secularity's concerns with *Gelassenheit* would be vindicated; only a holiness that overruled and repressed human flourishing could achieve the sanctity God demands of us. On the other hand, Nestorianism turns out to be the secular solution to the christological question. Here the humanity in Christ is preserved by keeping it at arm's length from the Person of the Son. To affirm the dignity of ordinary life, secularity has needed to sever its connection with the transcendental destiny of the human because it considers divinity and humanity to have a zero-sum relation. It has turned the gaze of ethics from humankind's destiny in the hereafter, to the engineering of human flourishing in the here and now.[23]

---

[23]Ancient heresies do not always have exact counterparts in modern tendencies. However, Aaron Riches has argued convincingly that much modern Christology,

From a Maximian perspective, Christ's hypostatic existence is both divine action within the world and an archetype for our sanctification. It is a divine pattern of making choices that humans need to make as a part of daily life. This is the fount of theological ethics that attends once again to the way in which Christ intentionally lived a divine life within the human register.

The Transposition of Eternal Sonship

The unveiling of hypostasis as the theological center of the Incarnation prepares us for a more detailed look at the hypostatic *unity* that Maximus envisioned and at how Balthasar translated this form into his own words. What Maximus intends as a formal description of the relation between the eternal Trinity and the hypostatic union lived by Christ on earth, becomes, in Balthasar, a highly dramatic description of Christ's utter submission to the Father in his mission to the world. With this we begin to see that this missional hypostatic descent and union not only unveils Christology as an ethical momentum within the church, but as a specifically nonresistant momentum. Here the absolute submission of Christ to the Father becomes visible as a complete submission to the conditions of humanity. Zero-sum Christology is no longer necessary.

The hypostatic unity of the Incarnate, Maximus came to see, was a unity created by the Logos between two natures that united the very characteristics that separated the person from other hypostases who shared in the respective natures. It's a hypostatic unity between that which distinguishes the Son from the Father, and that which distinguishes Jesus from other humans. This requires some unpacking. In the trinitarian debates around Nicaea, Amphilochius, and the Cappadocians had honed the phrase "mode of being" or existence (τροποσ τῆ υπαρχί) to describe the unique distinction of the three Persons vis-à-vis the one common nature of the Trinity.[24]

---

in its efforts to regain sight of the historical Jesus, tends toward a Nestorian solution. Aaron Riches, *Ecce Homo: On the Divine Unity of Christ* (Grand Rapids, MI: Eerdmans, 2016), 9–12.

[24]Balthasar, *Cosmic Liturgy*, 214. In his "38th Letter" Gregory of Nyssa formulated, in terms that would remain the standard, the relation between nature and person in

The three Persons share one common nature but each expresses or gives existence to that nature in a unique τροποσ that distinguishes the Person from the other two Persons. This was their hypostatic existence as Persons. However, what distinguished the Persons from each other was not something each Person held for itself in autonomy, but was rather the unique way this Person related to the other two.

What distinguished the Persons (their mode of being) was each Person's unique origin vis-à-vis the other two Persons.[25] Difference was secured in the unique manner in which each Person was established relationally with the other Persons.[26] What distinguished the eternal Son, the particular manner by which he gave unique expression to the common divine nature, was his being begotten from the Father. This eternal relationship of begotteness or dependence as the mode of being of the Son to the Father is picked up by Maximus and is massively important for Balthasar's Christology.

It was Maximus's insight to see that this trinitarian understanding of Person could be put to work in the christological question as well.[27] In the incarnation, of course, we are not referring to a unity of Persons within one common nature, but to the unity of two utterly different natures within one Person. However, Maximus was confident that the resolution of the christological problem would build on the work of Amphilochius and the Cappadocians following Nicaea. Unity, here now between two radically unequal and asymmetrical natures, could also occur hypostatically. As Mark McIntosh aptly summarizes, "the divine and human [natures] in Christ are united in enacting together that particular pattern of

---

trinitarian theology. See Christoph Schönborn, *God's Human Face: The Christ-Icon* (San Francisco, CA: Ignatius, 1994), 103.

[25]Maximus wrote in PG 91, 549D–552A,

> For we recognize the one and only essence and nature in the divinity, unfolding in three hypostases distinct from one another by their properties ... in particular by being unbegotten (the Father), by being begotten (the Son), and by emanating (the Holy Spirit): these properties ... denote the Persons in whom the one divinity resides, and who are themselves this one divinity (quoted in Schönborn, *God's Human Face*, 105).

[26]This simple sentence has massive implications for Balthasar's theology of unity in difference. The distance between Persons is a distance of love.

[27]Balthasar, *Cosmic Liturgy*, 214–15.

self-surrender, obedience, and love which is the mode of existence of the eternal Son, i.e., the pattern which distinguishes the Son from the Father and the Spirit."[28]

The incarnation is not the appearance of mere "divinity" in human flesh, but the appearance of this kind of Sonship: complete dependence on the Father.[29] Jesus Christ is the union of Divine Sonship with humanity. That is the unique personal expression of divine nature with which human nature is joined.

But now one step further. The Logos was not only differentiated from the Father and the Spirit, but Jesus was also differentiated from other humans as a fellow human. He shared in a common nature with them as well—but he gave expression to that nature in a way utterly unique. Just as the Logos gave unique expression to the divine nature, he also gave unique expression to human nature. He lived a unique instantiation of human nature (he was in every respect a *person* in the modern sense of that term) by transposing his Divine Sonship into human terms. What set Jesus apart from other people was his human expression of divine Sonship, the transposition of trinitarian Sonship into human terms of obedience, willingness to suffer, and utter love to the end, out of submission to the Father.[30]

The incarnation then is not merely the unity of two disparate natures, but of two unique takes, or expressions of the natures united by the Logos. In the incarnation, what differentiated the Son from the Father was exactly what differentiated Jesus from other humans.[31] The Logos is the unique expression of Sonship in the Trinity, and the incarnate One is the unique expression of trinitarian Sonship in humanity. The Son, in his very distinction

---

[28] McIntosh, *Christology from Within*, 40.

[29] "Insofar as he is God, he is eternal, infinite freedom; insofar as he is the Son of the Father, he is this freedom in the mode ('tropos') of readiness, receptivity, obedience and hence the appropriate response: that is, he is the Father's Word, image and expression." Balthasar, *Theo-Drama*, 1993, 2:267. See also Balthasar, *Theo-Drama*, 1994, 4:325–6.

[30] Here I am relying on the exposition of Schönborn, *God's Human Face*, 102ff.

[31] In his own *A Theology of History* where he makes use of this conception of the hypostatic unity between God and the world, Balthasar distinguishes between the *absolute* uniqueness of God and the *relative* uniqueness of Jesus as a man among other humans. The human uniqueness of the individual, which Jesus partook of, is analogous to the divine uniqueness of the Persons of the Trinity in their relations. Balthasar, *Theology of History*, 11.

from the Father, embraced human nature and united himself with a manner of being human that differentiated Jesus from other people. The distinctives of Christ's life are the revelation of the distinctive relationship Christ has with the Father. Here are Maximus's words:

> In those qualities through which the flesh of Christ distinguishes itself from other human beings [Jesus' manner of life], it did not distinguish itself further from the Logos; on the other hand, in those qualities through which it distinguished itself from the Logos, [being human nature] it did not distinguish itself from the rest of us. In those, however, through which it distinguished itself from us [Jesus' manner of life] it preserved the union, or, better, the identity, with the Logos in the hypostasis.[32]

Balthasar comments on Maximus's formulation, "the same is true in the nature of God: what distinguishes the Logos from the Father is, in the state of the union, no longer distinguishable from what distinguishes the incarnate Logos from other human beings."[33] The Son's eternal hypostatic relation in the Trinity is united with Jesus's manner of life. Sonship is given a human mode of existence, performed (unguessably) in every aspect of Jesus' human life. With this Maximian description, Balthasar says, formal Christology reaches its apex.

What Maximus has done here finally is show that the consubstantiality of the Son to the Father, his divinity, is in no way threatened but is rather revealed by the very depths of humanity that Jesus plumbs within his life and death. To be fully human for Christ is exactly to give full expression to divine Sonship. In the life of Christ, humanity becomes the expression of his eternal Sonship, his eternal yieldedness and readiness to be the Word of the Father. What he has also shown here is that the very existence at every step and choice of Jesus as the Logos incarnate reveals the Father's will. His entire existence is tuned to give expression in a human key to the will of God.

This we are calling Christ's defenselessness, yieldedness, or nonresistance to the Father. Divinity in its human expression is a "letting be" of the will of the Father. It is a humanity whose very

---

[32]Balthasar, *Cosmic Liturgy*, 247. From Maximus, *Epistles*, PG 91, 557A.
[33]Balthasar, *Cosmic Liturgy*, 247.

uniqueness from other humans, what sets Jesus apart as a unique human among other humans, is the manner in which his entire existence gives earthly expression to the eternal mode of being which is the Son of God. His eyes look constantly to the face of the Father, willing to give himself utterly in love for the Father. This is not merely humanity; this is divinity transposed now into a human way of being.

> We see in [Christ] a being whose whole bearing—down to the least word and gesture—reveals a human nature, but one that has been translated into a wholly different manner of existing. ... Everything that is truly human can be found in this new manner of existing, yet none of it is any longer "simply human" ... or "only human" ... but it appears as strangely "inhabited" ... by another. This "indwelling" is perceived at once as the most interior and intimate relationship possible in which God is tenderly concerned to preserve all that is human and natural and to heal it. ... Thus is this "new manner" of being, this "divine mode", this "way of existing thus and no other way" ... this new quality that has no effect on quantity, that promises to show us the way to the unity we are looking for.[34]

Christ's human life, his daily possessing of human nature in lordly, free manner, is not in competition with his divinity but is the very presence of that divinity in the world. Brian Daly summarizes this newly emerging dogmatic engagement with the texture of Christ's life thus:

> Just as *who* Father, Son, and Holy Spirit are is grounded in *how* they take their origin from each other and are related to each other, so it is the "how" of Jesus—how he came to be, how he acted—that revealed and even grounded the reality of who he was and what he was, and serves for us as an efficacious model of how we are called to live and what we are called to be.[35]

---

[34]Ibid., 215. Here Balthasar is exegeting Maximus's *Opuscala*; PG 91, 77AB, 108B, and *Ambigua*, PG 91, 1048B, 1048A, 1044D-1045A, 1052A, 1053CD, 1053B, and 1057A. Later we will pick up the thought given here that the nonresistance of the Son to the Father shows that "God is tenderly concerned to preserve all that is human and natural and to heal it," a nonresistance of God to the human condition.
[35]Davis, Kendall, and O'Collins, *Incarnation*, 165–6.

This has massive implications for theological ethics. As *hypostatic*, the divinity of Jesus is imitable. It is the utterly human, utterly nonpredictable actions by which Jesus offered himself completely to the Father. As we contemplate and imitate these human actions, we are entering into the very being of God for us in Christ.

In his lifework Balthasar takes up this Maximian formal "summit," describing the unity of humanity and divinity in Christ in order to extend it into a spirituality of *Gelassenheit* and, we could say, nonresistance. Christ is the answer, given in utterly human terms, to the gift of the Father granting him eternal life within himself as the Son. His whole mode of human life, the submission, humility, gentleness, and meekness as it differentiates him from other people is an expression of an eternal reception of being from the Father. Christ has been eternally yielded to the Father as the source of his being; he now gives that eternal "letting be" to the Father a human mode of expression in his long-suffering love. The nonresistance that distinguishes him from the Father becomes the very thing that distinguishes Jesus from other humans—his utter love to the end. Through participation in Christ, disciples enact this same pattern of meekness, humility, and self-gift, which was Christ's transposition of Sonship into human terms. Disciples share in the divine nature when they are united to the manner in which that divine nature is given human expression in Christ.

This is the first aspect of Christ's bidirectional nonresistance, his yieldedness to the Father lived as a human life. In this Chalcedonian definition, as interpreted by Balthasar, the eternal begotteness of the Son in his trinitarian distinction from the Father, becomes united with those aspects of Christ's life traditionally associated with nonresistant ethics—his suffering in the face of evil, and his willingness to love in the face of great debasement. Here in these nonresistant actions there is no dichotomy to be found between divine transcendence in divine origin and full humanity.

This is the dogmatic font of theological ethics for Balthasar. As Mark Yenson says:

> For Balthasar the shift toward a personalist ontology in Maximus, grounded in a diachronic Christology, means that Christology is henceforth more explicitly correlated on the one hand to Trinitarian relationality and on the other to historical particularity and finite freedom: in Christ, over and beyond the

two natures, we encounter the Son of God entering and assuming human history.[36]

Christ's explicit teachings about nonresistance, such as we see in Lk. 6:32-5, are given by Jesus so that "you will be children of the Most High." In Mt. 5:43 the same pattern of nonresistance is urged "so that you may be children of your Father in heaven" making you "perfect as your heavenly Father is perfect." By inviting his disciples to be nonresistant to the Father, as he was nonresistant to the Father, Christ beckoned them to live in that same vulnerability, love, and courage in the face of evil. This is the nonresistance of Christ to the Father that moved Christ into the crosshairs of the evil, which curses the human race. When we turn now to look at the Dyothelite/Monothelite debate, we can see more clearly that in this nonresistance to the Father Christ was also nonresistant to the human condition.

The Dyothelite Nonresistance of Christ to the Human Condition

Having seen that within Maximian neo-Chalcedonian Christology, Christ offers a human nonresistance to the Father by transposing and preserving his eternal Sonship, we now turn to the second move, which is to show that Christ offered a divine nonresistance to the human condition, preserving a genuine humanity. This is a key move in our quest for a gospel-formed ethic of pacifism. We are pointing into the mystery by which costly human love is elicited by a sharing in divinity. I want to show here that the dogmatic basis for an ethic that "resists not evil" is found in Christ's unwillingness to resist the full reality, even the depravity of the human nature he assumed. By adoring and entering this mystery, we become people who like Christ are open to the fundamental reality around us, willing to "let be" our enemy, not in the sense of giving approval to the enemy's evil designs, but in the sense of entering into the reality of the enemy's life with the intent of lifting *that*, along with the pain it causes, to God.

---

[36]Yenson, *Existence as Prayer*, 48–9.

One of the great theological struggles that Maximus the Confessor engaged in, and which eventually cost him his life, was the question of whether affirming two natures in Christ also meant affirming two wills. Was the will something inherent in the natures, and thus dual, or was it inherent in the Person, and thus singular? The Monothelite position argued that will was personal, and thus that Christ had only one will, a divine will. Dyothelitism (two wills), led by Maximus and Pope Martin, saw this as compromising the true humanity of Christ. If Christ did not also have a human will could this truly be a human obedience which he offered to the Father? And if Christ's was not a human obedience, has humans' disobedient instinct truly been taken in by our Lord and healed? The great christological axiom of the church fathers that only what is assumed is healed here makes its presence felt. But with two wills, the question of their unity becomes acute: Was it possible for Jesus to live *our* life as a sinless life without the divine will overriding the human will? As we will see, this debated focused scripturally on the Garden of Gethsemane and the struggle of Christ with the call of the Father.

We again enter what can appear to be an alien-sounding formality in our theological tradition. But as I will attempt to show, in the Dyothelite vision that eventually became the orthodox confession, the hypostatic center in Christology opens our eyes to the marvelous way in which God in Christ preserved (refused to resist) his human nature, and through that deified the human life offered in the incarnation. Christ's nonresistance to the human is not only a letting be but also a "letting be" unto deification. It is an openness and receptivity to the human with a view to raising it, sanctified to God. This is the intent of the bidirectional -resistance we are envisioning as gospel nonviolence—not only to love one's enemies but to be an ingredient in their deification, their participation in God. Nonresistance must have within it an evangelistic concern for the enemy, within its "letting be."

Dyothelitism we will show is a divine nonresistance to the human condition in all its aspects, the second direction in which Christ's yieldedness extended. A nonresistance to the Father and a nonresistance to the human condition are deeply united. Christoph Schönborn says of the Dyothelite achievement of Maximus:

The fight against Monothelitism constitutes a certain return to the realism of Christ's humanity, to this humanity's lowliest and humblest manifestations; it also brings a new and sharpened awareness that the reality of the eternal Word transpires foremost in his ultimate self-abasement. ... In the dramatic events of Gethsemane and Golgotha, the faith-filled meditation discovers anew the heart of our salvation; in the despised countenance of the Lord, it finds the true icon of God's love.[37]

Balthasar was keenly interested in the way a Maximian Dyothelite Christology resisted the Alexandrian (Balthasar would also say Asian or Buddhist) tendency to imagine the world absorbed into God and gave expression to the affirmation God shows to the world he has made. There is a solidity to the world, a dignity as created world that God was seen to respect and preserve in the events of our Lord's life. But this was not a respecting and preserving that left human nature alone. "Letting be" does not mean leave alone.

For this reason, Chalcedon's great word was "save" (σώζειν): the preservation of the peculiar character of both natures. ... For Maximus this word becomes the most central concept in the whole order of redemption, for it unites in itself both aspects of Christ's saving work: healing and rescue, on the one hand, and preservation and confirmation on the other.[38]

It is in part this tendency of dissolution into the divine for which spiritualties of *Gelassenheit*, nonresistance, and yieldedness to the enemy in love are critiqued. Is the world in all its earthy pain, frailty, and beauty finally something to be overwhelmed, absorbed, and forgotten in the divine ocean? But, on the other hand, it has proven to be difficult to resist this "dissolving" tendency without resorting to secularity. Secularity *is* one way of preserving the solidity of the world, but it does this by diminishing the ultimate divine destiny of the human.

This Maximian preservation and affirmation of the non-divine is a core dynamic within Balthasar's theology of beauty. The world in its radiance of the glory of God is not for that any less *world*. This is not a secular beauty but neither is it a Monothelite beauty in which the divine has to intrude violently to overcome the ugliness of the

---

[37]Schönborn, *God's Human Face*, 117.
[38]Balthasar, *Cosmic Liturgy*, 257.

world. The world is full of the glory of God, but that glory shines as the world's own glory. This also describes moral or spiritual beauty. The Dyothelite conviction is what Balthasar believes prevents his rather uncompromising theology of *Gelassenheit* from descending into anti-humanism. Here is an understanding of self-donation that preserves first, in order to give *itself* in love. Maximus, says Balthasar, gives all "'empty vessel' Christologies their correct interpretation as describing an active cooperation of the man Jesus that remains full-bodied in his *kenosis*."[39]

Maximus perceived the mistake lurking in the Monothelite assertion that, as there is only one Person who wills in the incarnation, so there must only be one will, and that divine. Monothelites worried that in Chalcedon's "without confusion" of natures and in Maximus's assertion of two wills in Christ, a compromise of Cyril of Alexandria's "single-subject" Christology had occurred. Two wills must equal two persons, they reasoned. According to Maximus, however, while the Monothelites determined correctly that unity of the natures/wills was a hypostatic, personal event, they drew from this the mistaken belief that envisioning a *natural human will* distinct (even free) within the Person smuggled in a Nestorian division into two persons. As Christoph Schönborn notes, there was still something in Cyril of Alexandria that saw the divine as superior in power to the human, which achieved its way because of its superior power, thus making impossible a genuine human will. This "could easily lead to viewing Christ's human nature as entirely passive, and only his divinity as active."[40] It is only with Maximus's Dyothelitism that the dignity of the human nature receives its fullest expression and single-subject Christology is able to resist the tendency to view the divine Logos as "wielding" humanity like a passive instrument.

Balthasar is mightily impressed by this Maximian preservation and it remains a distinct feature of his unity in difference theology all his life. It enabled him to see that unity between the divine and human occurs more deeply through the active, loving preservation of the difference between the natures yielding ultimately a deification of the human, than it does through a divine domination yielding a

[39]Balthasar, *Theo-Logic*, 2004, 2:70.
[40]Schönborn, *God's Human Face*, 119. Balthasar notes something similar about Cyril in Balthasar, *Cosmic Liturgy*, 228.

mixture of natures. Maximus sensed that if the divine in any way overpowered the human in Christ, the two must be on some sort of univocal plane—thus compromising divine transcendence as much as human authenticity. This is what we have referred to as a zero-sum understanding of God and the human. "The Logos does not exert some kind of extrinsic causality upon his human nature, the way Eusebius thought, but he operates *in* both of his natures."[41]

The occasion for this achievement came through Maximus's reading of the long-debated Scriptural account of Gethsemane. Balthasar wrote later in life about Maximus's discovery,

> more than two hundred years after Chalcedon!—that we cannot read the Agony in the Garden as if Jesus' human will had first balked at the imminent Passion and had then been overpowered and brought back into line with the divine will, but that on the contrary, it was none other than this human will that had to give its free consent to the Father's plan. Only thus is Chalcedon brought to its logical conclusion.[42]

We can see this human "letting be" of the Father's plan through Christ's "letting be" of human reality in several layers. First, at the most basic level, what is the "natural" will of this child of Adam that Maximus held to be distinct from the Person and which he was determined to preserve in his Christology? According to Maximus, the will is based in nature. The natural will of humans that the Logos assumed is a created set of desires and movements built into the structure of what it means to be human, by which humans were intended to move forward and ultimately become what God intended them to become. God had intended Adam to reach the divine destiny by willing and so created him with a will by which he would move forward. This was to be the necessary though not sufficient path by which humans attain the glory of being the image of God. Ian McFarland explains Maximus helpfully: "In short, because they are agents, human beings are *willing* creatures, which is to say, their movements are characterized by agency rather than being unconscious or automatic. In short, motion is not just

---

[41]Schönborn, *God's Human Face*, 119.
[42]Balthasar, *Theo-Logic*, 2004, 2:69–70.

something that happens to me; *I* move."[43] Or as Balthasar put it, "an intellectual nature is defined by its self-determination (αυτοξινητον) and its freedom (προαιρεσί)."[44] For Christ to affirm his human will inviolate in Gethsemane, therefore, is to determine that it is only by the authentic exercise of this basic human agency that the will of the Father will be carried out.[45] For Maximus, the Person "is the realization, the concrete living out, of a rational nature."[46] The Person brings a unique mode of action to the natural, created will without overpowering it. This Balthasar calls "the dynamic, actualizing aspect of being" that works within the created structures of nature.[47] The work of the Person is the "concrete realization, its 'liberation' by appropriation of the nature."[48] The Person takes the movements and desires inherent in the will and enacts them in unique ways. To have freedom in this view is not the ability to do good or evil indifferently but to be a rational agent who gives a unique, unpredictable expression to the created desires and ends that God has given as the natural end of the creature. What Maximus saw occurring in the Garden was humanity making its offering, at last. The fact that it was by the Son of God that humanity was making this offering did not diminish in the least that here was Adam offering that oblation that was always his to give.

According to Maximus, a person cannot be reduced to her nature/will, but neither can the person exist in absolute spontaneity above the nature/will.[49] The mistake of the Monothelites was to imagine only two options: either a completely detached "I" riding free above nature or an "I" bound by nature in such a way that

---

[43]Ian A. McFarland, "The Theology of the Will," in *The Oxford Handbook of Maximus the Confessor*, ed. Pauline Allen and Bronwen Neil (Oxford: Oxford University Press, 2015), 520. He translates Maximus's autoxi/nhton as agency. It literally means "power over oneself." However, this should not be taken in a Nestorian direction to imply that Christ had two acting centres coexisting within himself.

[44]Balthasar, *Cosmic Liturgy*, 260.

[45]The human will of Christ was necessary to his obedience, but not in itself sufficient for his vocation.

[46]Ibid., 262–3.

[47]Ibid., 263.

[48]Ibid., 227.

[49]Maximus's scholiast correlates the traditional distinction between "image" and "likeness" with the nature/hypostasis distinction. "Nature is that which is created according to the image, the plan of being. ... The hypostasis is that which was created according to the likeness, historical life." Ibid., 226.

human freedom is destroyed. Here Balthasar makes an interesting observation that gives us a clue as to how he sees Monothelitism operating in the modern context. Between Pyrrhus (a Monothelite) and Maximus,

> two ultimate conceptions of the person are on a collision course. For Pyrrhus, person can represent only an irrational dimension, beyond everything natural. He wants to preserve its absolute spontaneity and self-affirmation through negations. Thus, in many respects, Monothelitism is a precursor of the personalistic nominalism of the late Middle Ages and modern culture.[50]

Nature is here diminished.

> Nature, robbed of the inner dynamic of its own purposefulness for the sake of the [freedom of the] person, descends to become a marionette. The consistent conclusion of this subtle, intelligent heresy is a new kind of docetism and, so, the denial of the ultimate basis of the Christian message.[51]

But Maximus saw a paradoxical third alternative. The person could inhabit and carry out the nature in a free way. By insisting that theology see the active, human will "saved" at Gethsemane, Maximus was resisting the possibility that the hypostatic union of the natures would devolve into a voluntarist "I" riding detached over the now-assumed humanity of Christ. The Person of Christ inhabited the natures and gave expression to their inherent desires and predilections, yet did so in a free, lordly way. In this way, Christ truly offered Adam's obedience in the Garden.

I call this a divine nonresistance to Adam. It is an active openness to and appropriation of human nature, a willingness to allow—no, even more, to enable—the full expression of human createdness, even in the wretched conditions under which Christ encountered that human condition in the Garden of Gethsemane. Maximus argued that the Logos had empowered the fullest human life possible by entering into human existence, preserving the agential

---

[50]Ibid., 263. Balthasar expresses concerns about nontheological existentialism and Bultmannianism in this respect. Cf. Balthasar, *Theology of History*, 19–20.
[51]Balthasar, *Cosmic Liturgy*, 263.

capacity of humans and empowering human nature to its grandest and most natural expression—the willing of what God wills. This basic structure of the natural human is important for our linking of preservation with nonresistance because it shows that what Jesus did in allowing himself to be taken was a *natural* action, with the grain of basic creational humanity, as it unfolds in a sinful climate. His love was not some divine detour around human instincts but rather a full-throated natural, human yes to the will of God. But how can a human person *naturally* will what God wills when that leads to death?

Going to the next layer, Maximus was also determined that the Logos's action to preserve the depths of the human condition preserved and healed not only a prelapsarian human nature, but the condition of that nature under the duress of the curse. How was this preservation of humanity in Christ to be done while maintaining the Scriptural witness that Christ remained without sin until the end? This question was important for Balthasar. We know from Balthasar's personal work later in life that he, of all people, wanted his readers to grapple with the depths of the darkness, fear, and horror that descended upon the Saviour in Gethsemane and on into the holy triduum, and to see this not as destroying but rather fully expressing Sonship. So in what sense can we say that Christ was "made sin" for us?

At first glance, Maximus's view of the human will seems unlikely to include that kind of existential struggle. In conceiving of this natural freedom embraced by Christ, Maximus would have us remove all *gnomic* qualities. The *gnomic* will according to Maximus is not a separate will but a mode of willing exercised under the conditions of sinful existence. It's an expression of the will that waffles, apathetic and unsure of how to proceed. It dithers between good and evil seeking which to choose. This Christ could not do, according to Maximus. As the divine Logos, according to scripture, Christ would have had a clear view of, and would have embodied the will of the Father. The drama in Gethsemane did not revolve around discerning the will of God in foggy moral conditions. It was not the modern freedom of looking to the left and to the right, choosing good or evil.[52] In Ian McFarland's words, "Jesus is not

---

[52]It is helpful to understand that the ancient Christian understanding of freedom was not centrally about the ability to choose between various options in an autonomous

struggling *against* the power of sin, but *for* the upward call of God."[53] Balthasar agrees in a later essay:

> Jesus is not a man who happens to find himself on earth and from that point on gropes to find and do the will of God by reflecting on himself and asking about the purpose of his being here on earth. His existence is not a matter of chance. Rather his very existence itself is a result of his mission ... and thus of his obedience.[54]

The struggle of Christ had to do not with ignorance of his divine call but with the limits of the natural will, up against the seemingly impossible demands of the Father. This was the incarnate Son of God, loaded with the limits of human weakness struggling to give a natural, human expression to eternal Sonship, and thereby redeem this human condition for all the world. Jesus was struggling in the Garden with the apparent inability of his natural will to arrive at the destiny of his calling in God, within its own limits. He was being summoned to a task for which his natural desires were insufficient.

Jesus had the natural human fear of death and desire to extend life. This, Maximus insists, was not an evil desire, but it was a desire that could not in itself bring Christ to the fulfillment of his vocation. The desire for life was extended to a breaking point in the Garden. This also leads to the realization that what Christ took to himself (suffered) in the Garden was the consequences that humans had brought upon themselves for their sin. Christ did not consent to commit sin, but he consented to knowing in himself the effects that voluntary sin had unleashed in the world. It was not an evil desire in the sense of being a voluntary sin, but it was what Maximus called "physical sin," or the natural consequences of sin as distinct from "moral sin," which was the sin itself.[55] The terror of death was

---

way, but was rather about the ability to do one thing, which is obey the command of God.
[53]McFarland, "The Theology of the Will," 528. Emphasis in original.
[54]Hans Urs von Balthasar, *Explorations in Theology*, vol. 4, *Spirit and Institution*, trans. Edward T. Oakes (San Francisco, CA: Ignatius, 1995), 141. Balthasar detects an ambiguity in Maximus on gnomic will. What Maximus ultimately wants to ensure is the hypostatic clarity with which the Father's will is perceived. In some cases it appears that Maximus believed that Christ's natural will included a perfectly healed gnomic will, that is a will that does deliberate but habitually chose the right path to achieve its desire. Balthasar, *Cosmic Liturgy*, 269–71.
[55]Balthasar, *Cosmic Liturgy*, 196, 264.

an aspect of this punishment that God had ordered, and Christ's preservation of human nature preserved this also and appropriated it to offer a perfect offering to the Father. The divine hypostasis did not destroy this fear of death and longing for life, but rather supported and enabled its fullest expression. It was the glory of Christ's offering in the Garden to open up and offer this fear of death to God, to make it a key ingredient of his obedience in a way that far exceeded the undeified natural ability of the human.

But this is not yet enough. Balthasar says, "The healing of nature demands a descent to that tragic point in man, where sin, as opposition to God, has come into its own. For sin to be overcome from within, it had, in some way or other, to be found 'within' Christ."[56] Not only did Christ take on "physical sin" but in another Maximian distinction, he also took on voluntary sin, though only *relatively*, not ontologically. In a "relative appropriation," Christ makes his own what is another's through loving identification rather than through an "ontological appropriation" according to nature. "But since he could not make our sinful manner of willing his own ontologically, he assimilated it to himself through 'relative appropriation.'"[57] This higher assimilation Christ achieves in his role as head of the Mystical Body "by which he stands in a loving and therefore sympathetic relationship with the actions and sufferings of all his members."[58] Christ takes to himself the voluntary guilt of the world in the sins of the members of the Body, now borne in Gethsemane and on the cross. Thus, the depths of anguish in the Garden are seen as a deeply ecclesial reality in which Christ is suffering the sin in his members. Christ is intentionally, lovingly experiencing sin in this way, while remaining fixed on the Father's will.

The Son thus experiences the full human postlapsarian flight-instinct from death, as well as the stifling anguish of sin-guilt, while remaining fixed in a clear-sighted way to the Father's will to save the human race. The Logos, in step eternally with the Father's will, was calling the human forth in a venture of *self*-sacrifice, but a self-sacrifice that found no detour around natural desires, the fear of death, and a loving solidarity with the sinner to the point of

---

[56]Ibid., 263.
[57]Ibid., 267.
[58]Ibid.

making sin his own. This was the weight of what was secured in the Dyothelite insistence that Christ's human will not be violated or subsumed into divine willing.[59] The divine will did not overpower but rather deified the human will to its fiercest in order to offer itself as a human offering to the Father.

And this we are claiming is the unsearchable mystery of a nonresistance in two directions that we believe can form the dogmatic momentum of a gospel pacifism within a secular age. This is a divine response to evil that out-secularizes modern secularity with its unflinching affirmation of human existence, while out-spiritualizing the Monothelites with its resolute vision of the Logos living his divine Sonship all the while under conditions of humility, even debasement and suffering in love. The Logos does not abolish or subsume the human in order to achieve a divine obedience to the Father. Neither does he dominate it or violently direct it in an extrinsic way. Rather, in a perfect expression of Sonship, he takes this nature to himself, preserves and enables its deepest desires and fears, takes to himself in loving appropriation the way this nature has been lived sinfully by his brothers and sisters, and in that bitter night in Gethsemane and Golgotha offers this to God. This was how the Lord "resisted not evil" and loved his enemies, actively, personally, authentically, freely offering himself as a sacrifice for their sins.

In looking back over this Dyothelite witness, in Maximus but also in Balthasar, one is struck by the paradox at work here. God "preserves" humanity in the incarnation, but the humanity it preserves is a missional humanity willing to sacrifice itself for the other in costly love. The Logos preserves and dignifies the full, rational ground of human nature as the creature desiring to extend life but does this by offering himself in self-sacrificial, self-abnegating gift for his enemies. What the Logos preserves, affirms, and protects, of humanity, is not a neutral, secular human nature, but a human nature as it was created to find its deepest fulfillment in obedience to God. It preserves this obediential, creational response under the worst possible circumstances and offers itself in yieldedness to God. Here, in the furnace of Gethsemane, where the Sonship (begotteness) of the Logos assumes a willful, human nature and offers himself for his enemies, we find the spiritual and dogmatic center for a

[59]Balthasar, Cosmic Liturgy, 264.

non-secular, gospel pacifism. This pacifism goes beyond the abuses associated with *Gelassenheit* by emphasizing the preservation inherent in the offering of Jesus, but also goes beyond the secular solution to those abuses that consist of autonomous self-assertion and preservation.

However, there is one further question that we need to explore. How did the Person of Christ enable this very human obedience to rise so far beyond the limits of what human nature in its this-worldly existence desires?

Deification is the short answer. The Logos glorifies the human in Jesus and lifts it to union with God without diminishing its humanity. How this is visualized is the question of the *communicatio idiomatum* and its relation to deification and here we return again to the hypostasis now in its mysterious gospel-narrative form. Balthasar argues that Maximus is able to rescue the entire *Logos/Sarx* Alexandrian tradition of deification, which until that point had never quite been able to safely describe the union of the soul with God without falling into a dissolution of the creaturely, whether in Christ or in us. The two are intimately related.[60] Maximus, of course, did not originate the doctrine of the *communicatio*, but he provided a way to understand it that preserved both Cyril of Alexandria's divine single-subject Christology, and the Chalcedonian retention of Nestorius's concern for a genuine, free humanity. With the Dyothelite understanding of the preservation of the natural will, the deification of the humanity of Christ could be explained in a Christian way as an act of union that preserved the Creator/creature difference.

Maximus envisioned a mutual indwelling relationship between the hypostasis and the nature in the incarnation. Maximus saw the two as distinct, yet never imagined them apart, as some metaphysical composition. They formed a unity and passed over to one another in their unity the respective modes of their action. For the Son, divine nature involved certain patterns of relationship with the Father. Human nature also had certain distinctive ways of moving as we have already seen—by agential rationality in a fallen world. In its fallen condition, it also had forms of wretchedness that it underwent by nature. In the en-hypostasization of the natures, the Person shared in these distinctive movements of the natures without confusing the human and divine. Within the hypostatic event of

---

[60]Balthasar, *Cosmic Liturgy*, 274.

union of the natures, there was an exchange of these properties that nonetheless allowed the Logos to remain consubstantial with God and the human nature consubstantial with all humans.

What the hypostasis communicated to the human nature of Christ was the strength, first, to do what it was created to do according to its nature, but then second, to go beyond what could be naturally willed and to in fact give expression to eternal Sonship and what the Father willed in human terms. The Logos, far from overriding the human will, empowered it to finally will according to its nature, to "become what you are," as Balthasar says.[61] The result of this is that "through man's participation in God, mankind—man's creatureliness—itself is perfected." Further, "by bringing back human nature from the brink of destruction, by rescuing it ... he reclaims it from the self-alienation of its sinful desire 'to be as god' and presents it to itself ... returning each one of us to ourselves."[62] By being divinized, "the world is perfected as world."[63]

> It is only then, when God and man come closest to each other and meet in a single person that it becomes obvious before our very eyes that God is eternally, irreducibly other than man and that man may therefore not seek his salvation in a direction that implies an abandonment of his own nature.[64]

In this *communicatio* the Son shared in the suffering of the human and the human received a glorification from its union with the divine.

What this exchange of properties also ensured was that a true nonresistance to evil on the part of the Logos remained in the picture. Without the hypostatic *communicatio idiomatum,* the Son of God would not have absorbed personally the barbs of human violence. God would have remained untouched by human suffering in the face of evil. But in beckoning disciples to a costly forgiveness of their enemies, God is not demanding they pay the price for a kind of love from which God would be exempt if a Nestorian account were true. In Maximus's terms, God really was suffering the hatred of humanity. And yet on the other hand, resisting the Monothelite

---

[61]Ibid., 226.
[62]Ibid., 257.
[63]Ibid.
[64]Ibid., 256–7.

view, this suffering, which God partook of hypostatically, was
genuine love. That is, it was God sharing in *our* suffering; it was not
God suffering in his own nature. God in his own nature remained
untouched by pain but in this *communicatio* he experienced
its depths. The *analogia entis* remains in play, the ever-greater
dissimilarity between God and creature is true even in the Garden
while God is living the cost of love for his enemies. Because this
suffering was a suffering not in God's own nature but through his
exchange of properties with human nature, Christ's suffering is
the height of love, entered freely. In response to the Monothelists,
Maximus insisted that God remained free in his assumption of
human weakness and in his absorption of human hatred. Balthasar
points out:

> Death and suffering belong of necessity to human nature in the
> concrete, as an expression of its weakness and abandonment.
> Through the Incarnation, however, they become at the same time
> a kind of freedom, an expression of power. On the other hand,
> the unity of God's freedom and power with human suffering and
> death achieves that divine annihilation which subjects God to
> what is not God. The result of both is redemptive suffering. "He
> suffered, if one may put it this way, in a divine way, because he
> suffered freely."[65]

This *communicatio idiomatum* envisioned by Maximus moved
beyond the four adverbs of Chalcedon and now began to feel out
how a union could occur between two natures that was unconfused
and undivided. Chalcedon had mostly relied on negation and had
not described how the union of the two natures occurred. According
to the inquiry of our project, we could say that the strategy for
resisting the drift from *preservation* of the human to *secularity* is the
communicatio leading to deification. Christ, though utterly human
in all his life, did not become secularized. His human nature, while
preserved intact, was not left untouched by the eternal Sonship of
Christ but was taken into union with the Logos and lived as active,
human nonresistance to the Father. It's very uniqueness as a human
nature became the register, the expression of the Logos in its giving

---

[65]Balthasar, *Cosmic Liturgy*, 259. He is discussing and quoting *Ambigua*, PG
91, 1056A.

back to the Father. Thus Balthasar can say that in the figure of Christ we see one "who had the [natural human] ability to will ... which in its realization developed, not in the direction of becoming its own [human] hypostasis, but toward that of God [the Son], without however ceasing to be a genuine human ability."[66]

This it seems to me is a significant challenge for gospel pacifists to take up in the modern world. It introduces a strong *evangelistic* intent to our ethics, the desire not only to be nonviolent, but to somehow empower our enemy, through God's grace, through the divine love flowing through us, to rise in glorious union with the Father. Love in this sense is not just loving the person as a secular entity, as though such a limiting of the person were the "real" person. Divine love in the world loves the actual person in all his or her humanness, but this actual humanness is fully actualized only in deification. We love this person *in God* and *toward God*, which is this person's fullest humanity. Union with God is the intent of costly love for the enemy.

We have explored now the two directions to which Christ offered his nonresistance, to the Father and to the wretchedness of the human condition. He lived the perfect transposition of Sonship in terms of human self-abasing love, and he consented to the full weight of the evil arrayed against him by preserving and then deifying a natural will. In *Man in History*, Balthasar sums up this neo-Chalcedonian faith and brings these two into unity:

God ... uses man in all his [man's] existential doubtfulness and fragility and imperfectability as the language in which he expresses the word of redemptive wholeness. God, therefore, uses existence extended in time as the script in which to write for man and the world the sign of a supra-temporal eternity. Hence, the man Jesus, whose existence is this sign and word of God to the world, had to live out simultaneously the temporal, tragic, separating distance [from his own origin, i.e. God] and ... the conquest of [that distance] through ... elective obedience to the choosing will of the eternal Father.[67]

---

[66]Ibid., 228.
[67]As quoted in Aidan Nichols, *Divine Fruitfulness: A Guide Through Balthasar's Theology Beyond the Trilogy* (Washington, DC: Catholic University of America Press, 2007), 132.

Nonresistance as Patience in *A Theology of History*

I wish to complete our exploration of Balthasar in this chapter by looking at one of his writings, *A Theology of History*, to see how this neo-Chalcedonian dynamic was emphasized in Balthasar as *Gelassenheit*. It illustrates Mark McIntosh's observation that Balthasar picks up Maximus's Christology and renders it ever more concrete and personal in his development of a theology of mission.[68] *A Theology of History* is an extended reflection on how Christ figures the unity in difference between God and the world not only at the single point of his conception, but by his earthy, temporal acts of prayer, obedience, and waiting. To contemplate this cosmic work of reconciliation between God and the world, according to Balthasar, the believer is led to gaze in wonder at the daily unguessable choices of Christ as he walked through his days. Balthasar does this by attending to Christ's relation to time, the manner in which he received time (and indeed all of nature) from the Father and returned it in obedience, surrender, and self-gift for the world.

Balthasar transposes the Chalcedonian concern about Person and nature into the more modern concerns about singularity and universality in order to draw a theological ethic from the facts of Christ's life. The reception and return of time within the Son's earthly life form a cosmic reconciliation between "the factual, singular, sensible, concrete and contingent; and the necessary and universal." Because he represents the descent of the Absolute into the human register of a single, unique human being, he is both the universal "timeless" norm of history and the absolutely unique occurrence within it. He reveals the will of God for the world in all his particular acts and words, but also in his very existence. "All existences, both before him and after him, receive their meaning from Christ's existence."[69] As the norm of history he is "raised to a position of absolute dominance and hence, fundamentally ... the centerpoint of all persons and their history," something no other human can achieve.[70] But he is also a single unique existence within history, living as a particular person in a particular time, something

---

[68]McIntosh, *Christology from Within*, 42.
[69]Balthasar, *Theology of History*, 71.
[70]Ibid., 9.

that God did not *need* to do for his own life (thus fundamentally unguessable).

> The resulting formula is both daunting and mysterious. Daunting because it subordinates all the norms of this world, their study and application, to the "particular law" of the uniqueness of Jesus Christ as the revelation, in the concrete, of the free will of God for the world. Mysterious because it bases this claim to total lordship (*kyriotes*) upon a mystery which cannot be surveyed or judged from any point of scientific observation: the mystery of the hypostatic union of the divine and the human in Christ, which casts its light and its shadow, directly or obliquely across all the values of this world.[71]

For this reason, if we really want to grasp the mystery and meaning of Christ as the revelation of the Father, "there is no place for abstraction, for disregarding particular cases, for bracketing off inessential accidentals at the historical level of his life."[72] The very texture of Christ's earthly life in all its unique, existential variety, its being *this* and not *that* by the real-time choices of this Person in hypostatic union, is what reveals the eternal nature of the creator God and provides thus a universal norm. For theology has the task of preserving "the normative content shining out from the irreducible fact."[73] This unique Person is "a miracle undiscoverable and unguessable by philosophical thought."[74] One could not arrive at this universal truth by "exceptionally profound thought."[75] One can only contemplate it as it arises in history. Neo-Chalcedonian Christology thus serves to direct the theologian ever to the existent, to the unique occurrence within the historical life of Christ, and to draw from that contemplation a vision into universal norms that apply to life and faith.[76] And so Balthasar picks from the tree

---

[71]Ibid., 14.
[72]Ibid., 16.
[73]Ibid., 17.
[74]Ibid., 10.
[75]Ibid., 16.
[76]Balthasar then concedes that this Chalcedonian approach to history and meaning heightens "the historical pole of human existence" in a manner that lends credence or at least shows itself akin to existentialism in modern thought. But whether this theology is the basis for an existentialist philosophy or of existentialism as a

of Chalcedonian Christology the fruit for theological ethics. Any theology, in order to be truly Christian, must be anchored in the real-time choices of Jesus of Nazareth. Union with Christ occurs through a contemplation of the postures and choices of Christ.[77]

In a way familiar to those who read his work widely, Balthasar here demonstrates the peculiar "manner of existence" by which Christ reveals the eternal life of the triune Godhead. "It is the will of him who sent me, not my own will that I have come down from heaven to do" (Jn 6:38): this is an oft-repeated verse and motif within Balthasar's Christology. The "form of Jesus' existence" was his mission to carry out to the furthest extremity, the will of the Father. This has first a negative aspect: not my will. But this negative aspect is set within a larger positive, whereby Christ is willing to carry out with every part of his being and life, the mission laid upon him by the Father. It was of his "essence" as Son to receive "life," "insight," "spirit," "word," "will," "deed," "doctrine," "work," and "glorification" from the Father in such a way that he has it "in himself" and in such a way that he disposes of it on his own accord, but never in any way that it denies his core existence as the sent one.[78]

It cannot be overemphasized that this utter availability for the Father's will in Balthasar's thought is verily the genuinely personal authentic self-expression of Jesus. It is not something imposed on him externally. This is an earthly transposition of his eternal divine mode of existence within the Trinity. "It is indeed this receiving of himself which gives him his 'I,' his own inner dimension, his spontaneity, that sonship with which he can answer the Father in reciprocal giving."[79] This receiving is not the "reception of something eternally alien … but the bestowal upon him of that which is most his own."[80] He receives that which is most his own in the eternal begetting of the Father, but that which is most uniquely

---

secularized derailment of Christianity is of no concern to the theologian, Balthasar says, "the business of theology is not to keep one eye on philosophy, but, with its gaze obediently turned towards Jesus Christ, simply and directly to describe how he stands in time and in history as the heart and norm of all that is historical." Ibid.

[77] This is similar to what we described above with regard to the early Anabaptist understanding of nonresistance. Through a contemplation of Christ's choices regarding power, the believer is made one mind with Christ.

[78] Balthasar, *Theology of History*, 26.

[79] Ibid.

[80] Ibid., 26–7.

his own is, in his earthly sojourn, precisely his submission unto death, his utter, human assent to the will of God in the face of evil, both human and demonic. "His mode of being here on earth will simply be the manifestation in the created sphere, the translation into creatureliness, of this heavenly form of existence: existence as receiving, as openness to the will of the Father, as subsistent fulfillment of that will in continuous mission."[81]

It is this very existence as a being-not-for-himself that makes Christ's mode of existence available to his brothers and sisters. His "being as self never becomes a theme (and thus inevitably a problem) but only passes, down to its very roots into prayer." His being as such is an availability to the human community and is always a prayer to the Father for his fellow humans. "But through grace even the rest of the children of God may participate in this trinitarian love and surrender."[82] Here we can begin to see that the hypostatic unity, what Balthasar earlier called the summit of formal Christology in Maximus, has been transformed into a path, a sojourn by which the children of God enter into that manner of existence demonstrated in the unique life of Christ. As Balthasar would say later in *Theo-Logic*,

> This means that the Spirit will not simply interpret a teaching (let alone the mere letters of "Scripture"), but will guide us to the vital depths of what takes place between Father and Son, and introduce us into the hypostatic realm. Nor will this be a kind of guided tour for a group of tourists visiting an as yet unknown landscape or a fascinating underground grotto: we can only be introduced to the christological reality if we are prepared to be assimilated to it. This unveils the central Pauline aspect of this "guiding" by the Spirit: it makes us to be sons in the eternal Son, *filii in Filio*.[83]

---

[81]Ibid., 27. "All this manifests 'the absolute positive aspect of differentiation' in absolute Being, which implies that the hypostases do not possess the divine nature in common like an untouchable treasure; rather, the divine nature is defined through and through by the mode of divine being (*tropos tes hyparxeos*)." Balthasar, *Theo-Drama*, 1993, 2:258.

[82]Balthasar, *Theology of History*, 28.

[83]Hans Urs von Balthasar, *Theo-Logic: The Spirit of the Truth*, trans. Graham Harrison, vol. 3 (San Francisco, CA: Ignatius, 2005), 18. We will explore this pneumatic element of Christology in Chapter 5.

Balthasar thus takes Maximus's Chalcedonian Christology and demonstrates that this is the formal principle of Christ's daily, missional, handing over of himself for the Father's disposal, and that by this handing over of himself, Christ also draws others into the same mystery. I believe this is a significant rediscovery of how dogmatics function in Christian spirituality and ethics. The confessional witness of the church is not some freestanding set of rules or propositions but is rather the church's testimony to what occurred in the dark of Bethlehem, Gethsemane, and Golgotha, in a way that draws us in to personally appropriate those realities and have them give shape to our own obedience. Confession in its creedal sense moves seamlessly to confession in its martyrological sense. Theology and ethics are united in this mystery.

Balthasar goes further to highlight the crucial aspect of Christ's assumption of human existence in the mode of time: his unwillingness to "anticipate the will of the Father. He does not do that precise thing which we try to do when we sin, which is to break out of time."[84] Christ speaks of "the hour" that is coming but leaves its timing, nature, and occurrence in the hands of the Father. In sin we arrogate to ourselves "the long view," we try to gain a God's-eye view of the world, rushing ahead in the presumption that we already know what is in store for us. "Hence the restoration of order by the Son of God had to be the annulment of that premature snatching at knowledge, the beating down of the hand outstretched towards eternity, the repentant return from a false, swift, transfer into eternity to a true, slow, confinement in time."[85] This, says Balthasar, explains the high priority of patience in the New Testament,

> more central even than humility; the power to wait, to persevere, to hold out, to endure to the end, not to transcend one's limitations, not to force issues by playing the hero or the titan, but to practice the virtue that lies beyond heroism, the meekness of the lamb which is *led*.[86]

Patience as the virtue suitable to a contemplative attentiveness to the cadence of the Father becomes here the inner posture of

---

[84]Balthasar, *Theology of History*, 30.
[85]Ibid.
[86]Ibid., 30–1.

nonresistance. It is also the mode in which nonresistance becomes visible in the world. *Kenosis* becomes, in Balthasar, the willingness of the all-knowing Logos to live as a human with what knowledge the mission of the Father demanded and no more.

In *Theo-Drama IV*, Balthasar links Christ's willingness to patiently leave "the hour" in God's hands with the specific content of Jesus's teachings on nonresistance. When Christ urges his hearers to "leave everything, not to resist, to love their enemies, to follow him unconditionally, to take up their cross daily, to give away even what is most necessary (the widow's mite), to take the lowest place," he is urging them to allow their lives to be formed by "the overwhelming demands of a supratemporal scale of values."[87] Nonresistance in this view is the transposition, figured by the incarnation, by which Christians come to live the eternal begotteness of the Son as a refusal to anticipate or short-circuit the manner and cadence of God's self-revelation. Secularity is the disenchanting of time, the stripping away of the sense that time is given to the Christian for God's purposes. As the Christian learns like Christ to leave "the hour" in the hands of the Father, each moment is at once "our time" but also at the same time "God's time." In this sense there is a strong connection between the commands of nonresistance in Mt. 5:38-48 and the forbidding of worry and anxiety in Mt. 6:25-34. Both entail a "letting be" to the reality of the world out of yieldedness to the Father.

Christ has taken his Sonship and offered it in terms that we, through the Spirit, are able to imitate in our own lives. This is not the abandonment of the human, but rather the deification of Adam's created nature, even under circumstances of wretchedness and duress, even under the curse. What I am suggesting is that this Maximian, Dyothelite, Balthasarian perspective on the drama of incarnation is, through sanctification, the dogmatic momentum of gospel pacifism. Gospel pacifism in this sense becomes the Marian consent to the mystery of the incarnation, God's chosen way (unguessable!) to overcome evil with good. It is a participation in his patient yielding to the Father's cadence of saving drama.

---

[87]Balthasar, *Theo-Drama*, 1994, 4:233.

Implications

Nonresistance as developed in the Mennonite tradition is an unwillingness to use violence against evil. While this term has recently been criticized for resulting in an overly passive pacifism, we have sought to re-form it by situating it within the active defenselessness of Christ to his Father and the resulting defenselessness of Christ to the world. This we are suggesting gives gospel pacifism an abiding unity in difference within the world. Jesus's worldly nonresistance was an active embrace, in various modes, of the concrete existence of the world at a metaphysical, physical, relational, and spiritual level, which placed him in a confrontation with the cursed condition of the world. It also set Christ apart from the world. Christ's difference from his surroundings was secured by his nonresistance to the Father. It was in these day-by-day (or night-by-night) encounters with the Father that Jesus received his mission to move on to the next village to announce the Kingdom there also (Mk 1:38). Balthasar emphasizes that by this daily *Gelassenheit* Christ sojourned to the Mount of Olives and faced the evil of a gathering night. This was a divine patience by which Christ allowed the times of his life to be cadenced by the Father's will rather than the violent imposition of divinity on the world. This was in fact his divinity in earthly expression. As the church becomes conformed to Christ, it finds its posture vis-à-vis the world within Christ's unity in difference. Here the world is taken in and "preserved" but only in union with Christ with a view toward deification.

This could be considered the source of a *trinitarian* pacifism. It is a posture toward the enemy that is lived out in union with the one whose nonresistance to the sin of the world gave perfect expression to the trinitarian procession of Sonship, received from the Father. It has its source in the transcendence of God in his trinitarian being lived out in human conditions; however, we are not left on our own to extrapolate what such trinitarian life might look like. Balthasar has shown us that we learn such trinitarian life, as is proper for humans, by attending to the stories of Jesus in the gospels as he walked (not rushed!) through his days.

The pacifism of the church conformed to this pattern will be a missional nonresistance, in step with the objectives and modalities of the Son's descent into the world. It takes its shape as a posture of the announcement of good news. Gospel pacifism is not a self-standing principle within the world, nor is it the sum total of the good news. Rather, it is but a disposal of oneself to the Father for his purposes and methods of confronting evil through Christ. It is a disposal of oneself that is *natural*, offering Adam's gift in Adam's way to God. When God sets out to reconcile the world to himself, he did it in such a way that we could find an analogous participation in it.

This is a *scriptural* ethic that remains scriptural. This nonresistance will have a nonguessable, nonpredictable element, since it moves by its daily calibration to the scripturally given actions of the Lord as Christ walks the earth today.[88] This too shows us that gospel pacifism cannot erect itself as a portable principle. It is centered through contemplation on the living, moving, deciding, even lordly "I" of Christ giving a startling expression to the desires and movements common to the human community. To be a gospel ethic, pacifism must participate in this hypostatic lordliness, this transcendence via nonresistance by a day-to-day union with Christ as revealed in scripture. It must be tethered to the scriptural descriptions of the manner and method of Jesus, and see these scriptural dramas as figuring the world's history unto the end of time.

But this does not mean pacifism cannot be creative and confident in its response to new situations. It is not a rote *imitation* that we are after but a deification patterned after the actions of Jesus. There is a divine power for improvisation here. This too is part of a *hypostatic* basis for ethics, that each person, though connected by nature to Jesus is not simply a replica of Jesus, a cloned *hypostasis* as it were, of the incarnate. Rather, in the day-to-day "letting be" of the Father in our life union with Christ, we are deified to become the fullest expression of ourselves, a humanity that cannot be reached by the power of our human nature alone but is lifted by grace to become itself in a way unimaginable. In this deification we bring to the conjunction all our ideas and gifts, and all our days, these moments that our *ours* to give. These all find their highest realization paradoxically in the utter self-gift, which this deification elicited in the Second Adam.

The bidirectional nonresistance of Christ leads us to believe that deification as understood by Maximus and arguably as understood

---

[88]This nonguessable aspect does not need to look like an occasionalism in which every action is suspended pending a direct intervention by God. Virtue need not be the sequestering of human deliberation from the day-to-day guidance of God.

by the earliest Anabaptists[89] have strong congruences. In this view we become sanctified as we are drawn up into union with God and receive his divine energies for our benefit and his mission. As Alvin Beachy said about early Anabaptist views of grace, it brings about "a reversal of the incarnation in which the eternal Word becomes man in order that man may become God."[90] In bringing in this Maximian and Balthasarian understanding of deification, we can say that Christ's nonresistance is fundamentally open to his brothers and sisters. Because Christ did not assume a human nature inaccessible to us, but one consubstantial with ours, and even weighted with the punishment of sin, Christ's defeat of evil with love becomes the sanctity of the church in its own encounter with evil through the church's daily participation in Christ. His difference from us was not in the condition of his humanity, but in the clarity with which he saw and affirmed the will of the Father, empowering his human nature to do infinitely more than it could within its own limits. What Christ accomplishes by incarnation we are offered by grace. Christ embodied this embrace of the world as the head of the Mystical Body, the church, opening the door for his members to share in his unity in difference. This suggests that while our own nonviolence will be a peregrinating affair, it has as its final destiny the unity of humanity with God in heaven, where the infinite distance between our natures will finally be evident against the backdrop of love.

But it will be a peregrinating affair. Chalcedonian nonresistance by the church is not a possession the church can once take into its house, domesticate and guard in its pristine form. A truly bidirectional nonresistance continually exposes the church to divine judgment, and this divine judgment creates an exile for the church throughout her days. "If you invoke as Father the one who judges all people impartially according to their deeds, live in reverent fear during the time of your exile." (1 Pet. 1:17) In this unity in difference the church is always setting out again to a new country, always being exposed again to the infinite love of the Father who never rests content until the glory of his Son has shone through all the world's days, in all the world's cultures, and been embraced by

---

[89]Thomas N. Finger, "Anabaptism and Eastern Orthodoxy: Some Unexpected Similarities?," *Journal of Ecumenical Studies* (December 1, 1994): 76–83.
[90]As quoted in ibid., 76.

every man, woman, and child. There is here no earthly city for this ethic to rest in, though it finds many friends along the path.

In the previous chapters we saw the instability that secularity had created for a Mennonite gospel pacifism. What began as life achieved by the believer in union with Christ in the sixteenth century became increasingly imaginable through secular, instrumental means. It appealed to wider society through its promise of civility. In a secular age, Pharaoh's magicians imitate the signs of Moses and Aaron, and this is unsettling. We also saw that in its desire to affirm ordinary human life, secularity has questioned the way Christianity asks its devotees to sacrifice themselves for a life hereafter.

From the perspective we have arrived at here, could we not suggest that secularity enables a new and deeper appropriation of the Chalcedonian confession? The trajectory of secularity has been a process of humanity coming to itself, in more self-conscious awareness and intention. What was formerly intuitive and instinctive now becomes more explicit and conscious. Humanity is awakened. This is the turn to the subjective that has been much observed. This can lead to an idolatrous autonomy and individualism. But in the mystery that we have been pointing into in this chapter, this awakening to the self could be turned into a more intentional, whole-hearted giving of one's whole self to the Lord. As the power and dignity of the choosing individual comes into focus, this can become either a godlessness or a more heartfelt gift of the self to God and to the world. But in order for this to happen, the nonresistance must be bidirectional. As the self is understood and affirmed and awoken to self-consciousness, it can turn to offer itself more fully to God, or it can turn in on itself.

In a world in which Christ has been revealed humanity awakens to a new regard for itself. This new self-regard and wakefulness can either be conjured by Pharaoh's magicians (for a while) or it can be circled back into the mission of the Father through Christ. What we will see in the next chapter is the increasing polarization of a world in which Christ is revealed. But in this way, I do not think secularity is only an enemy to be resisted, nor is this project about going back to a premodern enchantment with the world. Rather what is called for is an offering of the gifts of the age to the Lord.

What can we say about this nonresistance in regard to the concerns of possible abuse raised by critics of the Mennonite tradition of *Gelassenheit*? Several points do come to mind. First, as envisioned by Balthasar, Christ's nonresistance to the human community around him was given shape by his nonresistance to his Father. If he set aside his own well-being, it was not out of deference to people around him clamoring to impose their agenda, nor out of some lack of self-regard, but out of a confident, personal vocation from his Father. Christ's nonresistance to the Father was precisely what gave him a resistance to beguiling human agendas. *Disinterestedness*, as Balthasar describes it in keeping with Ignatian discernment, is not compliance with the powers of the world but a transparency to the Father's choice and the steeling of the will to consent to and pursue it. It is this steeled will which enables the saint to follow her own vocation.

One might argue that this is merely a defense "in theory" and not a practicable solution for real people in abusive situations, but I think this is an important distinction nonetheless. *Gelassenheit* can only resist its abuses when it is a live, day-to-day, gift of the authentic self to God. Under God's direction the specific texture of a life lived in service for others is given shape. The more nonresistance is secularized into a merely human technique, the more it will lack this transcendent ability to stand against each individual's context. And so, churches who want to resist possible abuses can emphasize the need for individuals to not merely conform to the church's agenda, but to genuinely hear the call of God, and to give themselves for that call, rather than the call of clamoring and dominating voices.

While 1 Pet. 2:13 says to "accept the authority of every human institution" and then goes on to name emperor, slaveholder, and husband as examples of human institutions, this is not enshrined for the believer as a general "principle" of nonresistance. Rather this submission is enjoined "for the Lord's sake" and for "God's approval." It is only suffering "for doing what is right" that is approved by God. This suggests that what is in view is a nonresistance tethered first to a vocation to the Father that figures the submission to human institutions.[91]

---

[91]Balthasar was not immune from the criticism that his ideals of receptivity, yieldedness, and self-donation traded on perceptions of gender types that he read into spirituality. For a very negative appraisal of Balthasar see Tina Beattie, "Sex, Death and Melodrama: A Feminist Critique of Hans Urs von Balthasar," *The Way* 44, no. 4 (October 2005): 160–76. For discussions that seek more nuance, see Aristotle Papanikolaou, "Person, Kenosis and Abuse: Hans Urs von Balthasar and Feminist Theologies in Conversation," *Modern Theology* 19, no. 1 (January 1, 2003): 41–65; Jennifer Newsome Martin, "The 'Whence' and the 'Whither' of Balthasar's Gendered

Secondly, in *The Glory of the Lord*, Balthasar makes a distinction about *Gelassenheit* that is helpful and in keeping with the Christic pattern. For Ignatius of Loyola, abandonment of self to God occurs at the beginning of sanctity, rather than at the end, as it did for German mystics such as Meister Eckhart. Self-abandonment is the entry into a way that eventually produces a positive involvement in the mission of God. It is not the final culmination of spirituality but the means by which one is first rid of other sinful vocations or self-identities in order to find one's true identity and vocation in God.[92] For Christ, "having" is not in any opposition to "receiving."[93] He receives his Person and his mission completely from the Father, but not in such a way that he does not in the end have it in himself. This is confirmed in the gift of resurrection. What this form of self-surrender also provides, besides an active, self-affirming fruit in the end, is a resistance against a radical, independent assertion of oneself that could be the equal and opposite reaction of merely secular attempts to affirm the self.[94] But in this view of spirituality, *Gelassenheit* does not imagine the final dissolution of the self into God, but rather the detachment of the self from competing idols, which then allows one to give oneself authentically and wholeheartedly to God.

But perhaps we can better perceive a nonresistance that is resistant to Mennonite "worm theology" if we apply what we have learned here to the possibility of self-defense. Natural law, with its instinct for self-preservation and self-defense, has been a key problem for gospel pacifists; if self-defense is an ingredient in natural law, does grace simply dissolve nature at this point, overriding natural concern for tribe and self?[95] Such a dissolving of human nature could lend

Theology: Rehabilitating Kenosis for Feminist Theology," *Modern Theology* 31, no. 2 (April 1, 2015): 211–34.
[92]Hans Urs von Balthasar, *The Glory of the Lord: The Realm of Metaphysics in the Modern Age*, ed. Brian McNeil and John Riches, trans. Oliver Davies et al., vol. 5 (San Francisco, CA: Ignatius, 1991), 104.
[93]Balthasar, *Theology of History*, 26.
[94]Ibid.
[95]Here I am drawing on Paul Marten's essay, "With the Grain of the Universe." Cf. J. Daryl Charles, "Protestants and Natural Law," *First Things* 168 (December 2006): 36–7. The stance of pacifism, for Charles, demands that "redemption" triumph over and annul the structures of the world. Aquinas defends killing in self-defense as justified by natural law.

Therefore this act, since one's intention is to save one's own life, is not unlawful, seeing that it is natural to everything to keep itself in 'being,' as far as possible.

itself to the abuses *Gelassenheit* is accused of. Balthasar takes up the relation between Christ and natural law in *A Theology of History* in a way that closely resembles Maximus. Maximus, he said, "presents the natural law and the scriptural law, revelation in nature and revelation in history, as a tension between poles of equal value that mutually complement each other. The third law, which Christ gives and embodies, brings both of them to fulfillment and final unity, in that it simultaneously removes the limitations of both."[96]

In line with this Maximian, Chalcedonian formulation we see a new integration of self-defense within bidirectional nonresistance. The Logos, in assuming human nature and redeeming it did not abolish self-defense but turned it toward the final end of created being, which is the union of all things with God and through that with each other. To this end, it is entirely conceivable, along lines similar to Paul Martens's argument regarding the natural law of the equality of persons, that the natural desire for self-preservation is extended in the law of Christ to defend even strangers and enemies.[97] In Mt. 5:46 Jesus says, "if you love those who love you, what reward do you have?" Here Christ does not abolish care for one's own but points to its limitations in the Kingdom of God—it has no reward. As natural law, this preservation of one's own life is not sufficient to gaining the supernatural end of created life. In Christ's incarnated life this natural instinct to preserve one's own is accepted by Christ,

---

And yet, though proceeding from a good intention, an act may be rendered unlawful, if it be out of proportion to the end. Wherefore if a man, in self-defense, uses more than necessary violence, it will be unlawful. (Aquinas, *ST*, II–II, q. 64, art. 7).

[96]Balthasar, *Cosmic Liturgy*, 292. See also Balthasar, *Theology of History*, 14–15; Joseph Ratzinger, Hans Urs von Balthasar, and Heinz Schurmann, "Nine Propositions on Christian Ethics," in *Principles of Christian Morality* (San Francisco, CA: Ignatius, 1996), 100–102.

[97]

Drawing forward Christ as "the Lawgiver"—as the Word/Logos/Law made flesh—and demonstrating that the evangelical law entails external actions ... open[s] the possibility, internal to Aquinas's own argument, of appealing to Christ as the revelation of divine law that necessarily corrects the failures of human understandings of "good" and "evil" in the first principle of natural law, corrects misguided secondary applications of the first principle of natural law, and attempts to define external relations by human law alone... . For Aquinas, life lived according to the divine law must look different from life lived apart from the divine law for good theological reasons (Martens, "With the Grain of the Universe," 122).

but in his mission, the first Adam is pried open and broken apart to become the Second Adam. This "self" is broken and expanded now to include all his fellow humans—even as they exist in enmity to him. Christ embraces now the whole human community as his body. Christ does a fierce "self-defense" in Gethsemane but one that defends a "self" that is the mystical head of the Body, the new humanity, which includes his enemies. He reaches out to them inviting them to become in fact what they are in his redemption, his brothers and sisters. Even within natural law, self-defense includes the defense of one's family and tribe. That family to be defended is extended in the Garden and becomes catholic as Christ takes his stand with the sinner. As we will see in our final chapter, within the great exchange, the enemy is found within a new solidarity as "the brother for whom Christ died." Preservation within a Chalcedonian perspective is not merely the preservation of the self but the radical Christic preservation and inclusion of the enemy within the "self" to which self-defense refers. Christ turns this human will to secure life into a concern not only for himself, but to a concern for his brothers and sisters as head of the Mystical Body, even as these live as his enemies.[98]

Within this view of natural law and self-defense, we can say that nonresistance, if it takes its form and substance from the incarnation, does not simply demand the extinguishing of the self for the sake of the other, but it requires that the "self" or "one's own" which is preserved, empowered, and defended, be defined incarnationally to embrace in its "self," all those whom Christ called his own. What is "defended" is not the self only in its individual sense, but the self as the "Body" of Christ defined in Gethsemane. A bidirectional nonresistance does not demand the pure sacrifice of the self, but the inclusion of a naturally impossible family of humans in the self to be preserved.

Finally, in Maximus and in Balthasar, this inner furnace of Christic, incarnational *Gelassenheit* is the white-hot forge in which the whole world is reconciled. This is not only about individual salvation, or about the salvation of the church. The cosmic synthesis of all things in heaven and earth is wrought in the mystery of Christ's descent. There is the source of peace, unity, harmony, and perfection. We

---

[98]Maximus sees natural law as chiefly expressing the unity and solidarity that humans have with each other. Balthasar, *Cosmic Liturgy*, 298.

can conclude therefore that in spite of the violent phenomena under which the world labors now in both natural and human realms, its home existence, its most "natural" primal ontological reality leans in the direction of harmony and peace. Violence is a surd irruption, the abolishing of beauty. The world as creation is not fundamentally a violent place and thus it can be entered into with a posture of nonresistance. This is not a sentimental dream but the realization that God is utterly transcendent to creation and that its existence depends on the gracious and unifying action whereby all things live in God—the assumption of the human condition in Christ.

If the church should, in its own patterns of life and worship, also radiate some measure of peace and love, it will surely be living not only in step with the future of the Kingdom of God, but with the creation as it exists suspended in the hands of God. At its most profound level, to live peaceably is to be creaturely when to be creaturely is to be rightly ordered toward the eternal rest of being united in God. Worldly being, in its wholeness at an ontological level, is a form of nonresistance (a letting be) toward God, the Creator who bestows existence. It is an openness and malleability to the gracious Word of God's creative will. The cosmos does not endure through violence but through a union with the love of God as this has been shown in the Christic synthesis of the incarnation, in the Garden of Gethsemane, and the hill of Golgotha.

But is this incarnation ever a *provocation*, and to that word we now turn.

4

Provocation: Violence in the Theo-drama

We have glimpsed the reconciliation of the world in the forge of Christ's bidirectional nonresistance. This is nonresistance following the form and path of the incarnation. But a temptation lurks. In contemplating the Word's entrance into the human realm perfectly empowering a human response of praise to the Father even by a cursed tongue, we might naively be tempted to see everywhere a "peace" and "synthesis," to think that presently all manner of things should be well. This by itself would minimize the historical, agonistic, travail by which the Word in flesh delivers the world from its bondage to Satan through time. We must hasten then to view the provocation that the incarnation goads in the human community and to incorporate this dramatizing within our theology of peace as well.

The argument of this chapter is that for pacifism to remain a gospel pacifism within the conditions of secularity, it needs to be united to the incarnational descent of God into the world, *even as that descent becomes the very goad of violence.* We are describing a christological descent within Balthasar's theology—incarnation, provocation, convocation—that we believe offers a dynamic unity in difference in which pacifism can become a gospel pacifism. Here we say that Christ and his disciples are not only nonresistant to violence as a general occurrence but specifically nonresistant to the recoil, the kicking against the goads that Christ's own presence in the world provokes.

Within gospel pacifism there must be some theological account of why people attack one another. Secularity has not only offered pacifists an instrumental means to a secular peace, but a way of de-theologizing violence as well. Puzzling over the perplexing fact of violence has a long history and no one said it more eloquently than Erasmus of Rotterdam in *The Complaint of Peace*. After noting that such diverse entities as the planets and stars, body and soul, vine and stem, loadstone and iron, work together in harmony, and that furthermore "savage lions do not fight each other ... and the concord between wolves is proverbial," he marvels at the wretched human, lacking any natural equipment for war, seething to kill. Clearly the one creature who is born helpless and who has no personal weapons save his rationality and the ability to cooperate with other humans should be the most peaceful of all. But then:

> What Fury appeared with such harmful powers, to scatter, demolish, and destroy them all and to sow an insatiable lust for fighting in the human heart? If custom did not blunt first our sense of amazement and then our awareness of evil, who would believe that men are endowed with human reason who thus fight, brawl, and rage against each other in perpetual discord, strife and war? Finally they confound everything, sacred and profane, with pillaging, bloodshed, disaster, and destruction; no bond is sufficiently sacred to check them in their frenzy for mutual extinction.[1]

With the rising disgust at barbarity on the European scene during Erasmus's time, there is immediately the beginnings of a secularization of violence. Erasmus does not offer a theological account of killing beyond viewing it as a particularly wretched form of passion that Christians, inexplicably, partake in with more vengeance than the heathen. "Anger, ambition and folly" cause war and he begins to lay out the diplomacy, commerce, and rationality, which will lessen the rage for war over time.[2] In Erasmus, the gospel emerges as a "how much more"; if a heathen can be convinced by his own self-interest to sue for peace, "how much more" the Christian who receives the Eucharist. As Charles Taylor showed, this revulsion at barbarity eventually learned to do without the "how much more."

---

[1]Rummel, *Erasmus Reader*, 292.
[2]Ibid., 304.

Part of developing a response to violence that rises above secular explanations to become a gospel ethic, I believe, demands a christological account of violence.[3] In such an account, we look expectantly not only for historical evidence of where humans are indeed this murderous, nor only for a psychological account of the inner desires and fears repressed and unleashed as a person finally rises to kill, nor only for a sociological description of how community dynamics of competition and mimesis conspire to elicit violence. All of these answers must be respected in their own place. But here I am interested in the way the presence of Christ draws to itself these natural realities and leaps forward, exposing an unguessable truth in the roots of violence.

It is our argument here, following Balthasar, that violence is more than one particularly morbid example of the many ways humans sin. As Raymond Schwager points out, violence has a paradigmatic place within the biblical taxonomy of sins. This is exemplified in the description of the earth in Gen. 6:11: "Now the earth was corrupt in God's sight, and the earth was filled with violence." Sin here "is characterized with one single word: violence (hamas)."[4] At the other end of scripture we read regarding the fallen Babylonian harlot that "her sins are heaped high as the heavens," for she traded in human lives and in her "was found the blood of prophets and of saints, and of all who have been slaughtered on earth" (Rev. 18:5,24). Violence sacramentalizes humans' rebellion and alienation from God.[5]

What we will try to see is Balthasar's reading of violent history as occurring "in Christ." All worldly history is revealed in its truest and ruthlessly real state when understood as writhing in an encounter with the ever-present Jesus of Nazareth and his disciples who by the Spirit become his body in the course of the world's days. This writhing encounter is not the only dynamic Christ unleashes. We will

---

[3]Violence is, by now, an immensely broad term that has become not only a word for killing, pillage, and rape, but also racism, abject poverty, psychological abuse, "micro-aggressions," and the whole catalog of ways humans are bad to each other. My focus here is on violence as killing, but a fuller treatment of violence would go beyond to address "malice, and all guile, insincerity, envy and all slander" (1 Pet. 2:1). For a good discussion of the broad theme of violence in the New Testament see Thomas R. Yoder Neufeld, *Killing Enmity: Violence and the New Testament* (Grand Rapids, MI: Baker Academic, 2011).
[4]Raymund Schwager, *Must There Be Scapegoats? Violence and Redemption in the Bible* (Leominster, MA: Gracewing, 1987), 48.
[5]C.f. John R. Yeatts, *Revelation* (Scottdale, PA: Herald, 2003), 341.

see the other side in the next chapter. But in various ways, Balthasar shows us that in his ascension, Jesus never "left" the world, but presses into it now with relentless universality, in and beyond the church. Christ is stirring, goading, haunting, and provoking as the world desperately seeks to go on as though Christ is not there. The world in demonic personification would sooner destroy itself than accept the reality figured in Christ. It is the vocation of the saints to live in the crushing pressure between Christ and the world.

> That is why the message of Jesus as an eschatological message, cannot be surpassed even within the confines of world history, whether it is adopted or rejected by a majority of mankind or suppressed by eschatological counterdesigns, artificially imposed. On the basis of this eschatological provocation introduced by Christ, the drama enacted between God and mankind, and between men themselves as they put forward and defend their warring systems of meaning, is already a drama "in Christ."[6]

Our ambition here must remain modest. We cannot offer anything like a full accounting of violence in its causes, forms, and cures. This is not a full theological or biblical reckoning of murder and its place in the fall, atonement, and discipleship. We must leave to another time the way this view of violence is taken up by Balthasar to solve vexing questions in atonement theology. Using Balthasar's *Theo-Drama* IV as a prime text, I will show how Christ's embrace of finite, human life becomes a kind of virus in the bowels of the rebellious world, eliciting a gag reflex by which the world is brought to judgment.

Gospel pacifism responds only to such violence as Jesus himself provokes in his presence in the world. John H. Yoder said, "The good news is that the violence with which we heirs of Cain respond to our brothers' differentness is the occasion of our salvation. Were it not for that primeval destructive reflex, there would have been no suffering servant, and no wisdom and power of God in the cross."[7] To this Balthasar would respond: agreed; however, the reverse must also be said. The suffering servant, the wisdom, and the power of the cross have provoked a "primeval

---

[6]Balthasar, *Theo-Drama*, 1992, 3:32.
[7]Yoder, *War of the Lamb*, 32.

destructive reflex." A theme text in *Theo-Drama* IV is Jn 15:22 where Christ says, "If I had not come and spoken to them, they would not have sin." Sin is a response to the appearance of Christ. Or, as he paraphrases, "it is only when heaven is wide open that hell too yawns at our feet."[8] It is precisely the love (the nonresistance!) of Jesus that provokes violence and it is this violence that nonresistance responds to.

Regaining a view of violence as *theo-dramatic*, will, I believe, energize the church to pray, suffer, and love in the face of this violence with renewed vision for its role in the theo-drama. When violence is secularized and no longer envisioned as the response of a people or powers to the presence, known or intuited, of Jesus walking about the world, the church settles to remain at instrumentalism. To walk in this path is to know in one's body that when the world descends to its orgies of violence, it is roiling in a deeper, apocalyptic warfare encompassing the church in her offering as she watches with her Master: "Then comes the end, when he hands over the kingdom to God the Father, after he has destroyed every ruler and every authority and power" (1 Cor. 15:24).

The centerpiece of Balthasar's trilogy is the *Theo-Drama* in which he describes the action whereby God enters the human story, thereby setting in motion a saving drama in which the human community has a real role to play. In *Theo-drama* I he set out his dramatic categories by gleaning the insights of great dramatists in history. This he followed with *Theo-drama* II and III, titled in German, "Die Personen des Spiels" or "dramatis personae," in which he draw a picture of a human person strung with tension: "On the one hand the creature is manifestly free before God ... and, on the other hand this freedom is a freedom 'in Christ'—and it is only 'in Christ' that theological persons can exist at all."[9] Balthasar's *Theo-drama* IV is titled "The Action" and it is here that he reflects on the events of salvation history. The tension in this figure of the human, living a form of freedom as a creature, but finally denied true freedom except as it is "in Christ," is an inherently unstable condition. In fact, Balthasar says, it is "so explosive that it [is] bound to burst into flame in the conflagration of the action; accordingly, we begin

---

[8]Balthasar, *Theo-Drama*, 1994, 4:11.
[9]Ibid.

this volume 'under the sign of the Apocalypse.' "[10] It is this startling assertion that we wish to elaborate in this exposition of violence. Balthasar structures *Theo-Drama* IV around an interpretation of the Book of Revelation. The Book of Revelation unveils the larger cosmic "Action" in which infinite freedom (God) saves the world by entering finite freedom and spurring an apocalyptic drama.

Mennonite Interpretation of Revelation

Balthasar sets up our view of the "action" between God and the world in *Theo-Drama* IV by framing his soteriology in a reflection on the Book of Revelation. As such it can be placed beside Mennonite works on Revelation that have ventured into this territory. In the previous chapter on Chalcedon, it was safe to declare that we were bringing something relatively new to Mennonite discourse over pacifism. Here we are adding nuance and depth to considerable work already done.[11] It is perhaps not surprising that a tradition that counts Hans Hüt, Melchior Hoffmann, and Bernard Rothman

---

[10]Ibid. *Theo-Drama* is five volumes in the English translation we are using, but is four volumes in the German edition. The English volumes 2 and 3 are volume 2 in German.

[11]In addition to the main works mentioned below, see J. Nelson Kraybill, *Apocalypse and Allegiance: Worship, Politics, and Devotion in the Book of Revelation* (Grand Rapids, MI: Brazos, 2010), who sees the emphasis in Revelation on empire resistance through the church's worship. Thomas N. Finger's two-volume systematic theology used eschatology as its formal structure; *Christian Theology: An Eschatological Approach*, vol. 2 (Scottdale, PA: Herald, 1989). He reverses the normal order and *begins* with eschatology and ends with a discussion of the nature of God. See also Loren L. Johns, ed., *Apocalypticism and Millennialism: Shaping a Believers Church Eschatology for the Twenty-First Century* (Kitchener, ON: Pandora, 2000); and Yeatts, *Revelation*. Though not only the work of Anabaptist writers, Ted Grimsrud's *Compassionate Eschatology: The Future as Friend* (Eugene, OR: Wipf & Stock, 2011) contains a now-familiar interest in rehabilitating apocalyptic rhetoric from the violence for which it has often been harnessed. Nathan Kerr in his discourse-framing work *Christ, History and Apocalyptic: The Politics of Christian Mission* (Eugene, OR: Wipf and Stock, 2008), 131, applauds John H. Yoder as the paradigmatic apocalyptic theologian for holding that "Jesus lives, concretely and in history, a life-story that is entirely free from and irreducible to any pre-given 'historical' coordinates, and general or 'meta' principle that might serve to range the complexities and contingencies of his history within any universalizable scope or logic."

as its forefathers would take an interest in apocalyptic theology. Balthasar could lead Mennonite exegesis back to its dramatic roots in the Anabaptist apocalyptic fervor, to a time when the Word of God was understood to be a working, live, dramatic stirring of world events.[12] Recent works, however, rather than focusing on the urgency of an age on the brink of Parousia, turn the rhetoric of apocalyptic theology to shape discipleship in an age of militarism, destructive capitalism, and the ruin of creation. That is, rather than focusing on the Apocalypse as a window to Christ's action in history, now pressing in, and soon returning in glory, the focus is on the kind of endurance and faithfulness saints need to exhibit as disciples.

Among Mennonite commentators on Revelation, the exegetical work of Loren Johns's *The Lamb Christology of the Apocalypse of John* is significant and has opened a door for pacifist interpretations of Revelation. After an extensive description of the place of the lamb and lamb symbolism in the Ancient Near East, early Judaism, and the Old Testament, Johns describes the way the lamb imagery of Revelation is wielded by the writer as a rhetorical strategy to form his congregations in faithful nonviolent resistance. He argues "that the images of the lion and the lamb were created specifically to address competing visions of how the Messiah wields power."[13] The rhetoric of the Lamb's triumph "*unmasks* the power of violence." Johns moves interpretation of Lamb imagery away from a dependence on cultic Old Testament ritual sacrifice to be seen rather as a rhetorical device used by John to incite the church to suffer nonviolently, to "follow the Lamb wherever he goes."[14]

J. Denny Weaver is keenly interested in the Lamb of Revelation in the development of his *Nonviolent Atonement*. Following Loren Johns, he argues that "the confrontation of church and empire depicted symbolically throughout Revelation is a nonviolent confrontation"[15] dependent on the death and resurrection of

---

[12]Walter Klaassen, ed., *Anabaptism in Outline: Selected Primary Sources* (Kitchener, ON: Herald, 1981), 317–18. Which is not to say that our aim is to rekindle the chiliastic excesses of 1525, or 1534, in our time; only the lived awareness and expectation of knowing the world to live and move within the providential hand of the Word.

[13]Loren L. Johns, *The Lamb Christology of the Apocalypse of John: An Investigation into Its Origins and Rhetorical Force* (Eugene, OR: Wipf and Stock, 2014), 191.

[14]Ibid., 38–9.

[15]Weaver, *Nonviolent Atonement*, 33.

Christ. Christians participate in this victory through their testimony of death and witness and are never called there to fight violently. Further, "the supposed battle scenes are not really battles at all"; they are over before they begin.[16] Weaver seeks to demonstrate (with Johns) that expiation, particularly as interpreted by Anselm of Canterbury, cannot be supported by the Lamb Christology of Revelation. Rather, the Lamb is used in Revelation as an image of defenseless resistance, or rather, as a symbol of the nonviolent victory Christ won on Golgotha.

What should be noted in these authors is a unified interest in locating Revelation within the first-century confrontation between the church and the empire. This apocalyptic script empowered the relatively powerless early church to mount a resistance to the onslaught of the empire's idolatry. So, it is argued, contemporary Christians living the way of Jesus can believe that their costly obedience is in imitation of the Lamb's mode of conquest. What is emphasized, though, is the nonviolent ethic that the Lamb rhetoric elicits. Revelation for these writers is not so much a christological account of violence as a persuasion to Christian nonviolence. This is summarized well by John R. Yeatts, author of *Revelation* in the Believers Church Bible Commentary series: "The message of Revelation is developed around the primary symbol of Christ the Lamb, who overcame persecution, not by military force and political violence, but by suffering love and exemplary martyrdom."[17] Regarding the seven seals depicted in Rev. 6, Yeatts observes that they are "a series of six seal judgments portraying the inevitable progression in a world that trusts in military solutions to problems. The point is that war leads to civil strife, which in turn leads to material deprivation and finally to death."[18]

---

[16]Ibid., 34, cf. Johns, *Lamb Christology of the Apocalypse of John*, 20.

[17]Yeatts, *Revelation*, 26.

[18]Ibid., 27. Later in a discussion of the evil associated with the seals, Yeatts asks, "In what sense is Christ responsible for the evil in the world?" He replies that all power, though it comes from God is misused by humans with free will and this results in "war, civil strife, famine and death. Nevertheless, in the process, God turns this misuse of power into righteous judgement for breaking the laws of justice built into the created universe." Ibid., 136. What is lacking here is what Balthasar would call a genuine drama in which evil is both dependent and respondent to God's prior gifting of creation with freedom in Christ.

Each of the Mennonite writers noted here is concerned that salvation be kept ethical[19] and worries that any divine intent or sacrificial meanings behind "the slain Lamb" will fund the belief that violence can redeem the world after all, if not by inflicting it, then by suffering its abuse.[20] It may be the case though that an overriding concern to separate God as far as possible from violence leaves violence with only secular explanations. If the world's violence is not providentially goaded and commandeered, then there is perhaps nothing else to do than deploy the instrumentalist techniques that secularity uses to suppress it. Balthasar, I will argue, adds a vital dramatic description of the clash between the church and the world and enables gospel pacifists to see their ethics as participating in God's relationship with violence.

The Apocalypse as Divine and Human Rhetoric

This can be seen clearer, when we note a difference of posture between Balthasar's treatment of the Apocalypse and Loren Johns's *The Lamb Christology*.[21] This concerns the nature of images such as the "Lamb" used in Revelation. Johns's approach is to see the Lamb as a rhetorical strategy that John adapted from his historical-religious context and turned for his inspired purposes.

> The modern reader must determine whether the rhetorical force of a traditional image lies in John's *dependence* upon or *reiteration* of that image, along with its traditional world view, or whether it lies in John's particular *use* of and *redefinition* of that image—or even his repudiation of its traditional world view.[22]

---

[19]To riff on J. Denny Weaver's book, *Keeping Salvation Ethical: Mennonite and Amish Atonement Theology in the Late Nineteenth Century* (Scottdale, PA: Herald, 1997).
[20]Weaver, *Nonviolent Atonement*, 33. Also Johns, *Lamb Christology of the Apocalypse of John*, 161.
[21]I am highlighting Johns's approach not because he is unique in it, but because he is a leading Mennonite exegete who seeks a reading of Revelation contributing to a theology of peace.
[22]Johns, *Lamb Christology of the Apocalypse of John*, 14. Emphasis in original.

Johns adopts the second and possibly the third option. The instructive thing to look out for, in this reading strategy, is the unique "spin" John places on stock rhetorical devices within his tradition. For modern readers the task is to be aware of these images' rhetorical performance, both in the text and in their own discourse, and to thereby "keep it ethical" by utilizing the images in keeping with Revelation's intent. The emphasis here is on the constructive role of the biblical author in wielding rhetorical material for his own purposes in his churches. Johns cites Elizabeth Schüssler-Fiorenza as a guide for his own approach, who says the Apocalypse is a

> poetic-rhetorical work. It seeks to persuade and motivate by *constructing* a "symbolic universe" that invites imaginative participation. The strength of its persuasion for action lies ... in the "evocative" power of its symbols as well as in its hortatory, imaginative, emotional language, and dramatic movement, which engage the hearer (reader) by eliciting reactions, emotions, convictions, and identifications.[23]

Balthasar would respond, but does John the Revelator not *see?* Does he not *receive* a vision from God? Balthasar would be worried about an approach stated this way and the perspective he adopts instead forms an aspect in how he offers us a theology of human violence. Though he would not deny that John had a role in shaping the text, this approach would simply not be dramatic enough for him.[24] It fails to quite grasp the way in which these texts *are* the hand of God in the history and (at the same time) point to the hand of God in history. For example, he is pleased by the title of Austin Farrar's book, *A Re-Birth of Images,* but is critical of the

---

[23]Quoted in ibid., 155. Emphasis added. See also Fiorenza's essay *The Book of Revelation: Justice and Judgment* (Minneapolis, MN: Fortress, 1998), 181–203. According to Johns, the Book of Revelation "is primarily a book of pathetical persuasion," that is, it persuades "by exciting the emotions and imagination of the audience. Johns, *Lamb Christology of the Apocalypse of John,* 157.

[24]According to Kevin Mongrain's exquisite overview of Balthasar's dramatic theology, Balthasar saw a "Gnosticism" in biblical critics' desire to detach themselves from the drama of the divine event that these texts are and narrate the texts from above. "The idea that revelation can be narrated objectively is post-Christian in that it assumes God's interactions with humanity can be surveyed from a higher, neutral perspective." Mongrain, *Systematic Thought of Hans Urs von Balthasar,* 44. For Balthasar's understanding of Scripture see Oakes, *Pattern of Redemption,* 183–208.

THE LAMB'S PROVOCATION OF VIOLENCE

subtitle, *The Making of St. John's Apocalypse.* "Making" sounds too subjective.[25] According to Balthasar, John *received* a vision from God and the text needs to be interpreted as such. Balthasar, in his trilogy, makes much of the fact that drama (and discipleship we could say here) comes from contemplation, from beholding the glory of God beyond our own constructions, as it enters the world in surprising ways. Accordingly, for Balthasar, John "is not a dramatist, but someone commissioned to write down objectively the events shown to him."[26] The book unveils that God is the subject of such disclosure (*apocalypse*). The book itself functions as an act of divine providence, and the seer's human contribution is enveloped within that larger divine action. "An objective world of images exists in God; excerpts from it are communicated now to this prophet, now to that, until in the Apocalypse of John a kind of *summa* is distilled from it." The truth of the revealed images is "guaranteed by the fact that he is their Revealer."[27] God is the One doing the revealing and the book needs to be interpreted by the Christian reader as such. "Ultimately the book of Revelation, coming after all the other books of the New Testament, remains what it is: a window into the ever-greater world of God, which defies all attempts at systematization on our part."[28] The visions of the Apocalypse as presented by John in the book are themselves an intrusion into the world by God that John receives and which ricochet down the centuries. They also witness *to* an intrusion into the world by God. Thus the bewildering use of past, present, and future tense in the book. The Book of Revelation is God bringing the eschatological victory of the Lamb into immediate encounter with the church and the world at every "present" it faces. Joseph Mangina in his commentary on Revelation states what Balthasar also sees:

> We can thus see Revelation as a kind of "apocalyptic haggadah," a rehearsal, a narrative, a memory of an event that is past that is somehow not past, but our present reality, and that toward which all of history is headed. Time is not annulled but transformed. The Spirit traverses even to the end of time, but then returns,

---

Balthasar, *Theo-Drama*, 1994, 4:47n4.
[26]Ibid., 4:19.
[27]Ibid., 4:16.
[28]Ibid., 4:18.

bringing the end itself with him. The one who stands at both the beginning and the end is Jesus Christ.[29]

As the Spirit brings the reality of the Christ to bear on the world through this rebirth and unleashing of divine images, the world encounters Christ in his most drama-creating glory. Because of the scriptural revelation of Christ in the Revelation, the world is not permitted the stupor of denial; it can no longer claim that *past* events such as the crucifixion, ascension, and Pentecost, nor the *future* coronation of the Lamb as the Lord of history for all to see, are not of the most immediate, pressing urgency. Scripture actively works through all the world's days to unveil the victory of the Lamb in such a way as to inflict upon the dark powers the unimaginable assurance of their own demise as "the nations" arrayed against the body of Christ in the world.

It is for this reason that Balthasar is constantly downplaying scholarly interest in the discovery of precedents the Book of Revelation may have had in ancient culture, politics, or religion, though he does not deny that there is some truth in them. Revelation cannot be adequately understood only by exploring either first-century imperial realities and the church's response to Caesar, nor "end time" historical events and the church's response at that time to the beast. He is constantly diminishing any possibility of reducing it to "coded" referrals to historical epochs in the church's life, either ancient, modern, or future.[30] These interests fail to grasp the freedom of the divine Orator in remaking and unleashing these images, and of the historical impact that the presence of the supernatural had in the life of John and in the lives of Revelation's readers henceforth.[31]

---

[29]Joseph L. Mangina, *Revelation* (Grand Rapids, MI: Brazos, 2010), 31.

[30]Balthasar, *Theo-Drama*, 1994, 4:15, 16–17, 20, 20n7, 31n3, 33, 37, 38, 42. In this Balthasar is going against the stream of considerable historical-critical opinion. Adela Yarbro Collins writes, "Perhaps the hardest won and most dearly held result of historical-critical scholarship on the Revelation to John is the theory that the work must be interpreted in terms of the historical context in which it was composed." "Political Perspective of the Revelation to John," *Journal of Biblical Literature* 96, no. 2 (June 1977): 241. Richard Hays says, though, that this approach has yielded "surprisingly slight results" since so little can be recreated of the historical setting. Also, much of the material seems to be set in heaven rather than on earth. Richard Hays, *The Moral Vision of the New Testament: A Contemporary Introduction to New Testament Ethic* (New York: HarperCollins, 1996), 172.

31

The images of Revelation are Christ's "modes of appearance," his chosen manner of appearing within the world that is not any less "real" for being apocalyptic scripture.[32] An important sentence describing what is happening in the Book of Revelation vis-à-vis the churches, is that "the images are like a mysterious 'dogmatics' that stands, irreducible, over against the actualization of the Church's life."[33] This also points to a concern in Balthasar's work that will recur in this chapter—the encounter between God and the world is an "unguessable" event. It is genuine revelation, which cannot be deduced. This is Balthasar's understanding of the role of Revelation in divine providence and it is a crucial aspect of understanding theo-dramatic violence. Revelation's images are the God-revealed depths of history as it exists in dramatic encounter with the Lamb.

Liturgy and Slaughter

What is unveiled in Revelation is a crescendoing rhythm of liturgy and slaughter, or divine judgment, which evokes praise from the lips of saints.[34] The saints laud the judgments of God but are also on the receiving end of divinely goaded violence from their enemies. The victory of the Lamb is such that it seems to yield only more determined opposition, and so there is a deep irony in the lauding of the saints because the events they are celebrating inevitably escalate a *mega thlipsis* and intense pressure against them.

Balthasar goes through Revelation vision by vision to show that its function as scripture is to unveil this revolt, assert the divine wielding of the world's most demonic acts, and unleash the liturgy

---

Von Balthasar is compelled to argue that historical-critical scholars are historically naïve when they bracket out the presence of the supernatural in the lives of the author's who produced the canonical Scriptures. The historical critics betray their own ideals with their a priori bias that the supernatural was not a real historical presence for the authors of the canonical texts. Claiming to be a historical scholar while ignoring the real historical presence of the supernatural in a particular place, person, and time, von Balthasar would argue, is a contradiction. (Mongrain, *Systematic Thought of Hans Urs von Balthasar*, 123)

[32]Balthasar, *Theo-Drama*, 1994, 4:45–6.
[33]Ibid., 4:46. In other words these images function as theo-dramatic "keys" that work to expose the to and fro of history as accepting and rejecting Christ. They resist a secular understanding of history.
[34]Ibid., 4:56.

of praise which this mystery reveals. The seven seals "open up the stage of the entire world action." John is shown "the eschatological crisis toward which history is running, once it had been set in motion by the Lamb's breaking the seal."[35] Here world history is unveiled as theo-dramatic, spurred to action by the Lamb. Balthasar calls the first four horsemen "timeless dimensions" of fallen existence ("life is a fierce wrestling for superiority," "life is controlled by reward and retribution," life is a "justice," which is given to the world, and finally "life is destined for death")[36] that are nonetheless attributable indirectly to the Lamb's authoritative rule over time. These are aspects of the violent refusal of the world unleashed by the Lamb's opening of the seals. The fifth and sixth seals are more concrete; "injustice rules, and the oppressed cry out urgently for right to be restored: they have to be patient."[37] The end is both impatiently and anxiously awaited.

The series of judgments that are unveiled in the seven trumpets "give a fantastic portrayal of the demonization of human history."[38] Balthasar sees Rev. 11:15 to be a decisive marker in the book: "The kingdom of the world has become the kingdom of our Lord and of his Messiah, and he will live for ever and ever." With this enthronement we hear the third woe, which is "the immediate reality of God's mighty power and wrath and his judgement upon the dead."[39] As the Messiah appears on earth in greater clarity in Rev. 11:15 and in the birth of the Child in Rev. 12:2, now "the devil comes forth in person (as opposed to the mere smoke from the abyss and his demonic offspring in 9:1-21); a further stage is reached when he assumes concrete shape in the two beasts ... unmasking himself as the perverse mimic of the divine Trinity."[40]

A central conviction of Balthasar's interpretation is that there is a trajectory within the book. As Christ becomes more "concrete" or incarnated in the world, so also does the evil power of Satan. With every revelation of the intense suffering love of the Lamb comes the revelation of more pointed, vicious, and imitative violence against the Lamb. Each increase in the Lamb's pressure on the world is met

---

[35]Ibid., 4:71.
[36]Ibid., 4:30–1.
[37]Ibid., 4:30.
[38]Ibid., 4:33.
[39]Ibid., 4:34.
[40]Ibid., 4:34–5.

by a more knowledgeable, pointed, intent revolt. Revolt becomes more self-conscious and free. But in this heightened self-awareness, the revolt comes to consume the sinner and it increasingly overwhelms his own life. In this increased self-consciousness of revolt is an increase in divine judgment. He describes how the judgments described in Rev. 16

> show symbolically how the divine anger penetrates the sinner's whole interior and exterior milieu: it is a psycho-physical abscess... . Nor do these things lead to conversion but—as in the case of the Egyptian plagues, which in many ways serve as a "type" here—to an ever-greater hardening of the heart. The plagues are not institutions of mercy: they are judgement; they lay bare the presence, in souls, of the essence of evil.[41]

Judgment in Balthasar's interpretation is the incursion of divine fire into the world that brings evil out into the open and pushes it onto the stage, where its secret intent can no longer be disguised. "Sin becomes unbearable torment."[42] Each of these cross-sections "reveals the total theological situation of history with regard to the opposition of faith and unbelief."[43] Balthasar thus sees Revelation not as coded referrals to discrete world events, whether in John's day or thereafter, but as the divine manner and occasion of "rubbing it in," relentlessly pressing in the true reality of Christ to a world that violently refuses to accept it. The apocalypse of Christ drives the world to paroxysms of self-destructive violence within which the divine judgment of sin can be perceived. Scripture plays an ongoing role in theo-dramatic history by unveiling the Lamb whose presence provokes judgment.

Balthasar's reading of Revelation offers a perspective on the question of whether God is "violent." As noted earlier, Mennonite commentators have sought to show that the victory of the Lamb is a nonviolent one since it is by his cross that all the victories of Revelation unfold. As such Revelation has played a significant role in the discussion of whether "nonviolence" as it appears in Jesus's teachings and death can be seen as the revelation of God's

---

[41]Ibid., 4:37.
[42]Ibid.
[43]Ibid., 4:40.

nature.[44] Does God in fact kill people? J. Denny Weaver argues that
as interpreted by Christ, God does not kill and he goes to some
length to show that Revelation does not show God killing people
but rather that the divine "violence" in Revelation is only sinful
people bringing on themselves the consequences of their own sins.[45]

Balthasar would agree to a point but would find this a too
secular and neutral understanding of violence. He tries to take more
seriously the language of divine intention in the Apocalypse than
Weaver. The liturgy that lauds the work of God in the wake of the
destruction points to a deeper mystery than only the consequences
of human deeds being unveiled: "Here alone in the New Testament,
a resounding 'Hallelujah' greets the most terrible ruination there
portrayed (Rev 19:1, 3, 4, 6)."[46] Whether the destruction is wrought
by humans, demonic beasts, or by the wrath of the Lamb itself,
the response of the saints is to praise God and his judgments. This
implies a divine intentionality and action behind the judgment. The
slaughter elicits adoration. And yet the description veils over the
violence, often portraying it as already past.[47]

In short, we could say that for Balthasar, God is able to destroy
his enemies without "violation." God goads sinners to destruction
by giving them ever more freedom in the revelation of Christ.
Where there is no violation of God-given freedom there is no
violence. The divine involvement in the destruction of the wicked
without murderous guilt for the "ruination" depicted is explained
by Balthasar in terms of the motif of "handing over," a recurring
"*traditio*" (a surrender, giving up) that he sees in Revelation. This
traditio has its origins in the Trinity where in the *processio* of the
Father he hands himself over to the Son gifting the Son with infinite
freedom and glory. "For just as the Father has life in himself, so he
has granted the Son also to have life in himself" (Jn 5:26). The Son
uses this freedom (divinity) to reciprocate in gratitude. Within this
primal "*traditio*" is included every subsequent handing over. As we
will see in more detail in the next section, freedom, for Balthasar
carries within it a weight, a demand of return, or reciprocity. There
is no "neutral" way of having freedom. It has this hidden weight

---

[44]See also the extended discussion with various authors in, "Is God Nonviolent?"
Conrad Grebel Review 21, no. 1 (2003).
[45]Cf. Weaver, *Nonviolent God*, 35–53.
[46]Balthasar, *Theo-Drama*, 1994, 4:54.
[47]Ibid., 4:41.

within it because of its analogy to the primal *traditio* of the Son's eternal generation in the Father. To give someone freedom is to weight them with the beckon to participate in divinity, to return the gift in gratitude. The gift of freedom is thus a gift of love, and love demands to be seen as love.

The Son is handed over to creation, given for the world. This revelation of the Son in the world gives a freedom to the world, and again the weight, the expectation of return in gratitude and love. In the world, "the Lamb has the same authority to hand on gifts (*traditio*) to others."[48] The Lamb "is God's mode of involvement in, and commitment to, the world; the Lamb is both 'worthy' and 'able' not only to symbolize God's involvement but to *be* it."[49]

> This "handing over" is repeated more than twenty times in the Book of Revelation: the horsemen are given their insignia and hence their power; the first beast is given the power to wage war against the saints; the second beast is allowed to give breath to the image of the first beast; the angels too are given bowls of wrath and the power to hurt the earth, and so forth.[50]

All manner of agents are "given" freedom and power by the Lamb's revelation on earth, and this gift of freedom dramatizes created existence. It creates a situation in which the receiver must either accept the freedom as it is given, in loving surrender to God, or violently resist. The freedom that God gives in his trinitarian pattern is always interlocked with mission, the calling to return an offering of thanks and love. But this gift of freedom then places the world on the knife-edge of judgment. It must be accepted or rejected, and there is no alternative. This mission embedded in freedom, when turned upside down blasphemously by the sinner in the grip of beastly power, becomes an empowering to destroy itself. God in this way is "powerless," giving his power and freedom over to the world, both offering himself in selfless love for the salvation of the world and thereby also radically endowing the world with freedom— an endowment that issues out in both obedience and revolt. But

---

[48]Ibid., 4:52. Note that Balthasar considers the Book of Revelation to be written by the apostle John who wrote the Gospel of John. He sees continuity between the two writings.
[49]Ibid.
[50]Ibid., 4:53.

within this "powerlessness" of granting weighted freedom we see
the omnipotence of God, the refusal of God to countenance the
refusal of his love. In this reciprocity of loving revelation, gifting
freedom and sinful, grasping freedom leading to intensified revolt,
we see what Balthasar calls the "the specifically theological law
of proportionate polarization: the more God intervenes, the more
he elicits opposition to him." "The suffering by which God's
wrath accomplishes his work is a divine suffering; vengeance and
reconciliation are two sides of the same thing." The Lamb handed
over to the world brings fire, which both destroys and cleanses, both
reduces to ashes and purifies of sin.[51]

Here we see that the bidirectional nonresistance centered in the
incarnation that we saw in the previous chapter becomes an active
force in the world, spurring historical action by the powers of the
world. In Balthasar's hands, Chalcedonian Christology points to a
dramatic involvement of the Lamb in history, pressing in a trinitarian
dynamic of gifted freedom and expected reciprocity that sets the world
on a tense edge.

Thus, the argument of Weaver that in Revelation evil destroys
itself can be dramatized by showing a greater divine origin and
destiny in the freedom that humans are given. Any debate about
whether or not God is violent needs to understand *violation*
theologically. Violation is necessarily tied to nature and without
understanding the nature of something, one cannot determine
whether it has been violated. "Violation" occurs when the nature of
humanity as a God-directed inner agency and desire, arising as the
gift of freedom "handed over" by God is trampled and abused. This
God does not do. But it is nonetheless the case that God destroys
evil. To put it crudely, God can kill the rebel nonviolently, by stoking
and provoking the very nature of the human to either worship or
revolt.[52]

---

[51]Ibid., 4:61. He does an extensive tour of the presence of fire in the Old and
New Testament, showing how it both destroys and saves. The scene of Shadrach,
Meshach, and Abednego serves as an example of this dual function of the same fire.
Jesus is said to baptize with fire, bringing in one flame both the Spirit's power and
the stubble-burning furnace into which all who bear no fruit are cast. Ibid., 4:59–63.
See also Mangina, *Revelation*, 124.

[52]The whole question of "nature" and its violation needs to enter much more directly
into the debate about what constitutes violence, and into the question of whether
God is violent. The scriptures, Old or New Testament, would never concede that
God breaks the fifth commandment against killing/murder. God destroys but never

Balthasar seeks to define violation theologically, as the failure to preserve the triune structure within human response. Where God preserves this triune structure within human life, even goading it relentlessly, he cannot be said to be violent. God judges the wicked without violating this primal trinitarian analogy in the heart of human rebellion. By "handing over" power, God is taking away neutrality and actively setting humans on the knife-edge of decision; their very revolt is merely a perversion of the "reciprocity" with which freedom is weighted in the trinitarian processions and thus has an inverted Christic shape to it, an upside down divine mission. It is this inner mystery of the Lamb's suffering gift of freedom empowering the world's twisted mission that is lauded by the saints and angels. But of course, this judgment does result in much flowing blood, and giving even a hint of divine causality to it will raise a further question of theodicy.[53]

And God will not stop. As the Book of Revelation unfolds in succeeding "cross-sections" of divine judgment and human revolt, there is an increasing merging of God's judgment and human's violent resistance. This is more than God "permitting" human evil and suffering it. This is God revealing himself in the Lamb's love, which at the same time gives a greater freedom to the creature to revolt back—in fact, it goads the creature's response. God is providentially wielding human's evil response to the Lamb in such a way as to bring about the collapse of evil upon itself. In this way, there is a mysterious divine hand hidden within human violence. God is not simply anti-violence.

---

violates the sinner. But in order to know whether something has been violated, we need to return to a teleological account of nature. What is the nature of a tree? A cow? A habitat? A person? What is it created *for*? Modern evolutionary understandings of the world, as well as postmodern understandings of the person, have discouraged interest in nature, seeing no *telos* to the world but only inner-worldly change. Thus, we are not in a good position to understand violation. In a world where things do not have a divine creative intention behind them, a "what for," there can be no such thing as violence.

[53]This question Balthasar does not address here, namely, is this whole drama worth it, in the end? Was this whole theo-drama "necessary" for God in light of its apparent cost in the blood of his enemies? But see *Theo-Drama*, 1994, 4:191–5. Balthasar's *Dare We Hope: "That All Men Be Saved"* is perhaps his attempt to ameliorate our unease at the grand worship given to God in the wake of Revelation's judgments, by showing that God is extending the real possibility of universal salvation to the human community.

This elicits choruses of worship from the saints who sing hallelujah. God is extolled for his mighty acts of bringing down the mighty, venging the martyrs beneath the altar and drawing history ever closer to its summation.

Because these images have their source in the infinite love of God there is an ever-greater "raising of the stakes" in the divine–human encounter that escalates to a fever pitch.[54] "Within God's own self— for where else is the creature to be found?—and in the defenselessness of absolute love, God endures the refusal of this love; and, on the other hand, in the omnipotence of the same love, he cannot and will not suffer it."[55] God relentlessly intrudes upon the world in the bidirectional nonresistance of the Lamb, offering freedom in love and goading the human community to its hour of decision.

Violence then for Balthasar is revealed and understood "under the sign of the Apocalypse." What Erasmus called a "Fury" that "appeared with such harmful powers, to scatter, demolish, and destroy them all and to sow an insatiable lust for fighting in the human heart" is humankind in the grip of the Lamb. Only there is its ferocity and persistence believable, and there is its mysterious relation to divine providence glimpsed. Balthasar is seeking to reclaim Revelation from a detached, historical-critical or rhetorical-critical place within the church and submit to its action as divine vision. As such, Balthasar points gospel pacifism to understand violence as it is spoken of in the New Testament as a Messianic woe, something that must be endured, and that may even be goaded by the saint in union with Christ. Gospel pacifism becomes then the willingness to live a theo-dramatic existence and to endure the suffering of Christ's presence in the world. It becomes the church's proclamation of the nonsecular reality of the world's violence—its revolt against the Lamb.

The assertion of post-Christian[56] secularity can here be understood as theo-dramatic, an idolatrous refusal of trinitarian procession, and the apocalyptic imitation of the freedom of God in his tripersonal distinction. But what exactly is it about the Lamb that the world seeks to smother? What's to hate about outpoured love, victorious and crowned at last? To that we now turn.

---

[54]Ibid., 4:56.
[55]Ibid., 4:329.
[56]"Post-Christian" for Balthasar refers not to a world that has left behind Christ, but to a world in which Christ has appeared and which cannot shake off his memory, try as it might.

The Pathos of Humankind in Its Incarnational Form

What makes the Lamb such a disturber of the peace is closely related to the dynamics of the incarnation, which we discussed in the previous chapter. It is a Christic relation between God and the world (unity and difference) lived out as bidirectional nonresistance that, as the answer to a deep human dilemma, both scandalizes and attracts. In this section we will try to explain some of the psycho-spiritual realities that Balthasar sees as structuring human responses to infinite freedom revealed as love, and then we will show how these realities are synthesized or resolved in the incarnation—an action that gives the theo-dramatic results we have seen in Revelation.

It is helpful to note that Balthasar lived and worked during a time in the Catholic Church when the understanding of the relationship between nature and grace was deeply controverted. Karl Rahner is a constant presence in the background for these initial chapters of *Theo-drama* IV in which the apocalyptic backdrop to soteriology is being established.[57] Rahner argued for a "supernatural *existentiale*" within humanity. This was an apologetic approach to theology based on the incarnation that said Christian revelation revealed to modern people new, fresh, and fulfilling aspects of what had already been their experience.[58] This led to the famous possibility of "anonymous Christians," who, though they had not received notice of the gospel, at some level already lived and believed what it taught.[59] Balthasar here uses the "Sign of the Apocalypse" to situate the religious posture of a post-Christian world differently. He worries that Rahner's "supernatural *existentiale*" becomes

---

[57]Ibid., 4:75, 138, 142, 143, cf. 273–84, 471–2.

[58]Balthasar frequently contrasts his position here to the view that humankind is in some way prepared for God's revelation and that "the incarnation of God is the unique and *highest* instance of the actualization of the essence of human reality." Karl Rahner in *Foundations of Christian Faith*, quoted in ibid., 4:283.

[59]As Karen Kilby notes, the difference between Rahner and Balthasar on the issue of "anonymous Christians" is ambivalent. Balthasar accepted the possibility of salvation outside explicit Christianity. According to Kilby, at the base of Balthasar's criticisms of Rahner was the worry that he undercut the possibility of witness, martyrdom, and suffering for the sake of Christ. Karen Kilby, "Balthasar and Karl Rahner," in *The Cambridge Companion to Hans Urs von Balthasar*, ed. Edward T. Oakes and David Moss (New York: Cambridge University Press, 2004), 259.

something of a closed system lacking theo-drama.[60] Revelation, Balthasar fears, then becomes only the revealing of what was always the case within the structure of the human, rather than the dramatic confrontation of God with humans' refusal, and the unveiling of a rescue and healing that includes but goes beyond nature. For Balthasar, the incarnational likeness within humankind is not merely something already there, latent beneath the surface, but rather something that must be agonistically struggled for.[61] As opposed to Rahner, Balthasar is tuned to the inability, frustration, and hostility with which humans run up against the limits of their knowledge of God, and to the drama of spiritual union by which the incarnation comes to fruition in the saints. Balthasar believes that the liturgy and slaughter of Revelation reveals an agonistic psycho-spiritual dynamic within human existence issuing in both revolt and obedience depending on the person's response.

Balthasar understands human life to be enmeshed in a deep pathos and miserable dilemma. This pathos is the source of great anxiety and it lies at the root of human rebellion against the Lamb. Nature and grace, though resolved at the archetypal level in the incarnation, seem impossible to reconcile at an historical, existential level. It is this enduring struggle in human life that is the source of history's theo-dramatic quality, its quality as an encounter between infinite freedom and finite freedom.

Here is how this dilemma emerges: Humans can see that their lives are a fickle, relative affair. They live in the constantly shifting sands of time and their lives are but a moment in a stream. And yet, in spite of this ephemerality, humans show an unshakable intent to write the absolute upon the relative.[62] They seem endowed and determined to make claims and to desire fulfillment with much more freedom and gravitas than their immediate situation would seem to warrant. They make statements ("this is a true fact" or "I love you") that they fully intend to be absolutely and not just relatively true, even though they are "aware of living in the medium of time (and time is ceaselessly changing everything)."[63] Balthasar says, "This is the point at which man lifts himself above the animal, whose head

---

[60]Balthasar, *Theo-Drama*, 1994, 4:75, 78.

[61]Aidan Nichols, *No Bloodless Myth: A Guide through Balthasar's Dramatics* (Washington, DC: Catholic University of America Press, 2000), 155.

[62]Balthasar, *Theo-Drama*, 1994, 4:83.

[63]Ibid., 4:81.

does not rise above the water level of time. Man swims in the river with his head lifted clear, aware of Being's unlimited horizon, its truth and goodness."[64]

But this intent to raise the head above the water level of time is the source of a pathos, a dilemma in postlapsarian humans, because it is not at all obvious that these instinctive claims to permanence and truth rest on anything solid. "Man's historical situation in this world is in a state of permanent tension: he is constantly on the lookout for a solution, a redemption [*Erlösung*], but can never anticipate or construct it from his own resources; nor does he have even an intimation of it." There is no permanence or lasting truth to be seen in earthly life, and yet there *must* be. Life bristles with unresolved tension. Though flashes of "absolute" meaning seem to sparkle everywhere, humans find no key to put the pieces together in a satisfactory way. They find no intramundane way to justify their awareness of staking claims beyond the shifting sands of time. This yields frustration as well as hubristic attempts to force the puzzle to resolution by sheer power. That is the human pathos, anthropologically and phenomenologically speaking.

We can go one step deeper and see that this connects with something basic in Balthasar's idea of freedom, which he had described in great detail in *Theo-Drama* II. Balthasar's philosophy of infinite/finite freedom is a vast complex, but for our purposes we need to see finite freedom only in its basic structure of two pillars that coinhere and create the unique situation that humans find themselves in. On the one hand is the pillar of self-determination, *autoexousion*, the freedom to choose and move.[65] In this is self-possession, the unique "I" that situates the person in the world in distinction from others. We are humans who in and of ourselves as created beings have a measure of goodness, meaning and power available to us. It is our possession.

The first pillar of freedom as autonomous motion, however, only comes to be through a second pillar, which is freedom as "consent" or indifference. The "I" receives its unique self-possessing autonomous motion not by shutting itself off to others but by recognizing that

---

[64]Ibid., 4:82. For Balthasar this swimming with the head clear is something inherent in what it means to be human, but also something that is heightened in history as God reveals himself in human freedom. Secularity is a time of sharpened self-consciousness about many things.
[65]Ibid., 4:141–2, 149.

it is only one being of many and that it depends for its existence on these others. My "I" is established in the recognition of others on whom I am dependent, such as my mother.[66] Ultimately this is the recognition that existence is a gift from others. My existence thus is a unique self-possession, but nevertheless a self-possession I receive from others. This pillar of consent is genuinely freedom, not just the limitation of freedom; it is the open path by which the person moves out and achieves unity with the farthest destiny of the creature, full unity with God. By consenting to the other I become freer. This second pillar points beyond the self and is thus a "dynamism" a "setting forth for a yonder shore" that is meant to point finite freedom in the direction of its home within infinite freedom.[67]

Here is how this happens. As I recognize that I receive my existence from others, I soon also see that these others do not have existence in themselves either; they too have a derived, consensual existence. This becomes a never-ending regression since within mundane life no origin or destiny for my life or any other life can be traced. My finite existence, while undoubtedly a good I possess, is "groundless"—that is, nowhere can I find either its origins or its ultimate destiny within my mundane experience. I cannot see where I came from nor where I am ultimately headed—this is obscured by my finitude. Such freedom "is bound to affirm its indebtedness."[68] My life is derived and my existence as an "I" with autonomous, self-possessing motion comes into view when I recognize this dependence.[69] Another way of saying this is that "man exists in two poles that cannot be torn asunder; he is always himself *and* his neighbour" and yet in neither can he find the ultimate ground for his being as a person making absolute claims.[70]

---

[66]Ibid., 4:100. Balthasar's oft-used description of the mother's smile that awakens the child to consciousness, freedom, and love is apt here. See Balthasar, *Love Alone Is Credible*, Cf. 76. To be awakened to consciousness by a mother's smile it to realize at a foundational level that my self-conscious existence is granted to me and drawn from me by consent to the goodness of being.

[67]Balthasar, *Theo-Drama*, 1994, 4:139.

[68]Ibid.

[69]Ibid., 4:139, 150. "What is consciousness? It is being [*Sein*] that is aware of its indebtedness to a source beyond itself; discerning being [*Sein*] and 'letting be' [*Sein-Lassen*], it affirms everything that is, or may yet be, in being." Ibid., 4:139.

[70]Balthasar, *Theo-Drama*, 1994, 4:79.

Now let us bring back this pathos that we discussed above, in which humans reach for solidity and a fulfillment that does not seem explainable in purely mundane terms. True fulfillment only comes in the unity of the two pillars of *autoexousion* or self-determination and consent to the other. But the pathos arises because of the "groundlessness" of freedom. After the fall, humans have refused to believe that freedom is "groundless" within intramundane existence, and that, as such, existence is dependent on the goodness of a Creator. Humans have sought to be like God, having the ground of their being in themselves. Humans grasp hold of the *autoexousion*, the autonomous "I," but lie to themselves about it, convincing themselves and others that this self-possession is self-originating and not dependent on consent to the other. In arrogating to themselves the "absolute" they inevitably diminish what in God is a unity of power and goodness (self-giving), shrinking it to pure power alone.[71] In other words, when humans arrogate God to themselves, they arrogate his power, but not the utter self-giving goodness, which is the mode of operation for this power. This results in the violent "demonic" nature of humankind in rebellion against the Absolute. It is self-possession (power and self-actualization) without consent to the other. Where power exists without goodness we find violence. "Wherever in the world we find great, powerful symbols of the absolute, they either come from the field of war or are pressing in that direction."[72]

The two poles of *autoexousian*, self-determination, and "not without the other" locate the instability, and often desperation—pathos—that pervades the human community.[73] We are in quest, searching for our ground and destiny, but we also resist acknowledging the precariousness of such derived life. In this we can see that a refusal to recognize one's dependence on God is of a cloth with one's refusal to recognize one's dependence on fellow humans. Modern dilemmas in reconciling the individual and the collective stem from this refusal to see the whole fulfillment of nature in grace.

But now we must take a third step and show that the incarnation is the fulfillment of this two-pillared human freedom:

---

[71]Ibid., 4:107.

[72]Ibid., 4:108.

[73]Balthasar discusses death, freedom power and evil as four "wounds of existence" that render the problem of existence unbearable. Ibid., 4:77.

Having reached this stage, we can venture the Christian affirmation that man, the first Adam, was created with a view to the Second. Not only with a view to God; though true, this is an abbreviation that does not do justice to the creature's authentic autonomy. Man was created with a view to the God-man; in him, the equipoise between the absolute and the relative, which man cannot discover, has been established. True, this equipoise comes from God, since it is his Word that becomes man, but not without the earth giving her noblest fruit to cooperate in the Incarnation.[74]

God, "in his freedom, has reserved to himself the gift of synthesis; he will present it to mankind and, in so doing, reveal both who he, God, is and who the authentic man is, the man who exists in the totality of his self."[75] In the incarnation God "solves" the pathos by showing that true human *autoexouosian*, or self-determination comes from full consent to God beyond the world. In order to appreciate what Balthasar is doing here regarding the "Second Adam" we need to remind ourselves of some of the main features of Chalcedonian Christology that we learned in the last chapter. There we learned that the incarnation was the perfect transposition into the humblest human terms of the Son's eternal hypostatic "letting be" of the Father, his reception of Sonship as his differentiation within the Trinity. Within Christ's nonresistance to the Father, eternal begotteness becomes in the human field the meek, loving, self-giving, nonresistance of Christ to the human community, even in its manifestation as an enemy. As this Person, Jesus was the fullest expression of divinity in human terms, and the fullest expression of humanity in divine terms. It is this understanding of the incarnation that is structuring Balthasar's view here of pathos as the desperate attempt to achieve a synthesis apart from where it is revealed in Christ.

The Son in eternity has his own Person through a consent to be begotten from the Father. This eternal letting be and being let be is the divine pattern for an analogous human freedom that also has these two poles. By this eternal hypostatic becoming of the "I" through consent to be begotten from the Father, Christ incarnates

---

[74]Ibid., 4:110.
[75]Ibid., 4:78.

and lives in human receptivity, meekness, and self-giving love even the wretchedness of the human community. Christ lives a life of "consent" to his divine origin and through that a "consent" to the human community of which he is now a part. In this way, the incarnation provides a structure for the fulfillment of human freedom. This is the unguessable synthesis to the pathos of human freedom that the incarnation unveils in history.

In the Gethsemane and Golgatha desolation he lives this perfect two-pillared freedom from within the above-described pathos in which humanity struggles to see how its life has divine meaning. Christ experiences humankind's anxiety and desperation in the veiling of his eyes from the Father. He experiences the conditions created by the cursed refusal of humans to return thanks to God as the sight of his Father is obscured. His cry of alienation from the cross is the cry of all humans who no longer see the God-fulfilled meaning of their lives, who no longer see any solid and absolute truth beyond the chaotic events around them. "Father, forgive them, for they know not what they do" (Lk. 23:34). But it is from this place of human desolation that Jesus nevertheless obeys his Father.

Here is the great exchange: the Son experiences the repulsive corruption of the trinitarian procession, which had been shriveled in humanity to a revolt, but gives to that corroded nature his infinite freedom, his eternal begotteness. Through his utter obedience to the Father he is able to lovingly walk through the hatred unleashed by humans. Thus, Jesus is both the revelation of the deepest pathos of human life played out on the trinitarian stage and also the fullest revelation of the trinitarian mutuality played out on the human stage. As such he is the event of its resolution— in his self-gift to the Father and to the world, Christ achieved the reconciliation of all things. He achieved the very height of human freedom by surrendering himself unreservedly to the Father, the ground of all being. Violence is the rebellious abhorrence for the way Christ achieved the resolution of this human pathos. It is this Christic dynamic within human freedom that figures violence as a christological phenomenon in history, a phenomenon shaped by this trinitarian synthesis in nonresistance. Violence thus becomes the post-Christian refusal of the mystery of Chalcedonian Christology as it was unveiled in the Son's human conformity to the Father's love for humanity on the cross.

The Violent Rejection of the Incarnation

As the revelation and enacting of this reconciliation of the two pillars, Christ has set himself in the cross-hairs of a human community that in so many ways refuses his answer. We do not have the space to illustrate how this whole embrace of the human pathos by Christ slowly escalates during Christ's life and eventually yields the crucifixion. Christ in this Chalcedonian formulation of the two pillars takes our place as our representative, and in the great exchange suffers the pathos in our place, draining the bitter cup of wrath that this pathos brings upon itself. This is all described in "the action" of volume IV of the *Theo-Drama*, and Balthasar brings together many models of the atonement through this incarnational atonement theology.

What we are concerned with here is not so much the way this escalation incorporates various aspects of atonement, but simply how Christ's presence, both in his life, and subsequently in post-Christian history, draws to itself the hatred of the human community. Balthasar believes that the more openly Christ is revealed as this unfathomable synthesis within the world, the more humans become conscious of themselves in their historical nature. Christ wakens humans to themselves but also to their radical God dependence. Over time in the post-Christian era, where Christ presses in, there people become more conscious of their self-possessed autonomy. Freedom is latched onto and exalted. This we can see is the trajectory of secularity where humans become self-conscious choosers, charting their own path beyond the flowing stream of time (or tradition, class structure, or tribe). Christ awakens humankind. But where the second pillar (consent to the other, and the Father) is refused, this growing self-conscious autonomy only heightens anxiety and fear because it becomes ever-more obvious that this freedom is unsupported within mundane life, there is no ground for it.

The revolt against Christ is an attempted severing of the incarnation's unity of self-possession and consent before God. It is a refusal of what Christ's synthesis means for the fulfillment of human destiny. It is the grasping of heightened human power along with the rejection of human "consent" to the other. It is a refusal to acknowledge that this, finally, is the only possible human fulfillment of freedom. It is a refusal of human limits, "a neglect of man's relativity and time-bound nature; in Christian terms it involves a disincarnation, a flight from time and presence."[76] For Balthasar, this is what characterizes life in secularity: an unprecedented freedom as autonomous motion coupled with an unprecedented refusal of the second pillar, consent. There is thus the heightened vision and temptation to "be like God" in opposition to human creatureliness. Because this heightened vision and self-consciousness nevertheless fail to achieve their goals, it occasions a surging anxiety and desperation yielding to violence.

Balthasar sees this refusal to be a kind of Gnosticism. Gnosticism for Balthasar is not only an early-church heresy, but a perennial temptation inherent in a post-Christian world. Kevin Mongrain argues that for Balthasar, Gnosticism is a sweeping illness that in any of its forms takes exception to the earthiness of the incarnation on the one hand, and on the other hand, to the fact that humankind needs outside, divine help in achieving gnosis. It rejects the historically contingent events of the biblical narratives as too earthy, it is "disdainful of the Christian claim that the eternal God entered time, becoming incarnate in a human being, suffered, died, and was resurrected as a spiritual body."[77] It also rejects the utter dependence of humankind on God and latches onto human-only ways of achieving transcendence and power. It is any attempt to have deification without the incarnation. What the Gnostic worldview then substitutes is divinity without Christ. For Christ and the church, the very end point of divine expression was the assumption of human flesh in humility and meek devotion to God. But in alienated humankind, Gnosticism seeks divinity by assuming a godlike stance within the world. "Gnosticism becomes synonymous with the claim that the eventual full rational discernment of all the laws of nature and history will allow the human race finally to take away the sins of the world and establish a universal reign of peace, justice, and happiness of earth."[78]

Secularity in its more malicious forms and Gnosticism are thus closely related for Balthasar. The creature in the throes of the revelation of God incarnate grabs hold of the freedom embedded in this revelation and "tries to arrogate divine nature to itself without

---

[76]Ibid., 4:145.
[77]Mongrain, *Systematic Thought of Hans Urs von Balthasar*, 36.
[78]Ibid., 138.

sharing in the Person who is always endowing, receiving, pouring forth and giving thanks for that nature—and who embodies its self-giving."[79] Instead of responding in step with the trinitarian pattern of gift and return, finite freedom "changes it into a calculating, cautious self-preservation."[80] According to Balthasar, the intent of God to live out deifying love under human conditions is met with a demonic intent to live out hate under godly conditions. It is not met with a demonic intent to "become flesh." Rather, it is met with a mockery of incarnation and the worship of disincarnation.

In the post-Christian era—where the world's relation to God has objectively been framed by Christ alone, but where humans refuse this synthesis—"man's openness *to* the upper realm becomes a purely anthropological fact that belongs henceforth to the immanence of horizontal world history."[81] People resist the intensification of the pathos revealed by Christ and seek desperately to solve it, after all, along purely human terms. Hence people's tendency to "attribute absolute significance to relative fragments of meaning in history and to commit themselves utterly to such constructions" is heated to a degree that can only be described in the liturgy and slaughter of the Apocalypse.[82] This is the titanism of post-Christian humanity and it emerges directly out of the pathos described above.

In Balthasar's view, after Christ's incarnation, humankind can no longer sustain the comfortable naiveté of an existence suffused with the warm glow of the gods. The numinous path of paganism is foreclosed[83] and in this sense the revelation of the Christic synthesis is the source of secularization for Balthasar. As the one who "solved" the pathos through yieldedness to the Father, Christ has objectively taken all glory and divinity from the gods (thus "disenchanting" nature) and has revealed that this glory can only be found in self-giving, creaturely existence offered to the Father.[84] If humans resist *this* answer to their pathos, their only option is radical and violent

---

[79]Balthasar, *Theo-Drama*, 1994, 4:328. The reason the creature can so casually reject the "whence" of this freedom is because of its freedom, its *autoexousian*, the gift to be self-determining in a limited way.

[80]Ibid.

[81]Ibid., 4:72.

[82]Ibid., 4:73.

[83]Ibid., 4:438–9.

[84]Ibid. This is similar to the argument of David Bentley Hart, whose indebtedness to Balthasar is well known, though he does not mention him in this case. "God and Nothingness," in *I Am the Lord Your God: Christian Reflections on the Ten*

secularization, the desperate fulfillment of human life on its own terms. It cannot be fulfilled any longer by "the gods." Humans will attempt to orphan the achievements of Christ and replicate them apart from the whole synthesis he achieved.[85] "Particularly where Christ's claim is put provocatively by his followers, pillorying the oppressive forms taken by the state, economics or racist fanaticism," this secularism will act "in a positively anti-Christian way."[86] This vision, refusing God's answer to the pathos from beyond this world, guarantees itself "by the greatest possible use of all worldly force (for example, vast stockpiling of arms, police, propaganda, concentration camps)."[87] And this "possibility of concentrated power," which drove the powers to crucify the Savior has since then "increased beyond all imagining. ... Weapons produced on the pretext of being for mankind's redemption would suffice to destroy the entire world, not just once but many times over, and their material potential conceals the spiritual potential of the 'plan' that opposes the redemption effected by Christ."[88]

One aspect of this grand attempt is the transformation of technology. Before the post-Christian era, technology "referred initially only to the technological improvement of the instruments that serve man," but in the modern era (following Hegel) humans, "having jettisoned metaphysics—gained control of the political and ethical realm and changed society's entire life into technology. To this technology the autonomy and dignity of the individual were sacrificed."[89] Where technology once was a fragment, a small piece of the puzzle, now it becomes a totality. Violence for Balthasar includes technology disembedded from its creaturely role and enslaved in post-Christian desperation to synthesize nature and grace. It is turned into a refusal to exercise holy endurance, an impatience at the long-protracted process by which God is giving the world its unity in difference. What this yields is modernity's destruction of creation. All of this violence is a rejection of the manner in which Christ has reconciled all things in heaven and on earth.

Commandments, ed. Carl E. Braaten and Christopher R. Seitz (Grand Rapids, MI: Eerdmans, 2005), 55–76.
[85]Balthasar, *Theo-Drama*, 1994, 4:439.
[86]Ibid.
[87]Ibid., 4:441.
[88]Ibid.
[89]Ibid., 4:91.

This then is an attempt to read modern life through the apocalyptic, dramatic lens offered by the Book of Revelation. At the beginning of his venture into theo-dramatics, Balthasar wrote this dense paragraph, which aptly sums up this dynamic. In it we find a perspective of Christ-haunted[90] life in the world. Worldly existence dwells under the weight of glory:

> Essentially [worldly existence] is an opening-up or a closing-off to the presence of some light that radiates from existence. Seeing or not seeing; letting be or violently overpowering, imprisoning, extinguishing. In oneself or in others. Confusing the power of what seems, shines, radiates gratis (which equally implies surrender and powerlessness) with the power of possession and the urge to dominate. The confrontation of these two kinds of power, the succumbing of the vulnerable, defenseless power to the force of arms, revealing, as it succumbs, the inseparability within it of power and powerlessness. The vessel shatters, and finite speech with it, thereby opening up to an infinite speech that acts and suffers in it.[91]

In a Christ-haunted world, existence cannot be a neutral dithering placidly between good or evil. Christ in his unguessable, startling synthesis of human existence never departs but presses into each moment of the world's days, giving to being a light that radiates in from beyond. Where this is the case, human life can only be "an opening up or a closing-off," a "letting be or a violently overpowering." In this milieu where a stark *autoexousian* or self-determination is presented by Christ, there will be a constant temptation to grab hold of that freedom and use it now to dominate what can only be had as the free gift of the Father. In this violent clash, the defenselessness of the saints, while appearing to be weakness, will, because of its Christic posture open up an infinite speech of omnipotent power within the world.

---

[90]To steal a line from Ralph Wood's title, *Flannery O'Connor and the Christ-Haunted South* (Grand Rapids, MI: Eerdmans, 2005). Flannery O'Connor's fictional characters are often an apt demonstration of humankind weighted with divine freedom leading to violent revolt.
[91]Balthasar, *Theo-Drama*, 1993, 2:30.

The Church and Provocation

This dramatic understanding of the relentless incarnation of Christ can be extended by what Kevin Mongrain sees as Balthasar's *corpus triforme* understanding of the incarnation. In this perspective of the incarnation the Word takes human form both in the Old Covenant, in the earthly life of Jesus, and in the body of Christ, which is the church. In this three-phase manifestation of God in human form, the world is confronted in a way that elicits historical change.[92] The incarnation has a pedagogical function within the divine economy, not only appearing among humans but gradually shaping, forming, and directing believers in the trinitarian love made manifest and real in the Christ event. This too is the church's divine incarnational vocation.[93]

As such, the church, Balthasar will argue, is a key phase in the incarnational unveiling of God and in the pedagogy of the human community. Ethics (faith, hope, and love) within this *corpus triforme* are a disciplining in the posture of incarnation.[94] But the question for our concern here with disincarnated violence is, in what way does the church too experience or bear within its body human resistance against this divine path and pattern? Is there also within the church both adoration and revolt? First, the church's long-suffering experience of the provocative incarnation mingles it with the "historical" Jesus of Nazareth and his journey to Jerusalem and the cross. The church participates in Christ as he is sent to follow God's will to the very end of time. Which means that saints "follow his will into the abysses opened up by his provocation, with all the monsters that lurk and slumber there."[95] The saints live in the fault line between the two tectonic plates of the world and the Lamb and express by their own prayer and lament the pressure created by this grinding collision.[96] This is "the central object of faith's pondering

---

[92]Mongrain, *Systematic Thought of Hans Urs von Balthasar*, 29. Mongrain argues that this *corpus triforme* view of the incarnation is an Irenaen understanding of the incarnation that Balthasar used across his work.

[93]Mongrain is arguing that Balthasar has an Irenaen understanding of the effect of the incarnation in the world.

[94]Mongrain, *Systematic Thought of Hans Urs von Balthasar*, 127.

[95]Balthasar, *Theo-Drama*, 1994, 4:436–7.

[96]To borrow an image from Darrell W. Johnson, *Discipleship on the Edge: An Expository Journey through the Book of Revelation* (Vancouver: Regent College Publishing, 2004), 181.

on this drama" that yields the texture of Christian ethics: "It is as the *slain* Lamb that he won his victory; it follows that his disciple's struggle cannot be an armed one, except their armor be the full panoply of faith (1Th 5:8; Eph 6:14f), and especially the 'endurance and faith of the saints (Rev 13:10).'"[97]

> In the Book of Revelation, there is only one way to combat the trinity of hell, which is the final shape of evil: believers must bear witness in their lives and in their blood, thus fully incarnating their faith as they pit it against utter, satanic dis-incarnation. ... This eschatological opposition between the apparent omnipotence of evil and the apparent mortal powerlessness of believers cannot be dismissed as a mere vision. It is genuine prophecy.[98]

But this paragraph leads immediately into a section in *Theo-Drama* IV titled, "The Church's Form: Beautiful and Marred." This raises for us the question of whether divinely goaded *disincarnation* can also happen within the church's life, or whether it is only the world's reaction *against* the church? The church, according to Balthasar, does not only stand with Christ in regard to this provocative finger in the world's side—the church itself is provoked, scandalized. Balthasar sees the church in history not only standing with Jesus, but also participating, at some level, in the world's revolt against him. "Her history—past-present and future—is almost inevitably tragic" as she straddles in her existence a bundle of tensions she finds almost impossible to manage.[99]

In this section, Balthasar does not attribute violence to the church (though he concedes in other places the violence of church history). Balthasar seems willing to grant that the church itself is sinful,[100] though he still describes an *immaculata* over against this divided,

[97]Balthasar, *Theo-Drama*, 1994, 4:58.
[98]Ibid., 4:452. Balthasar believes that in a world where a "secular" synthesis appears successful it will become increasingly difficult to be a Christian, since the Christian must relativize it all in the name of the incarnate One. Cf. Balthasar, *Theological Anthropology*, 191.
[99]"The realms of "time and eternity," the "already and not yet," of "visibility and invisibility," of "obedience and freedom," of "the order instituted by Christ and the authority and inspiration of the Holy Spirit in each of the Church's members," of "tradition and constant newness," and of "rootedness in the Old Covenant and of that which transcends it." *Theo-Drama*, 1994, 4:453.
[100]Ibid. Cf. Balthasar, *Glory of the Lord*, 1:569–70.

heretical, and sinful body.[101] Of chief concern for Balthasar in this section is "the domestication of faith" in which "faith is overtaken and hollowed out by knowledge." This is a Gnosticism that seems to increase in intensity with every new revelation of the genuine Word of God in history. Wherever there is revelation there is an increased temptation and possibility of securing from it a "law" of history, a bird's-eye view now of the way things must be.

A Mennonite steeped in the *Martyrs Mirror* would probably emphasize more bluntly the way in which the church itself has murderously opposed the intensified incarnation of the church in daily life. The church is the body of Christ and as such participates in his suffering love, but can it carry out at the same time (in other places) the disincarnating severing of its members? It seems to me that Balthasar's own theology points to this possibility in "the church beautiful and marred." The church itself wrestles with the radical freedom that Christ has infused into worldly life and is constantly tempted to batten down the hatches and secure by its own strength what revelation it believes now to be in its possession.

Going beyond the examples Balthasar uses, we could extend this to say that any time the church seeks a success in the world that does not follow from the life, death, resurrection, and ascension of Christ in kingly power, there is this *Gnosis*, a secularizing tendency to secure the benefits of Christ without the life of Christ. This success could be achieved through modern managerial methods, media savvy, a Constantinian use of state power for ecclesial ends, or simply the church's enjoyment of a cultural appreciation of one aspect of the church's ethic, such as personal self-control and improvement, individual freedom, or nonviolence. But as the body that always opens itself to the events and power of the incarnation, this Gnostic temptation in the church can be struggled against and overcome.

And this, prophetically, will be the salvation of the world. It is the fruit of the divine determination to love the world in complete incarnate offering, by which God saves and judges the world through its finite freedom. It is as the body of Christ that humankind truly has its way, its fullest freedom, its greatest offering to the salvation of the world. Both by violently rejecting and by lovingly accepting this onslaught, humanity, "guilty as he is in God's sight, lie[s] passive

---

[101]Balthasar, *Theo-Drama*, 1994, 4:456.

and anaesthetized on the operating table while the cancer of his sin is cut out."[102]

Balthasar and Yoder Together

Having demonstrated the theme of provocation in Balthasar's Christology, it may be useful now to draw some comparison between the emphases of Mennonite theologian John Howard Yoder and the vision of incarnational provocation seen here in Balthasar. I believe that taken together, these theologians are greater than the sum of their parts. These theologians had much in common.[103] Both theologians were seeking to help the church grapple with what it means to live with little cultural and political power. Both were seeking to guide their respective churches in developing theological resources for a renewed engagement and openness to the world. Both saw the "Constantinian" adoption of worldly power by the church in the fourth century to have been a disaster to the witness of the church.[104] It is unlikely that Balthasar could be outdone by Yoder in his assertion that it was

> fundamentally important to note that nowhere in the New Testament does the slightest ray of divine glory fall upon the structures of the state. ... There is nowhere even the faintest suggestion that the state should take on the form of an earthly reflection, a reproduction or representation of the heavenly Jerusalem and its eschatological glory.[105]

Both believed that violence was a decisive symptom of the church's failure in this worldliness. Both noted that there was in the modern post-christendom church the temptation of another sort

---

[102]Ibid., 4:318.
[103]I am not aware of either of them ever mentioning the other. They both lived in Basel during the 1950s and were connected to Karl Barth during that time.
[104]Yoder's critique of this is everywhere. Balthasar is more subtle, but he mentions this explicitly as the pretext for his book, A Theological Anthropology, vii. See also Balthasar, Engagement with God, 82–93 and Theo-Drama: Prolegomena, trans. Graham Harrison, vol. 1 (San Francisco, CA: Ignatius, 1989), 37–40. This is discussed in Long, Saving Karl Barth, 224–6.
[105]Balthasar, Glory of the Lord, 7:502.

of Constantinianism, a progressive application of the "principles" of the cross to the unconverted world as a political and tactical instrument.[106] Both believed that the culmination of saintliness in history was not worldly triumph or progress but probable martyrdom.[107] It is not difficult to see a kinship between what Yoder called "methodologism" and Balthasar's understanding of Gnosticism:

> according to which theology consists in a theoretical or meta-level discussion concerned primarily with the question of the proper elucidation and interrelationship between an allegedly agreed-upon collection of central concepts or loci, and which can in principle be justified to anyone on the basis of the internal logic of the system itself.[108]

Balthasar was constantly wary of any abstractness or speculation in theology. And so, both theologians believed that by a fresh openness to the appearance of Christ in his humanity, the church could resist both the old and new Constantinianism and be the provocateur of the world's judgment and salvation.

But the provocation of Christ in the world highlights what we can see as a mutually beneficial difference between these two writers. Perhaps we might be permitted to dust off an older, discredited terminology in Christology one last time and suggest that Yoder sees the provocation from below while Balthasar sees it from above. For Yoder, what provokes the world to violence like the crucifixion is the radically "upside down" political reality of Jesus and his community, the concrete ethical practices of the church in obedience to the example of Christ. Yoder's most famous book, *The Politics of Jesus*, can be read as an extended essay on the real-world provocation which the ethical vision of Jesus for his community of disciples presented to the powers of his time. Jesus takes up space in the moral arrangement of the world—political, social, economic space. Jesus's ethic presents an either/or to the world whom Christ

---

[106]Yoder, *Politics of Jesus*, 236.
[107]Balthasar, *Theo-Drama*, 1994, 4:447; John Howard Yoder, *The Original Revolution: Essays on Christian Pacifism* (Scottdale, PA: Herald, 1977), 33.
[108]Chris Huebner's description of Yoder's understanding of "methodologism"; "Mennonites and Narrative Theology: The Case of John Howard Yoder," *Conrad Grebel Review* 16, no. 2 (1998): 23.

calls to substitute his powerlessness, forgiveness, and generosity for
its own might, violence, and security. For Yoder, Jesus is not killed
by people who mistook him but by people who understood him and
recognized him as a threat to their real-world pretensions.[109]

According to Yoder, the church has often rejected this provocation
in its own life, seeking ways to sidestep the jagged edges of this
humanity of Christ, either by contextualizing Jesus as a product of
his time, by spiritualizing his message, or by locating the real intent of
Christ in an atonement that is chiefly the forgiving of personal sins on
the cross. By these evasions, the church's ethics have been coordinated
with other sources; "common sense and the nature of things."[110] For
Yoder, it is congregations living now according to this revolutionary
scriptural ethic that attract the scorn of the world and participate "in
the triumphant suffering of the Lamb."[111]

We have adverted earlier to criticisms of Yoder's theology as one-
sided. It is unrelenting in the concreteness of its ethic, but numerous
readers wonder finally whether Yoder's church really needs Christ on
an ongoing basis of spiritual union. Paul Martens expresses strongly
what for other readers is a more vague suspicion:

> Throughout his corpus, Yoder has sought to unite the gospel with a
> social style, with a particular politics. But perhaps it is also true that
> to accept fully the synthesis offered as "the politics of Jesus" is also
> to explode the sought after unity of Jesus' gospel with a particular
> politics. However he phrases it—whether as the unity between
> medium and message, deeds that "say", "gospel" as a secular term,
> practices that a social scientist could recommend, or any other
> form of this same principle—the culmination of Yoder's decades
> of theological and ethical reflection appears to be the same: Yoder
> seems to leave us with a Jesus who has become merely an ethico-
> political paradigm that opens the door for a supercessive secular
> ethic.[112]

A. James Reimer described Yoder as having an "inadequate
recognition of the ritualistic, cultic, mystical, and sacramental

---

[109]Yoder, *Politics of Jesus*, 59–60.
[110]Ibid., 20.
[111]Ibid., 244.
[112]Martens, *Heterodox Yoder*, 141–2.

aspects of the religious experience."[113] Yoder, it seems to me, has read Jesus correctly as far as he goes. I would simply say that he lacks a sensibility for the incarnational relation of yieldedness, prayer, and contemplation with which Jesus sought his Father and the path which that "vertical" nonresistance opens for the church's sanctity. This lack of concern for spiritual union in daily *Gelassenheit* creates the suspicion that God for Yoder is "only" about ethics. It also creates the impression that the only thing provocative about the church is its moral achievement of Jesus's ethics, rather than pointing to how Christ might also be present (provocatively) within the church's sin as well. The grace that manifests in the undeserved acceptance of the sinner, is also a provocation to the world, and it is not emphasized greatly in Yoder's work.

Balthasar, we might say, comes at provocation from above, as something intended and enacted as the theo-dramatic intent of the entire plan of salvation originated in the Father's love. Its primary texture emerges as a trinitarian analogy in the human condition. As God descends into human affairs, a hidden "solution" is planted within the world that grows in fruitfulness and in its ability to provoke scandal. What is precipitated in the world is a spiritual more than an ethical crisis, although ethical dimensions are always present. It is not so much Christ's moral teachings in themselves but his relationship with the Father and his insistence that this submission in humble earthiness is the divine plan for the cosmos that elicits the anger. Thus, for Balthasar, the provocative nature of the incarnation is often a hidden affair; it is the unseen presence of Christ in the saintly, but often "secret" nuptiality of the contemplatives that goad the powers to revolt against Christ. There is less emphasis in Balthasar on the church's compassion, generosity, and the radical reorienting of its power structures to reflect Christ's powerlessness. It is not the exalted discipleship of the church that is a burr in the world's saddle, nor the countercultural way the church structures its power, but the hidden presence of Christ in her humble presence and prayer.

Frederick Bauerschmidt, however, fears that Balthasar's "fear of Titanism lead[s] him to underplay the fact that Jesus has given his followers a way that is, by God's grace, in fact *livable*—albeit stumblingly—in this world, and livable not just for individuals, but

---

[113]Loewen, "Reply to A. J. Reimer," 172.

for the community of disciples as a whole."[114] Balthasar, he argues, "does not really pursue the opening that his own theo-dramatic approach makes for a new political theology" and that "Balthasar's comments on the political significance of the cross seem, frankly, banal." Balthasar is so concerned that the cross not become a tactical instrument in the creation of human community that he fails to show its genuinely incarnational presence as an alternative human community, structured by a new economics, hierarchy, and reciprocity. Kevin Mongrain responds to Bauerschmidt by pointing out what our work here has seen clearly; Balthasar's theology of the incarnation does not permit any either/or between the vertical, spiritual realities and earthly, political realities. It also has an intensely political drama within it that Balthasar explores with his treatment of Revelation. But Mongrain and Bauerschmidt both agree that Balthasar's location in an upper-class Switzerland did not give him the sensibility he needed, nor the proclivity to explore how theo-dramatics interacted with social evils beyond the Marxist messianism that was his frequent target. These writers tend to think Balthasar would be helped by not only critiquing Moltmannian progressive liberation theologies on the left for their gnostic appropriation, but applying a critique also to destructive capitalism on the right. I think that would help, but from a Mennonite perspective we might suggest that Balthasar extend his theo-dramatic provocation vision to congregations, communities of Jesus who, through their participation in Christ's yieldedness to the Father, allow their structures, polities, and ethics to reflect the Sermon on the Mount and Jesus's destabilizing of power in the church. In this way, a Mennonite will need to go beyond Balthasar and insist that the incarnation of Christ takes up form in the *Nachfolge* of believers in congregations of discipline and peace.

In neither of these theologians is there any reason to exclude the other on this front. Balthasar, while he does not linger long on the ethical practices of the church, certainly sees sanctity as a manifestation of Christ in his body.[115] There is no reason why this could not be spelled out with greater emphasis. It could also be said that Balthasar is so keen to emphasize the Augustinian

---

[114]Frederick C. Bauerschmidt, "Theo-Drama and Political Theology," *Communio* (September 1998): 547–8.
[115]See especially his essay, "'Beatitudes' and Human Rights."

peregrinating, fragmentary life of the city of God that he does not match his exalted spirituality of individuals with a comparable congregational life. Likewise, there is no reason why Yoder's *Politics of Jesus* could not be extended beyond the "body politics" of the church to acknowledge the hand of the Father at work eucharistically in the assent of the church to Christ's suffering in the world. Yoder could have written about the limits of "ethics" and the need for prayer, hidden sanctity, and a fruitfulness (grace) beyond moral communities of Jesus worshippers, but he rarely did. I would suggest that Yoder's understanding of provocation from below, and Balthasar's understanding of a descending provocation could join together to issue in a fuller testimony to scripture's clear affirmation of both aspects. It would be a fuller reflection of the incarnation. Yoder's concrete ethical practices of the church could be seen together with Balthasar's mystical presence of Christ in hidden sanctity and prayer to more fully embody the Chalcedonian mission. They could both compensate for idiosyncratic insensibilities in the other. Yoder can help the church prevent an amoral, apolitical spiritualism, and Balthasar can help prevent a moralistic secularity from creeping into our ethics. In this way, both Christ's relentless embrace of human affairs and his gesture to eschatological completion of all things in God would find a more adequate place. They would in this way together more fully account for violence as christologically goaded.

Implications

If pacifism is to retain its theo-dramatic place within salvation history and be a gospel pacifism, it needs to consider Balthasar's understanding of violence within Christ's encounter with the human community. This is again an immersion in the Chalcedonian mystery of the event in which God took human nature to himself and consented to the implications. Within this Chalcedonian mystery, a figure is planted deep within the world, a presence that goads a Satanic revolt unto the destruction of the world. This is an aspect of the figure of Christ in history. A theology of history is the church's attempt to speak of this Christic figure in the world. What is its shape and how has this world warped and twisted itself to be rid of this presence? How has Christ's presence drawn to itself the glory and worship of the world?

There are several implications of this that can now be drawn out. First, what can we say about violence from within this place between God and the world? All violence is here a Messianic woe, the travail of a world in the labor pains of Christmas.[116] Violence is theologized by seeing it as a response to God via a response to the "other." This does not make it any less human. "Just as you did it to one of the least of these who are members of my family, you did it to me" (Mt. 25:40). And this must include all violence—personal, communal, and national—all "violation" of the humanity of another. Violence is the rebellion of humanity against God sacramentalized. It is the sinful response of the human community in its rejection of the kind of life that God provides. Violence disbelieves that God is truly the providential Lord of creation who will in the end be shown to be faithful to the things he has made.

This also sheds light on the primal frenzy that violence seems to crescendo toward. Warcraft in the modern world seems unable to rid itself of religious, sacrificial underpinnings and rarely remains content with limited, rational ends. I have not discovered any writing of Balthasar's that considers the just-war tradition of the church. However, his descriptions of the violence in the world's encounter with the Lamb show us why just-war theory, which is the attempt to chasten war to rational, proportionate ends, runs so contrary to the post-Christian mind. Secularity of course seeks mastery over its warcraft as it seeks to dominate all areas of life, but violence in the theo-drama is not a rational, carefully measured act of judgment upon evil, as just-war advocates intend it to be. Humankind, which refuses both the Lamb's powerlessness and its glorious divinity, attempts to be secular, yet discovers that within a purely secular frame, the vigor required to prosecute war is lacking. This is not to say just-war prudence should not be sought, but only that secular, rational explanations for the fury demanded in war fail to satisfy a post-Christian mind. Stanley Hauerwas, in particular, has pointed out the sacrificial, mystical-religious nature of American wars.[117] People will not fight for their country as cynics, Hauerwas writes, and the modern nation-state inevitably reaches past rationality to

---

[116]The slaughter of the innocents in Bethlehem by Herod is thus a paradigmatic symbol of evil. It is humanity lashing out at itself in a fear-based attempt to rid the world of this defenseless threat to human power.

[117]Stanley Hauerwas, "Why War Is a Moral Necessity for America or How Realistic Is Realism?"

more primal, cultic justifications for war. To secularists, the all-out claims of good versus evil and the securing of cosmic righteousness by the "ultimate sacrifice" seem more adequate to the demands and costs of war than more scientific language. Balthasar's view of history as occurring with such immediate intensity before the Lamb's coronation gives material, objective content to this tendency to ramp up rhetoric to all-out sacrifice for cosmic righteousness. Balthasar sees the military-industrial complex as profoundly theo-dramatic.

A theological understanding of violence reminds us that while violence might be repressed, suppressed, sequestered, or managed instrumentally (barely), it cannot be healed other than by consenting to Jesus's obedience to the Father, and the subsequent glory. To truly address violence in a Christian way must involve an irrepressibly *evangelistic* vison that seeks to persuade unbelievers to cast their lives on God through Christ. This is peacemaking with a view to deification, the union of the person with God. By this Christ brings healing to our fraught human community.

Second, we can also see secularity from a new perspective. Secularity is not a neutral stance within humanity. Secularity itself is Christ-provoked. Christ has entered history and in his lordly freedom to be the Son of God within worldly conditions has planted within the human imagination a way of being human that is personal, intentional, awake, and free. This consciousness is unleashed in the world as the church grapples with this new personal existence.

A post-Christian world (a world in which Christ has appeared in the flesh) does not have the option to go back to an earlier imbedded, enchanted mindset, in which the gods coinhered with the cycles of nature and the human person was immersed in the flowing stream of time. In Christ, the self has now raised its head above the stream. The self can now either be Christ-awake, radically free through a yieldedness to the Father, or it can attempt to mimic this awakening from a stance of antagonism to God. This attempt to mimic Christian freedom, according to Balthasar, will necessarily be more intentionally anti-Christ the more Christ is revealed. In this sense, secularity becomes "secularism," the aggressive disincarnation of life to secure a way of being human that is radically and gnostically autonomous.

Titanic post-Christian secularity also becomes hyper-anxious. As the self increasingly claims control of its own destiny, its inescapable vulnerability to the ephemeral and shifting sands of time are thrown into its face with gut-wrenching urgency. *I am awakened to self-mastery and thus awakened ever more frighteningly to my own vulnerability.* Technology in a titanic mindset makes this hyper-anxiety clear. Modern technology, beginning with the telegraph, has increasingly transported humans telepathically beyond their bodily presence in one place to become larger than human. With the internet a human can now live sprawled across the globe seemingly exerting power far from home. But this consciousness of the self projected in global grandeur immediately has its pathetic vulnerability thrusts into its face. We are anxious not because we are the tiny primeval peering up into the cosmos, but because we are gluttonous titans sprawled across the globe who only half-believe our own delusions of grandeur and realize when the sun sets that this control is all a sham.

Third, this has implications for Christian faithfulness in a secular age. In this apocalyptic view of history, the church is involved in the world not first by seeking worldly power, or by convincing the world to notice the church's relevance. In a post-Christian world rather, the church is already involved in the world to the extent that the Lamb unveiled before the world is incarnate in the church's life. Saints must have patient faith in this presence. Gospel pacifism becomes in essence the act of prayerful consent to the live unveiling (apocalypse) of the Lamb at the heart of the church and the Spirit-led consent of the church to be conformed to the figure of this Lamb. By being united to the Lamb, the One from whom the world cannot lower its eyes, the church just is in the world and is rejected by the world. As the church is united ever deeper with her slain Savior through through baptism, Eucharist, evangelism, and worship, through the way its own structures of leadership and decision-making mirror the manner of Jesus, and through the way it speaks its own judgment against sin, it is "caught in the cross-fire" of the world in its business with the Lamb. The church becomes involved in the world not first by its political action (though that is not excluded), but by its union with the Lamb who is now pressing in against the kingdom of this world, goading the world's kickback. In this theo-dramatic view, there is no divide between worldly involvement and spiritual union.

We cannot reject secularity in toto since this would be a rejection of the Chalcedonian Christ. Secularity draws from Christ's "letting be" of human nature, and from Christ's *hypostatic* freedom from human nature. Secularity has received this human freedom from its centuries-long tutoring in the church's witness. If secularity is theo-dramatic in this way, it provides an opening for the offering of the full, authentic self to the Lord. It opens up conditions for a more committed, active, participation in fellowship that has become alert to ways in which embedded realities like gender, race, and class subverted love in un-self-conscious ways. The awakening of the self is not in itself an anti-Christian phenomena and needs to be embraced in this way as one possible way God is creating the worldly conditions for a more personal, active Christianity.

And yet, there is a profound instability about secularity as well, a hazard which Balthasar has shown us. Where humanity accepts its own freedom, but rejects the way such freedom is acquired and sustained in Christ's consent to the Father and in defenselessness before the "other" of his brothers and sisters, it becomes anti-Christ in a way that is also much more awake and intentional. Human rebellion against God leaves behind its ignorance and now becomes personal. Secularity includes within itself the hazard of "disincarnating" the figure of Christ in ways that quickly become demonic.

As a truly theo-dramatic ethic, pacifism must be deeply suspicious about the gains of secularity without wholesale rejection of secularity. As an ethic stripped of Christ, secularity has the capacity for a violence inconceivable in older, more pagan ontologies. As Balthasar has pointed out, the mind-blowing willingness of the modern nation-state to annihilate the whole world in a quest for its own security is the outcome of a deep insecurity and anxiety within the secular mind. Humanity here chooses to be the master of its own destiny even if this entails annihilation. This is the demonic rejection of the "nonresistance" by which Christ found freedom by consenting to the "hour" held in the Father's hands, and by that nonresistance made space for the "other" of the human community, even in all its wretchedness.

Secularity in this sense exists on the knife-edge of judgment—will it consent to Christ in worship or will it descend into self-annihilating titanic revolt? The church in its faithfulness must also submit to being the occasion of this judgment on the world. It receives this judgment into itself and knows itself to be the place where the powers of incarnation and disincarnation join arms in battle. This inner judgment then becomes part of the church's evangelistic witness. It bears witness to the power of the incarnation within its own midst and proclaims this good news without establishing itself as a self-standing institution in the world. By its proclamation of the need for all to trust in Christ it divides the crowd, eliciting both worship and revolt. We shall explore the act of the church's judgment more fully in the next chapter.

But this also means that we must be utterly Christ-centered in whatever "political theology" we envision. In no sense can the church's politics be orphaned from the real-time movement of Christ in the world taking up union with his saints. Christian "political theology" can never be content with universal "Christian principles" or even "middle axioms," to use a phrase from John Howard Yoder, that can be severed as durable, self-standing meeting places where Christians can leave behind their union with Christ to engage productively with others. What *is* capable of engaging productively in the world in solidarity with nonbelievers is not a "middle axiom" but a Chalcedonian Christian. A baptized, catechized member of the body of Christ can *be* the incarnation of Christ living in profound solidarity with people of all faiths to accomplish goals all have in common as humans. In the presence of this nonresistant person *in* Christ, Jesus is involved in the world, in whatever realm it may be, science, education, politics, homemaking, and so on. The member of the body of Christ can be a seed within the world, often hidden, even as Christ was and is hidden. "But he sternly ordered them not to make him known" (Mk 3:12). This may be a seed that lies dormant in the ground for centuries before the Holy Spirit waters and brings it to life.

This apocalyptic understanding of the Christian's involvement in the world brings a new urgency to the repeated assurance in scripture that true saintliness suffers in the world at all times. There is a suffering for the saint in secularity that must be endured. This is first the embarrassment of Moses and Aaron realizing the irrelevance of their imitable sign in Pharaoh's court. Within the conditions of secularity, the church will be matched and even out-matched in its ability to be moral. Why now cast your life upon the God and Father of our Lord Jesus Christ when a superior morality can be achieved through secular means? This is the suffering of faith in an ambivalent place, seeking to be faithful without the dignity of being found worthy to be attack and opposed. The Christian ethic receives not the shouts of "crucify him," but a yawn in an age that has taken to itself the treasures of the Christian inheritance and secured them in instrumental ways.

To adore and contemplate Jesus in the face of this yawn requires the anointing of the Spirit.[118]

But if Balthasar is correct, titanic secularity will not tolerate the nonresistant saint for long. As someone who lived through the twentieth century's monstrous secularities of both the right and the left, he was acutely tuned to the way post-Christian control of history could go. The more the figure of Christ is revealed in saintly devotion and ecclesial life, the greater will be the recoil of post-Christian society against the Lamb. And so, within this view, while not every secular society will mimic a Stalin or a Hitler, secularity will always have a taste for these kinds of gigantic efforts at human self-mastery.

In Chapter 1 on Mennonite rhetoric on pacifism, we showed that "nonviolence" was not the bottom line for Anabaptists such as Michael Sattler, Pilgram Marpeck, and Menno Simons. Rather, pacifism was dependent on a *Nachfolge Christi*, the imitation, participation, and solidarity of the believer with the meek, incarnate Christ. It was this union with Christ that determined the saints' approach to violence rather than the ideal of "nonviolence" as a detached principle. Balthasar's approach to the Lamb's confrontation in the Book of Revelation offers us a retrieval of that approach to Christology. It assumes that the church will very much be in the world, a constant reminder to the world that Christ still presses in. The church surrenders to following this Christ throughout its days. It is the violence in the interchange between the Lamb and the world that will be met nonresistantly. The Lamb's breaking of the seals unleashes a turn of events that results in the dark power's self-destruction. However, since this is the Lamb that is fighting, and since the saints are called to wait and endure, an ethic of openness to the deeds of the Father through the suffering Christ become the modus operandi of Christian ethics. We turn then from provocation to convocation.

---

[118]Did God give Pentecostalism to the world at just the moment the church needed to assert its unique vocation in the face of a secularity threatening to completely imitate the people of God? Sociologists such as David Martin have pointed out the way in which Pentecostalism is a Christianity goaded by the realities of secularity. It is a mobile, egalitarian, personal, and powerful Christian resistance to a secularity that had defeated traditional expressions of Christ. See David Martin, *Pentecostalism: The World Their Parish* (Hoboken, NJ: Wiley-Blackwell, 2002), and David Martin, *Tongues of Fire: The Explosion of Protestantism in Latin America* (Hoboken, NJ: Wiley-Blackwell, 1993).

5

Convocation: The Church and the Lamb

The Ecclesial Contours of Mennonite Pacifism

In seeking a dogmatic momentum for pacifism, we are examining three aspects of the incarnational descent of the Logos into the world. We are claiming that pacifism, to be a theology of peace, must be united with Christ who travels this path into the far country. It adopts his posture toward the Father and toward the world. It experiences the backlash of alienated humankind, knowing the fellowship of Christ's sufferings. In each of these aspects confession and ethics are joined together as the contemplative, adoring gaze of the church before her Lord.

Having considered the hostile reaction that this love elicits, we come now to the final phase of this descent into flesh, the appearance of glory in human conditions as the church. Here at its most incarnated fulfillment, pacifism blossoms as real-life ecclesial love. Trinitarian love opens out to enemy love, which opens out to fraternal love.[1] What we are seeking in this chapter is an emphasis in ecclesiology on the contemplative union of the church with the enemy love of God out of which fraternal love in the church emerges. This is the convocation that mirrors the provocation of Christ in the world. The argument of this chapter

---

[1] I use the term fraternal love to refer to the love between sisters and brothers in the church community. It's not perfect but it's better than "brotherly."

is that the fullest participation of the church in the incarnational descent of her Lord is a participation in God's judgment of the world through Christ.

Before we wade into Balthasarian terrain again, it is important to say a few things about the relation between pacifism and the church in the Mennonite story. It is stating the obvious to say that for early Anabaptists, the rejection of the sword was an ecclesial reality. Peter Reidemann, in a 1545 Hutterite confession of faith, says, "Christ, the Prince of Peace, has prepared a kingdom for himself, namely, the church, and has won his kingdom by shedding his own blood. Therefore, all worldly warfare in this kingdom has come to an end. ... Therefore, Christians should not take part in war, nor should they use force for purposes of vengeance."[2] Here the church was to be the place where the atonement of Christ founded a peaceful nonresistance toward evil for the body of Christ.

In the sixteenth century, the practice of this was often dependent on a "two-kingdoms" theology, which drew a severe ethical division between the world as ruled by the state and the church as ruled in the "perfection of Christ."[3] The church was to be free in its reverence for the Lord. The sword had a legitimate place in the hands of the state in the worldview of these Anabaptists, but the church (including *all* members) was to be a unique, heroic mission set free within the world to live in union with Christ's atonement. Because of this two-kingdom theology and the brutal reality of politics in the sixteenth century, it was difficult, if not impossible, for Anabaptists to participate in the magistracy and in several other vocations in society. In these spheres the "missional" ability of a Christian pacifist to influence society was minimal. And yet, these "two-kingdom" pacifists were vigorous in propagating their faith abroad in a way that few other churches of the time were.[4] John H. Yoder argues

---

[2]Riedemann, *Peter Riedemann's Hutterite Confession of Faith*, 134–5.

[3]The term used in the Schleitheim Confession in 1527. Friedmann, *Theology of Anabaptism*, is a thorough interpretation of Anabaptism as a "two-kingdom" theology. I recognize that there was diversity in Anabaptism, especially in the 1520s. However, few Anabaptist leaders that survived past the Münster episode articulated a theology of culture for involvement in societal leadership.

[4]For a description of Anabaptism's surprising missionary activity see David Almon Thiessen's MCS thesis, "The Church in Mission: Factors That Contributed to the Sixteenth Century Anabaptists Being a Missionary People" (Regent College, 1980). See also Arnold Snyder's description of "the communication of Anabaptist ideas" in *Anabaptist History and Theology*, 167–84.

that the unique evangelistic fervor of these beleaguered Christians arose precisely because of their refusal to avail themselves of the state's coercion. "In the sixteenth century, established Protestantism generally disavowed the concept of world missionary outreach ... [because] the numerical fusion of church and society made it simply unthinkable that the Christian faith could be propagated in another form than in the extension of political and cultural sovereignty of Christendom."[5] Anabaptism, in this view, displayed a freedom from the world that permitted its life to be calibrated to Christ. It did not need to pace itself to the expansion of any nation and thus was free for mission. Evangelism was thus the pacifist mode of the church's expansion.

A key ecclesial aspect of early Anabaptist pacifism was its belief that the difference between church and world lay in how judgment was to be enacted. Walter Klaassen says of early Anabaptists, "the sword is almost always opposed, not to nonviolent resistance, but to the ban." When Christ took the sword from Peter, he gave him instead the power to peacefully bind and loose in the church. This form of ecclesial judgment entailed "a totally new life orientation in which all human relationships are governed by patience, understanding, love, forgiveness, and a desire for the redemption even of the enemy." One of the basic problems of the sword for the Anabaptists, according to Klaassen, was "that killing a person destroyed any possibility of improvement or repentance" and amounted to "a usurpation of the divine prerogative."[6] Anabaptist thinking insisted that Christian judgment conform to the judgment of Christ and further those ends for which he died. In the Schleitheim Confession, for example, the entire discussion of the sword revolves around the kinds of judgment Christians can or cannot render. "In the perfection of Christ, however, only the ban is used for a warning and for the excommunication of the one who has sinned, without putting the flesh to death,—simply the warning and the command to sin no more."[7] After exploring various ways in which worldly judgment fails this test of daily connectivity to the judgment of Christ we find this conclusion:

---

[5]Yoder, *Priestly Kingdom*, 118–19.
[6]Klaassen, *Anabaptism in Outline*, 265–6.
[7]Wenger, "Schleitheim Confession of Faith," 250.

In brief, as is the mind of Christ toward us, so shall the mind
of the members of the body of Christ be through Him in all
things, that there may be no schism in the body through which
it would be destroyed. For every kingdom divided against itself
will be destroyed. Now since Christ is as it is written of Him,
His members must also be the same, that His body may remain
complete and united to its own advancement and upbuilding.[8]

Church discipline then was intended as a pacifist mode of judgment
expressed toward other Christians for the sake of Christian
participation with Christ. The church's refusal to use the sword
anywhere in or out of the church was rooted in this calibration with
the judgment of Christ. In this premodern setting, it remained the
case that only churches that practiced this peaceful judgment could
practice nonviolence. The church was in this sense not "defenseless";
it had peaceful practices of church discipline.

According to this interpretation, evangelism and church discipline
were Anabaptist modes of living gospel pacifism in union with the
judgment of Christ. Because the church had no coercive powers
at its disposal to further itself, it involved itself in evangelization.
Evangelism was the church's announcement of God's judgment
on the world—both in his loving suffering and in his fiery wrath.[9]
Because it had no coercive power for its internal protection, it
developed a theology and practice of church discipline.

But the danger of this judgment becoming "worldly" or merely
human was a constant reality. Pilgram Marpeck, for example, wrote
four long letters to the Swiss Brethren on matters related to church
discipline. He accuses them of running ahead of the Spirit of Christ
and prejudging outside the parameters and pace of salvation. "By
their fruits (He does not say by the blossoms or the foliage) you shall
know them," he writes, which means that a hasty, harsh, and human
judgment must be avoided.[10] Whoever, therefore, "establishes,
commands, prohibits, coerces, drives, punishes, or judges before the
time the good or evil fruit is revealed, lays claim to the authority,
power, and office of the Holy Spirit of the Lord Jesus Christ and,

---

[8]Ibid., 251.
[9]Anabaptist missionaries were frequently prophet-chiliasts who sensed the end of the
world pressing in, and who rallied people to join the elect who would be spared.
Snyder, *Anabaptist History and Theology*, 167–8, 175.
[10]Klassen and Klaassen, *Writings of Pilgram Marpeck*, 323.

contrary to love, goodness, and grace, runs ahead of Christ."[11] Arnold Snyder argues that it was the eclipse of an imitative, Christ-tethered form of judgment in favor of a form more focused on a vision of a pure church that eventually caused the problems the Dutch Mennonites experienced in the later sixteenth century in their obsession with shunning.[12]

However, separatism from society was the outcome of Anabaptism in its sixteenth-century context. At this ecclesial level, Mennonites, at least until the twentieth century, did not often see their pacifism as evangelistically active in the world. It was rather a "stance" or a privilege, accorded to them as Mennonites where this could be secured, which exempted them from the exercise of worldly judgment. According to the seventeenth-century *Martyrs Mirror*, the defenseless Christian might be a leaven, witness, and provocateur in society, but there was little thought that Christians had a mission to translate their peace theology into the worldly structures of society beyond the congregation.[13] For Mennonites in Europe and in North America, ecclesial pacifism was more a reason for separation than involvement in the world.

With the founding of twentieth-century parachurch organizations such as the Mennonite Central Committee in North America, Mennonites began to discover ways to translate their pacifism into mission beyond the church. This was abetted by the mid-century emphasis, borrowed from biblical scholars such as Oscar Cullmann, that God was Lord of the whole world and not only of the church, and that therefore the convictions of the church in these matters needed to be published abroad and established in society in instrumentalist peacemaking. This enabled a more missional pacifism.[14] It fueled

---

[11]Ibid., 324.

[12]Snyder, *Anabaptist History and Theology*, 384–90.

[13]Van Bragt, *Bloody Theater*, 14.

[14]In Cullmann's view, the church was at the heart of the kingly reign, but the reign extended beyond the church to include the state which, though unconscious of it, nevertheless also existed under Christ's direction. See J. Denny Weaver, ed., *John Howard Yoder: Radical Theologian* (Eugene, OR: Wipf and Stock, 2014), 151–4. Leo Driedger and Donald B. Kraybill call this shift in Mennonite peace theology the most significant theological transformation in church–state relations for the twentieth-century Mennonite church. Yoder's later *Politics of Jesus* was only the concretization of this new frontier. See Driedger and Kraybill, *Mennonite Peacemaking*, 121, 147; Bush, *Two Kingdoms, Two Loyalties*, 197–204.

an evangelical urgency to the practice of pacifism. Now the church possessed a much-needed medicine in a violent world.

But this urgency to leaven society with nonviolent witness could also make the connection with ecclesiology more tenuous. It could have the effect of exporting pacifism from the church and from the lay person. Was pacifism now something only for specialists involved in international peacemaking and societal activism and leadership? If pacifism was now carried out in ways shared by many people outside the church, how was this still ecclesially formed?[15] As we pointed out in Chapter 2, a pattern of secularization is tempting wherever the church seeks to embed the gospel out in the world in the daily walk of the laity. It comes to be questioned whether such action is truly dependent on the church at all.

But with (or perhaps because of) this tenuousness, twentieth-century Mennonite peace theology sought all the more to emphasize the organic connection between pacifism and ecclesiology. Yoder was a key part of this and his work plows important ground for our work in this chapter. Here the church was described as that place on earth where the Kingdom of Christ takes up a visible, political reality, and where the defenseless power of the cross meets sociology.[16] The church, Yoder says, is the social form of the gospel in this world.[17] If anything, the church plays a more central role in the refusal of violence than ecclesiology did for early Anabaptists.[18]

Stanley Hauerwas, a close follower of Yoder's theology of the church and its connection with nonviolence, argues that "keeping theological ethics theological" means beginning and ending ethics in and for the church. For Hauerwas, "Christian beliefs about God, Jesus, sin, the nature of human existence, and salvation are

---

[15]MCC calls itself "an arm of the church" and requires that its workers "have active membership in or demonstrated commitment to and participation in a local Christian church." However, baptism is not required. See https://mcccurrentopenings.secure. force.com/recruit/fRecruit__ApplyNotice?page=AboutServingwithMCC.

[16]Yoder emphasized that his goal was not to create an unpopular church, or a minority church, or a countercultural church, but a church with "fidelity to the jealousy of Christ as Lord." Yoder, *Priestly Kingdom*, 86.

[17]Yoder, *Original Revolution*, 108–9.

[18]J. Alexander Sider and Jonathan R. Seiling, trans., "Theologian in Contradiction: An Interview with Hans-Jürgen Goertz on John Howard Yoder's Radical Pacifism," *Conrad Grebel Review* 33, no. 3 (2015): 378. Is it also the case that ecclesiology itself is a modern invention? This is the argument of Nicholas M. Healy, *Hauerwas: A (Very) Critical Introduction* (Grand Rapids, MI: Eerdmans, 2014).

intelligible only if they are seen against the background of the church." As Christians "we believe we not only need a community, but a community of a particular kind to live well morally."[19] The task of the theological ethicist, according to Hauerwas, is to give some account of the difference that being in the church (with its peculiar stories, rituals, traditions, and beliefs about Jesus) makes for ethics. Ecclesiology is the theological component that makes ethics theological ethics, and the church is the school of virtue in which believers are trained in peace. Hauerwas has asserted the need for a tradition of practices (much more so than Yoder)[20] by which the church passes the reality of socially embodied salvation from generation to generation. For Hauerwas, the church is the school of gospel pacifism.

However, in developing a framework for an ecclesial basis for pacifism, one must also hear a recent criticism of Hauerwas expressed by Nicholas M. Healy. Healy argues that Hauerwas has elevated the church as an ethical community by using "social-philosophical theories" rather than first-order reflection on God. Hauerwas, he claims, is partaking of a view of the church that is rooted in Frederick Schleiermacher's understanding that "the function of Christian Churches is to mediate Christ's particular experience of God through their patterns of life. Thus the lived experience of a Church is prior to—and to some degree normative over—its interpretation of scripture and doctrine."[21] Accordingly, Hauerwas has located the church vis-à-vis dogma in such a way that dogma has become dependent on the church rather than vice versa. The chief ecclesial concern for Hauerwas is apologetical, or the use of the church to make Christian ethics intelligible and attractive in the world. "His account of how we come to belief and what makes it an attractive possibility is treated not in terms of the attractiveness and cogency of a Christian account of who God is and how God

---

[19]Stanley Hauerwas, *Against the Nations: War and Survival in a Liberal Society* (Notre Dame, IN: University of Notre Dame Press, 1992), 42–3.

[20]Gerald W. Schlabach, "Continuity and Sacrament, or Not: Hauerwas, Yoder, and Their Deep Difference," *Journal of the Society of Christian Ethics* 27, no. 2 (2007): 171–207.

[21]Nicholas M. Healy, "Ecclesiology," in *The Cambridge Dictionary of Christian Theology*, ed. Ian A. McFarland et al. (Cambridge: Cambridge University Press, 2011), 154. This is similar to the accusation leveled against Hauerwas by Nathan Kerr in *Christ, History and Apocalyptic*, 109.

relates to us, but largely in terms of what we do as the church."[22]
This places heavy demands upon the church to be something that it
almost never achieves and it locates the core of theology in what the
church can manage to demonstrate with its ethics.

It is not my task to adjudicate whether Hauerwas is ecclesiocentric
in the way that Healy contends, but this accusation does signal
a warning for us in developing the dogmatic basis for a theology
of peace in its ecclesial form.[23] Any description of the church here
must be rooted in God and in what God has wrought. It must be
genuinely incarnational in the Chalcedonian key we described
earlier, where the priority of God in his mission is paramount,
thereby securing the genuinely earthy, perduring, and sojourning
nature of the church without dissolving it into God. The church
must be structured, empowered, judged, and limited by God and
God's action in Christ. The statement, "Let it be with me according
to your word," becomes the posture of incarnational ecclesial ethics.

But as this incarnational reality, it must also be a genuinely earthly
community, susceptible to investigation as a "social phenomenon."
We could say that the church is a "social phenomenon" deified to
express humanity's overdue praise to God. Are these "phenomena"
taken into God's salvific mission and do they become transparent to
the Spirit whose work it is to choreograph this mission within the
relationship of Christ with his Father? This is Balthasar's question
for ethics. It is not difficult to find references within Hauerwas's
writings that display an openness to this dynamic, even though
dogmatics has not been fully explored in his writings.[24]

---

[22]Healy, *Hauerwas*, 56.

[23]It is doubtful that Hauerwas would agree to Healy's description of his theology,
never mind his evaluation of it. For a retort to Healy's very critical introduction
see P. Travis Kroeker, "Hauerwas: A (Very) Critical Introduction," *Modern Theology*
32, no. 2 (April 2016): 300–302. Kroeker maintains that Healy has misunderstood
the ways in which Hauerwas's understanding of the church is theological, and not
merely theoretical or sociological.

[24]Hauerwas has been a mighty and vocal opponent of ethics divided from theology.
It would, however, be fair to say that though Hauerwas is insistent that ethics be
done in close fellowship with theology and that the best moral theologians are those
immersed in the church's "story," he has assumed the writings of others like Karl
Barth for this rather than explicating the dogmatic tradition himself. For a description
of his commitment to a *theological* ethic, see the section "Who are Christians? The
Christian Story" in Stanley Hauerwas, *The Hauerwas Reader*, ed. John Berkman and
Michael Cartwright (Chapel Hill, NC: Duke University Press, 2001), 54–181.

What we are seeking then is a deepening love for the enemy, which comes from the missional vocation of the church in cadence with the judgment of Christ. Balthasar offers an ascetic understanding of Christ in the church that views the believer as coming to mingle in Christ's incarnational loving judgment of his enemies. This is where the missionality of pacifism is founded, and we will argue that it is a helpful ecclesiology of pacifism. We turn now to Balthasar to grasp his vision of fraternal love in the church and the way this issues in a kind of Christian judgment.

Balthasar's Theology of Love

Balthasar's writings are filled with a theological vision of love and this vision shapes his view of the church. He writes in *Mysterium Paschale*, "Born of the utmost love of God for the world, the Church herself is essentially love. What she is, that she ought to be: her essence is her unique commandment (John 15:12.)"[25] All of Balthasar's writings could be described as an attempt to receive the vision of the love of God and to understand what this means for a church apprehended by that vision. Nicholas J. Healy states, for Balthasar "being—creaturely being and trinitarian being—unveils its final countenance as love in the death and Resurrection of Jesus Christ."[26] This is the source of his ethics and we will see the extent to which neighbor love is bound up with the incarnation for Balthasar's ecclesiology.[27]

It is in love where the analogy of being between God and the world most clearly becomes visible for Balthasar.[28] In *Love Alone Is Credible*, for example, Balthasar explains something central to his theological aesthetics, which is that God's revelation becomes

---

[25]Balthasar, *Mysterium Paschale*, 134.

[26]Nicholas J. Healy, *The Eschatology of Hans Urs von Balthasar: Eschatology as Communion* (New York: Oxford University Press, 2005), 211. This is not the Nicholas M. Healy referred to above in the context of Hauerwas. Both have written about Balthasar.

[27]Joseph Ratzinger, Hans Urs von Balthasar, and Heinz Schurmann, "Nine Propositions on Christian Ethics," in *Principles of Christian Morality* (San Francisco, CA: Ignatius, 1996), 79, is a helpful distillation of the intensely Christocentric nature of ethics for Balthasar. For a good introduction to neighbour love in Balthasar's writings see Steck, *Ethical Thought of Hans Urs von Balthasar*, 112–21.

[28]This is explored in Balthasar, *Love Alone Is Credible*.

credible and intelligible to us as we perceive and respond to it as love. In this gift and reception and regift of love, God becomes someone who can be known and believed in. Christian fraternal love is figured in profound ways by the love of God. As humans become more radiant with God's love they become not only more fully human, but also able to grasp the nature of God, which is love. Divine love and neighbor love come into tight-knit harmony. In the incarnation, the analogy of being, structured by love, is exposed in history-turning potency. Here the action of God in love comes to be expressed in the most-human neighbor love of the Son of a Jewish virgin.

We should emphasize that the contemplation of divine action and being is the decisive element in Balthasar's understanding of human love.[29] Contemplation is a prayerful inner longing, the receptive attentiveness of the believer to the beauty of Christ in the world. In contemplative prayer, the texture of the incarnation in its self-giving and sacrificial reality is received through the spiritual senses.[30] This is union with Christ. The loving contemplation by the believer of the Word of God as it appears in the world is itself a form of love that both transforms the person and extends the person's love out to the neighbor. Prayer, for Balthasar, is the opposite of violence.

29

If revelation were not love, then a receptive disposition of pure letting be—which is intelligible only as the attitude of love that allows itself (as faith) to be led beyond all desire for self-knowledge—would be inhuman and unworthy of God, and God's revelation itself would not be able to instill such an attitude as an answer to his Word. Love can accord a priori (and therefore as faith) only with love, never with nonlove. (ibid., 83)

[30]Balthasar's theology of the spiritual senses has been described recently by Mark McInroy. McInroy shows that Balthasar was concerned throughout his theological anthropology to demonstrate that through grace, humans can perceive divine glory, and that this God-given capability is not the end point of mysticism, an elite achievement granted only to the few, but rather how all believers can be transformed to embody the love of God. McInroy describes Balthasarian spiritual senses in a way that supports our contention that the spiritual life is figured by the incarnation. Spiritual perception includes sensory corporeal perception but sees "the depths within the form." This is the unity in difference of contemplation patterned in the incarnation. *Balthasar on the "Spiritual Senses": Perceiving Splendour* (Oxford: Oxford University Press, 2014), 186.

But it is also through loving our neighbor that we contemplate the love of God. "That is why we can speak of our brother, not as 'Christ in disguise' but as the 'sacrament of Christ.'"[31] Contemplation of Christ and neighbor love mutually nourish each other.

> The eyes of Christian love are full of faith and of faith's contemplation; they have a luminosity which discovers and lights up a supernatural depth in whatever and whomsoever they fasten upon: this sinner, this unattractive and insignificant person, this avowed opponent of the Church and of Jesus Christ is in reality my brother; Jesus Christ has borne his sins just as he has borne mine (which means that there can be no accusations on either side); his unpleasant characteristics are a burden he is obliged, willy-nilly to drag around with him, and although I cannot see it, this burden has some connection, through God's grace with the total burden which weighs on the shoulders of Jesus Christ.[32]

In the trial, which the encounter with the other brings, some dimension of Christ's agony presses into the experience of the believer.

We are seeking a form of enemy love that includes but goes deeper than the instrumental techniques the world has discovered to reduce violence and develop a just society. Balthasar was concerned to describe a form of love that "is not written against a background of merely interpersonal relationships and motivations for conduct, but against the background of a unity that lies above the persons, overlapping and embracing them all."[33] In these general introductory remarks about love for Balthasar, we can see that a contemplative, prayerful attentiveness to the Word of God in the world is the basis for a spirituality of "letting be" by which the believer enters the mystery of God and becomes transparent to God's love. This is a

---

[31]Hans Urs von Balthasar, *Prayer*, trans. Graham Harrison (San Francisco, CA: Ignatius, 1986), 215.

[32]Ibid., 216. Helmut Harder notes that though Anabaptists rejected the sacramental system of the medieval church, they retained the sacramentality of the church as a whole. The church became the one sacrament of Christ. See the unpublished *Historical and Theological Essays Presented at the International Catholic-Mennonite Dialogue 1998–2002* (Winnipeg, Manitoba, 2002).

[33]Balthasar, *Glory of the Lord*, 7:447.

good beginning to understanding gospel pacifism as a prayerful reception of God's love as it unfolds in the world.

The Expropriation and Appropriation of the Believer in Christ

With those introductory comments on Balthasar's understanding of love, we seek now to understand the way the Holy Spirit interacts with the cross of Christ to make a path for a church of enemy love in the Balthasar's thought. This is not only conceptual. What we see here is a theology of *ascesis*[34] by which the believer is lifted from self-regarding egoism and mingled with the descent and glory of Christ. It is through this ascesis that the church rises to offer a judgment not of a merely human sort but as a judgment embraced within Christ's judgment. This is the vocation of the church, to become so pentecostal that its judgments become conformed to the judgments of Christ.

It is helpful once again to exposit a specific section of writing in Balthasar where this comes especially to the fore. "In Laudem Gloriae" is the final section of the last volume of *The Glory of the Lord*, Balthasar's seven-volume theological aesthetics. As such, it describes a kind of climax or fulfillment of the appearance of glory in the world.

First, a word about theological aesthetics. Theological aesthetics for Balthasar is that work of theology that seeks to describe the appearing of God within human perception.[35] It is "a 'coming to see' the form in which God's Word comes to us, gives itself to us and loves us."[36] It describes a "knowing" that is taught to the disciple by the manner of God's appearing. Balthasar is concerned to do theology as though God had spoken first, and to work "in the power of the divine love which draws near to us and enables us to receive itself."[37] This is a significant and central feature of

---

[34]The practice of Spirit-enabled self-discipline for the sake of union with Christ.
[35]"What is here called 'aesthetic' is therefore characterized as something properly theological, namely, as the reception, perceived with the eyes of faith, of the self-interpreting glory of the sovereignly free love of God." Balthasar, *Love Alone Is Credible*, 11.
[36]Balthasar, *Glory of the Lord*, 7:389.
[37]Ibid.

Balthasar's theological aesthetics: *divine glory establishes the conditions of its own reception.* Divine glory is self-interpreting in the way it transforms the believer to adopt a posture matching the manner in which the glory is displayed in the world. We do not bring to divine revelation a secular competency, knowledge, epistemology, or theological method that prepares us to know God. Rather, God in his appearing tutors our senses and conforms them to the figure of his appearing so that there is a consonance between our knowing and the Lord. It was Balthasar's conviction that modern theology had lost its way by obscuring the theological order by which we come to know. Christian theology (and the church itself) begins when God appears in his glorious beauty. The appearing of this glory draws the church into existence and elicits saintly life, including the theological task itself. The church's shape is figured by the manner of divine appearing.

How is divine glory displayed in the world? *The Glory of the Lord*, Balthasar's seven-volume series on theological aesthetics, is a vast complex, but in the section "In Laudem Gloriae," Balthasar says divine glory radiates out in divine *expropriation*.[38] God's appearing is God giving himself over. A divine expropriation occurs as the Son gives over possession of himself to the Father in humble descent. For Balthasar this handing over by the Son is already an inner-trinitarian reality that finds expression in the history of salvation in the incarnation. We saw this trinitarian dynamic in the previous chapter in our discussion of the divine *traditio*. The Father gives divine being (freedom) to the Son who offers himself back in a gift of free gratitude. When the Son does this through the manger, the cross, the grave, and the ascension, we have the matchless appearance of divine beauty in the world that not only draws the saints' gaze but also draws them into all the worship, mission, prayer, and action of the church through all the world's days. There is here an inexhaustible depth within the form of the Son's appearance. This splendor of self-gift shines forth eternally, even if this beauty is radiated through the "ugliness" and horror of the cross. The splendor is love.

This divine expropriation becomes the archetype and inner spiritual momentum of a responding human expropriation. God gives being (freedom) to us in Christ and we offer it back in a gift of free gratitude. This offering back of the self to God is a

---

[38]Ibid., 399ff.

self-expropriation. Christians are "raptured" beyond themselves through the contemplation of the manner of divine love as it appears in worldly conditions. For this reason, there is in all of Balthasar's spirituality an awareness of ecstasy, of being drawn forth to participate in the dynamic that is unfolding in the outpouring of God's love. As the glory of the Lord appears before the saint, her eyes are lifted from the self and fixed on the beauty of love. This is not a pure selflessness but rather the engagement of the self with what appears. This is rapture, a drawing away from self-absorption through the gaze of the soul on Christ to give itself even as Christ has given himself. This rapture, because it is a conforming to something beyond itself, does not come easily—it involves a long and painful dying to oneself in order to become conformed to the glory made visible.[39] But this ecstasy is the fulfillment of what it means to be human—this is no human dissolving in the ocean of God. This ascesis is the sanctifying way the saint is transfigured in the ecstatic expropriation of the self. Faith, hope, and love are the human responses appropriate to the manner of the appearing of divine glory in the world. They are postures effected by the divine glory, attuning the believer to know God.

But this is not merely an individual matter between the believer and God. Here at the end of *The Glory of the Lord*, Balthasar suggests that the consummation of divine glory's entrance into the world is not the return of such glory back to the One, as was suggested in neo-Platonic philosophy. Rather, he argues:

> The final point of the outpouring of God's love ... is the dawning of the divine love in what is not God and what is opposed to God, the dawning of eternal life (as "resurrection") in utter death: not the dawning of the divine "I" in the non-divine "Thou" but the dawning of the divine I-Thou-We in the worldly, creaturely I-Thou-We of human fellowship.[40]

---

[39]This is analogous to the appearing of any beauty before our eyes.

> The demand the beautiful itself makes to be allowed to be what it is, the demand, therefore, that we renounce our attempts to control and manipulate it, in order truly to be able to be happy by enjoying it: all of this is, in the natural realm, the foundation and foreshadowing of what in the realm of revelation and grace will be the attitude of faith. (*Glory of the Lord*, 1:153)

[40]Balthasar, *Glory of the Lord*, 7:432.

In this quote we can begin to see a Balthasarian ecclesiology of enemy love. The final summit and fulfillment of divine glory descending into the world is God's love of his enemies taking form in the creaturely "I–Thou–We of human fellowship." The response of the church to God's entrance "is the inherent and logical end of an act of glorification begun by God himself."[41] Because of this, the church's life, "above all the mutual love of Christians, is an act of praising God not only in an external way, but with an inherent relationship to the essential glory of God."[42] The words "external" and "inherent" are key here. Balthasar is envisioning the closest possible relation between the archetype of expropriation (divine self-giving) and its type (human self-giving), without collapsing the difference. The church in its earthly, perduring visibility in mutual love is the glory of God become incarnate. The incarnate God is its archetype.[43] The church in its very nature is a rapture, a coming out of egoism, elicited by the beauty of God's appearing "in what is opposed to God." The church's fraternal love is precisely this mode of rapture from egoism, the conditions created by divine glory itself for the reception and assimilation of divine glory. Christ-figured fraternal love between enemies, we might say, is the epistemological condition established by God for his own reception in the world. As the church is formed in this way through contemplation, the church has a divine consonance with its Lord. The world will know the glory of God as it is lived out as enemy love in the church's I–Thou–We.

This it seems to me is a beautiful replenishing of nonviolent ecclesiology: To be a gathering of enemies in fraternal love matching God's appearance. All of the church's being and action is nourished in this vision by gazing into the glory of the Lord. Adoration here blends seamlessly with action, as both are figured by the church's conforming to the beauty appearing. They are the divine beauty's creation of the conditions for God's appearance on earth. They are nourished only on this appearing.

As expressed above, the "glory" of the church is her participation in divine self-expropriation, in the Son's dispossession of his own

---

[41]Ibid., 7:399.
[42]Ibid.
[43]This has similarities with Pilgram Marpeck's understanding of the church formed by the "outer" and "inner" aspects of Christ. Klassen and Klaassen, *Writings of Pilgram Marpeck*, 378–9.

will in surrender to the Father. In Balthasar's view, the Father/
Son relation is not jealously guarded by God. It is a complete act
of hospitality that the world, even as enemy, is invited to mingle
in.[44] Bringing a human fellowship into being within this mystery
between Father and Son, Balthasar says, is the work of the Holy
Spirit: "Since the Spirit himself is the glorification of the love
between Father and Son, wherein God's true glory disclosed itself
to us, it is likewise only he who can bring about glorification in
the world."[45] The church lives in the pentecostal "space" between
Father and Son. In keeping with his Augustinian theology of the
Spirit, Balthasar holds that the church is in fact an earthly, Holy
Spirit manifestation of the love between Father and Son. As the
church is brought into the Father/Son relation at the point where
Jesus "breathed out his spirit," the church becomes a partaker of this
divine trinitarian love. By the Spirit's work, the church is "raptured"
out to participate in cruciform triune love. Here Christopher Steck
captures Balthasar's sense:

> The Christ-event has really become, through the Christians'
> incorporation into Christ, their story, not just epistemologically
> (i.e., the lens through which they interpret their lives), as it might
> seem in some works of narrative ethics, but ontologically, as the
> fruit of the Spirit's power to "liquefy" the Christ-form, to use von
> Balthasar's language, by stamping it into the lives of his followers.[46]

---

[44]God "is the opposite of a strict lord who demands that what he has lent out should
be given back to him intact and untouched. He is the sower who ... watches to see
what will come from the union of divine vital power in the world that receives it."
Glory of the Lord, 7:432. The church is the incarnation's obedience and love sown
in the world, and God now becomes "latent," God watches "contemplatively" to see
what fruit the world will yield with the seed of the Word of God within it. Ibid., 7:419.
[45]Balthasar, *Glory of the Lord*, 7:389. This is very close to the centre of Balthasar's
pneumatology as described much more fully in *Theo-Logic*, 2005, esp. 3:157–64.
Balthasar believes that the Spirit is both the expression of the love between Father
and Son (after Augustine) and also the fruit of the love. The Spirit is the "Gift"
(162) namely, the love that is given between Father and Son, and it is also the excess
(160), a fruit which is nevertheless not external to the love. When believers receive
this "Gift" (162) in salvation they receive the relation of the Father and Son, which
is divinity itself, deification. "The Spirit should be called *donum doni*, that is, the
Father's love, given to the world in his Son and 'poured out into our hearts' through
the gift of love in the Spirit" (162).
[46]Steck, *Ethical Thought of Hans Urs von Balthasar*, 89.

This is why the church's true form is mutual love. The Christ-event of love offered to the Father is "liquefied" into human community as eucharistic, mutual love through the Spirit.[47] The church's fraternal love is a Spirit-led mingling in the dynamic that unfolded between Jesus and the Father.

Believers come to know from the inside "the establishment in Christ ... and, in the same breath, in us too ... the whole extreme tension between powerlessness in the lostness of death and the supremely mighty power of God's resurrection."[48] This lived Christic tension is the very dynamo of God's love in its incarnate form. It is this pneumatic inclusion into the tension that is a wellspring for an ethics that is more than merely instrumental and worldly. It is an earthliness set within the Father/Son relation.

> The Spirit of God is sent to change this possibility into a reality. He shows the world that the poverty of the Son, who sought only the glory of the Father and let himself be robbed of everything in utter obedience, was the most exact expression of the absolute fullness, which does not consist of "having", but of "being=giving." It is in giving that one is and has.[49]

Soteriology, pneumatology, and ecclesiology thus come together. In the entrance into this divine community (Balthasar calls this divinization[50]), the church participates in the incarnation and is conformed to the inner dynamic of the mission of Christ in human flesh. "In order to draw near to God, one must not move so much as a step away from the Incarnation."[51] We become people who love at great cost. Hence "man enjoys an inner participation in the attitude of divine selflessness, and he is able, like Christ, to give an incarnated form to this attitude in giving away his own goods."[52] This is the divine pedagogy that trains the soul to receive the glory of the Lord.

---

[47]Hans Urs von Balthasar, "Spirit and Institution," in *Explorations in Theology*, vol. 4, *Spirit and Institution* (San Francisco, CA: Ignatius, 1995), 237.
[48]Ibid., 7:394.
[49]Ibid., 7:391. Balthasar discusses a communion of the saints rooted in the *pro nobis* of Christ's offering in Balthasar, *Theo-Drama*, 1994, 4:417–23.
[50]Balthasar, *Theo-Logic*, 2005, 3:75.
[51]Ibid., 3:78.
[52]Balthasar, *Glory of the Lord*, 7:429.

This is then a church taken up into the momentum by which God the Father loves his enemies through his Son and brings them into the relation between Father and Son through the Spirit. Here the divine "I–Thou–We" is transposed into what was not God, what was even opposed to God. In this Spirit induction into the Father/ Son expropriation, the saints become united with the one who died as their representative, in loneliness.

To sum up what we have seen so far: The Spirit creates the church by bringing (enrapturing) the human community into the glory of God revealed in the love of Jesus for the Father, lived in utter extremity in the cross and resurrection. The Father/Son relation is lived out by Christ as a hospitality for the enemies of God on the cross. The Spirit brings the church into this Father/Son relation. The church just is the Holy Spirit–created conditions for grasping that act of divine expropriation. An ascesis occurs whereby the human community has its eyes lifted from itself and beholds the glory of God. This beholding is a form of contemplation that involves the complete transformation of the church's life so that it can indeed apprehend, from the inside, this act of God.

I am suggesting that this ecclesiology is a worthy momentum for a church seeking to grasp what enemy love means within a secularity that often seeks to hive off Christian postures and run away with them as self-standing principles of nonviolence or peacemaking. Here fraternal love has both a vertical and horizontal axis in the relation between the Father and incarnate Son shown in scripture. This is an involvement in the world which is the condition by which the appearing glory of God in the world can be truly grasped and mingled with.

But we need to see more clearly how this is ecclesial enemy love.

The Brother for Whom Christ Died

We have already seen Balthasar's suggestion that the culmination of divine glory in the world is the incarnation of God in what is opposed to God. Balthasar situated the severe commands of the Synoptics regarding love for enemies within the solidarity of Christ with humans, especially Christ's human enemies. What we can see in the subsection "The Brother for Whom Christ Died" within "In Laudem Gloriae" is that Balthasar saw Christ's commands of the Sermon on the Mount and the Sermon on the Plain immersed within the larger trinitarian drama of God reconciling the world to himself. In this dramatic setting, these commands become constitutive of the inner mystery of the church.

He begins to explicate enemy love in this way by describing the transition from the old covenant to the new covenant viewed from the perspective of Christ.[53] There was already in the old covenant both the command to love God and the command to love the neighbor, but before the Incarnation their unity could not yet be fully grasped. The demands of neighbor love there were limited by a too-narrow understanding of God's election of Israel. There "God is 'obliged' and summoned to punish Israel's enemies; he hates the evil-doers, and the Israelite has the right and the duty to join God in this hatred."[54] The love of neighbor was severely limited because God's election of humans was seen as limited.

Though this particularism was already questioned in the old covenant, Jesus proclaims "the lordship of God, the dominance of God's will and act and disposition not only in Heaven but also on earth, and God's victorious superiority to all that men contrive in the depths of their hearts." The horizon of Christ's expansion of the apparent limitations to the covenant is God's lordly goodness to all creation. "All the apparent limitations in Old Testament ethics derived from human deductions from the incomprehensible election of one and not of another."[55] But these "human deductions" needed to be overcome for God's covenant promises to Abraham to be fulfilled. The full Creator intent of God for the whole world needs to break open *within* God's covenant with Israel.

The commands to love the enemy in the Sermons entail a closer calibration of the church with the steps of divine love into the world, rising beyond merely human self-enclosed calculations. The Sermon

---

[53]This transition is a recurring point of discussion in Balthasar's writings. For Balthasar, Jesus was an unanticipatable fulfillment of the old covenant, in whom none of the old covenant forms were left behind. He broke them open, making them transparent to God's missional intent in the world. For a discussion of Balthasar's approach to the old and new covenant, see Todd Walatka, "Theological Exegesis: Hans Urs von Balthasar and the Figure of Moses," *Pro Ecclesia* 19, no. 3 (2010): 300–317.

[54]Balthasar, *Glory of the Lord*, 7:435.

[55]Ibid., 7:435–6.

on the Mount cracks open the election of Israel. The commands in
the Sermon on the Mount presuppose this dilation of the loving
intent of God on the earth. In the "antitheses" (Mt. 5:21ff) of the
Sermon on the Mount, the limitations of the old covenant are
exposed and opened "making them transparent to the original total
will of God."[56] Here the exaltation of the Creator God comes to
define redemption's limits (or lack thereof). God is "your heavenly
Father, who makes the sun rise on the good and bad alike, and sends
rain on the righteous and on sinners" (Mt. 5:45). "This exalted
state is kingly; to imitate it, it is necessary to be exalted above the
covenant relationship between two unequal partners—a perfection
is required that corresponds to that of your heavenly Father."[57] In
withholding redemption from God's "enemies" Israel was sheltering
itself within its own enclosed system. That is a Gnostic failure,
in Balthasar's terms. It makes absolute what was only a human
construction.

A fundamental equality now emerges to view. The universal love
of God the Father "which had to present itself first in the old covenant
as a kingly freedom of election, goes to its end in Jesus' partiality for
the sinners, tax collectors and harlots, the lost and the rejected."[58]
In Christ the election of God is now known as coterminous with
the Creator sovereignty of God. These bracing demands in the
Sermons are thus unanticipatable readings of divine election, lifted
by revelation above the humanly deductible limits of neighbor
love. Gnostic human ideals and constructions end up fragmenting
and dividing the human community rather than offering unity.
These commands of unreserved love and defenselessness abolish
any appropriation of God that is severed from the revelation of
divine self-expropriation. They break open a conception of unity
in difference that falsely proclaims divine assent to human gnosis.
Balthasar is showing that the commands of nonresistance are the
redemptive revelation of the truth about nature or creation. God's
creative intent for the world is brought into view by the redemptive
incarnation of Jesus.

---

[56]Ibid., 7:436.
[57]Ibid. See also Balthasar's essay "The 'Beatitudes' and Human Rights," in Hans
Urs von Balthasar, *Explorations in Theology*, vol. 5, *Man Is Created*, trans. Adrian
Walker (San Francisco, CA: Ignatius, 1989), 445–6.
[58]Balthasar, *Glory of the Lord*, 7:437.

Here Balthasar writes this vital sentence:

The works of love must certainly remain (Mt 7.21), but within the framework of the disposition of the Father and the Son: deriving from the heavenly simplicity of the Son's transparency to the Father, which leads to the simplicity of his Cross in which it is made concrete—for it is there that Jesus does not resist the one who is evil, it is there that he lets himself be struck on the cheek, gives even his cloak, goes two miles, and loves his enemies (Mt 5.39ff).[59]

We return here to the bidirectional nonresistance of Christ, issuing out into a bidirectional unity in difference of the Christian. The nonresistance of Christ to the Father becomes a "transparency" to the Father's unlimited election of the least, the last, and the enemy, what we have been calling a bidirectional nonresistance. "The works of love" are lifted out of a merely human context and limitation and taken into the "heavenly simplicity of the Son's transparency to the Father" and, through this participation in the Trinity, become concrete, human enemy love to the ends of creation. These commands become, as it were, sacraments to the Father/Son relationship on the cross, displaying as that relation does the Father's love for the least and the last enemy. They witness to the cross as it displays the Father's absolute lordly freedom over the tribalism of the world's gnostic constructions.

In submission to the sovereign lordship of God's love over the earth, Christ goes forward in his life from birth to resurrection and ascension overstepping boundaries to humanly perceived election that had been set in far too limited and particularistic a manner via human deductions.

The internal and external boundaries that had been set for love (sabbath ordinances, laws of purification) are very deliberately broken, the solidarity with sinners is provocatively stressed ... and Jesus goes towards his death without averting his gaze, in order to live out his motto, to serve rather than to be served, to the end and "to give his life as a ransom for all."[60]

---

[59]Ibid., 7:437–8.
[60]Ibid., 7:438.

Christ says, "'What you have done to the least of these you have done to me', because I stand with my whole being behind the least, whose burden of poverty, hunger, tears, and oppression I have superabundantly taken upon myself."[61] This is the "communion established by God, not merely promised from afar, not merely afar, not merely offered, but really bestowed on humanity as a whole."[62] This boundary-breaking is Christ's total availability to the Father's will for the world. It is a breaking open of Israel's too-cramped understanding of divine election.

This can be included now in what we said earlier about the Spirit's role of bringing the church into the dynamic between the Father and the Son on the cross. It is this real incarnational (not abstract or hypothetical or merely "eschatological") communion of solidarity with the least and farthest, beyond human deduction, into which the Spirit brings the church when she is drawn into the trinitarian relation. To be a pentecostal church is to be a body that lives with real-time, spiritual, concrete immediacy the breaking of Gnostic, humanly deduced notions of election in the Son's utter solidarity with enemies on the cross. The life of the Spirit church is now the real presence, the incarnation of this solidarity of Christ with the world, in the world. "From now on, one's fellowman—whether friend or foe—is 'the brother for whom Christ died' (I Cor 8.11; Rom 14.15)."[63] Here the "protological, apparently impartial love of God has arrived, by way of the Old Testament predilection of the 'chosen', 'beloved' Israel, to its eschatological end."[64] Each individual now stands in a new place. Christ has "born the guilt of this human 'Thou' and has died for him, and therefore can identify himself with every individual at the last judgement."[65]

This exploding of the Gnostic horizons of election is an unguessable revelation of judgment. It is the judgment of God now seen not through human categories but through the cross cracking open these cramped distinctions and exposing them to the matchless love of God for the enemy. This judgment of God in its eschatological form shapes the church's approach to each person, friend or foe.

[61]Balthasar, "'Beatitudes' and Human Rights," 446.
[62]Hans Urs von Balthasar and W. J. O'Hara, "'Communio'—a Program," *Communio* 33, no. 1 (2006): 161.
[63]Balthasar, *Glory of the Lord*, 7:439.
[64]Ibid.
[65]Ibid.

Here the judgment of God is already pronounced upon the Son of God and this Son, as the brother of all people, becomes for them the path toward a new election, or solidarity with God.

This hope was the source of Balthasar's humanitarian ethics. Balthasar, who was often nervous about issuing grand social agendas for the church to implement in societal change, was nevertheless quite clear about the mission of the church when this was tethered contemplatively within the offering of Christ to the Father. There was a hope for humankind articulated in the cross, and this hope needed to "move into all the other structures of human society":

> It remains a significant sign that Christian involvement in its most resolute forms has always been initiated with a persistent and sometimes almost stubborn preference for places where, from a human and worldly point of view, there is no more hope, or the involvement no longer seems worthwhile. For example, in caring for the dying, for life grown old and worn out, for the incurably sick, the mentally ill, and the handicapped, where not even a smile of thanks is ever to be expected, we should not ask whether such undertakings make sense or are worthwhile, for they were undertaken ... in a consciousness that, in an involvement of this sort, the Christian understanding of hope sometimes becomes visible in its pure form.[66]

It is both the burden and the hope of the church to be figured by this overcoming of a particularist election in Christ. It is a burden because the world is deeply sinful and throws up a mighty resistance to the church's bidirectional nonresistance as we saw in the previous chapter. And this resistance is not only "in the world" but in the church as well because the church struggles to be conformed to this election. It is also a burden because for Balthasar, the entrance of the glory of God into the world is not a "merely forensic justification,"[67] an eschatological, "not-yet," or "*simul justus et peccator*" kind of righteousness,[68] but a concrete earthly holiness that impinges on

---

[66]Balthasar, *The von Balthasar Reader*, 413.

[67]Balthasar, *Love Alone Is Credible*, 103–4.

[68]Balthasar also has a form of this Lutheran emphasis, but, like the Anabaptist critique of Luther, resisted its tendency to envision a righteousness that was theoretical, or hovering somewhere above the daily sanctity of the believer. Christ does impute righteousness to us, but it is real, human righteousness, in battle with lingering sin

the world, we might say, an inch at a time.[69] This is the pedagogical work of the Spirit discipling the church to perceive the entrance of divine glory into the world.

But this real and present burden is also the hope of the church. The church is that community that surrenders itself to be figured by the unsurpassable horizon of God's election. How is the church to live under this daunting challenge? Balthasar can be very circumspect about how possible it will be to accomplish what he in one place describes as the beatitudes' human dignity using the beatitudes' attitude of total reliance on God.[70] This may be exceedingly difficult and never perfected. But as the pilgrim church is able, and as empowered by the Spirit, it will take concrete steps to live this way and not that way in response to this revelation. The inability of the church to live according to this vision results in suffering rather than in despair, in patience, and modesty rather than in conjuring some worldly justice per worldly standards. It results in what Balthasar describes as a Christian anxiety for the world stemming from its union with Christ, which is the missional center from which ethics would proceed in the world.[71]

In *The Christian and Anxiety*, the shape of this hope is felt where the church "constantly demands too much of natural man by asking him to imitate Christ." This entire path forward of coming to unite

---

and effecting real communion between the saints. See Ibid., 103–14; Balthasar, *Theo-Drama*, 1994, 4:417.

[69]This distinguishes Balthasar's approach to the Sermon's lofty commands from the "agape theology" approach used by several twentieth-century Protestant theologians such as Reinhold Niebuhr. For Balthasar the Sermon's nonresistant commands as located in the theo-drama do not constitute some "impossible ethic" meant to drive one to pure grace. The solidarity of Christ with the enemy is itself an objective reality, the truth within the world that is to be reckoned within one's interactions. This trinitarian location of the enemy is the truth about this person; it is not some ideal or purely vertical assertion unrelated to the justice that this person deserves from us. Christians, if their work is to correspond to this revelation, will seek to work out, by the Spirit, a prudential life according to this truth. Cf. Niebuhr, *Interpretation of Christian Ethics*, 35–62. See also Anders Nygren, *Agape and Eros* (Louisville, KY: Westminster, 1953).

[70]Balthasar, "'Beatitudes' and Human Rights," 455–6. See also a book Balthasar's theology of the poor: Todd Walatka, *von Balthasar & the Option for the Poor: Theodramatics in the Light of Liberation Theology* (Washington, DC: Catholic University of America Press, 2017).

[71]Hans Urs von Balthasar, *The Christian and Anxiety*, trans. Dennis D. Martin and Michael J. Miller (San Francisco, CA: Ignatius, 2000).

with the archetype, Christ "will always appear, and rightly so, to be an exorbitant demand, an excessive strain, and thus a threat to and the destruction of natural man and his laws and limits."[72] The path from the old covenant to the new is trod by each person the church beckons into her solidarity. But in all this the church's "sole desire" is that the person "might dare in faith to go beyond his own nature." And to this end God has, "by becoming a visible man and founding the visible Church," given believers the "abundance of visible helps as found in the organs and functions of the Church":

> Ecclesial office and the men who exercise it; Sacred Scripture as a tangible word; the sacraments as definite forms and vessels of the salvific encounter between man and God; tradition, which enables the believer to align himself with the past; the example of the saints and of all fellow Christians who have a living faith; the firmly established order of the Church year, which takes the believer in and leads him gently from mystery to mystery.[73]

Further, in an essay Balthasar wrote setting out the agenda for *Communio*, a journal he cofounded, he describes the way the Lord's Supper especially is the spiritual means by which people are drawn into the solidarity of Christ with the world:

> The reality of Jesus' eucharistic self-communication at his Last Supper and in the communion of those who take part in the meal which is established ... [is] not in any sense magical, but sacramentally objective and inseparably constituting both communion with God in Christ and communion with one another (1 Cor 10:16ff); this opens out a possibility of living for others which exceeds purely human capacity because it is a sharing in Christ's vicarious suffering for the Church (and thereby for all men) (Col 1:24), involving sharing a common lot with the Lord ("live with," suffer with," "be crucified with," "die with," "be buried with," "be raised up with," "be made alive together with," "be glorified with," "be fellow heirs with," "reign with") which all along is open to a universal human participation, and

---

[72]Ibid., 149–50.
[73]Ibid., 150.

for that reason alone explains and justifies the difference between "Church" and "world."[74]

In summary, this is the way in which Balthasar sees the radical commands of nonviolence within the Synoptics to be united with the larger purposes of God in Israel and in Christ, tearing down boundaries that had till then been human constructions that undersold the love of God. It is by one's inclusion in the covenant between Father and Son that one comes to have this form of neighbor love. Here the divine love of God for the world becomes the neighbor love of the believer for the enemy. The synthesis this presents between "vertical" love and "horizontal" love is "absolutely creative" and could not have been pre-guessed by any philosophical ideal or principle. It attests to the freedom and lordly sovereignty of God over creation and "it is identical with the unique christological synthesis itself, as this is given expression by Chalcedon."[75] The Chalcedonian definition, by describing the matchless unity of God with human flesh, exposed to view the way God chose to become a brother to every human person. The church is that human fellowship created by the Spirit to give fleshly embodiment to this unconditional embrace of the human enemy *in Christ*. Its structures and activities are pointed to inducting believers in real ways into this reality. This I–Thou–We of human fellowship is the earthly summit of the glory of God.

It seems to me that this vision of the church as an aesthetic conformity to the solidarity of God with the enemy speaks a strong word to the church in the secular age tempted to achieve what solidarity it can using instrumental human means. The church in secularity is tempted to turn its adoring gaze from the Creator's unsurpassable election unveiled in the cross and settle back again for "gnostic" human achievements that are attainable without this divine exposure. It is tempted to settle for mere "human rights" and secular notions of "inclusion" when through divine revelation and grace an election of the human community is beckoned that includes but infinitely transcends what can be accomplished through nature. It settles for a narrow enacting of horizontal solidarity because vertical solidarity has become too divisive, elusive, or demanding.

---

[74]Balthasar and O'Hara, "'Communio'—a Program," 162.
[75]Balthasar, *Glory of the Lord*, 7:441.

It is interesting that in an age where vertical nonresistance is occluded, human nature itself begins to fall out of view. A trademark secular value such as human rights depends on a substantive belief about the reality of human nature that is impervious to the accidents of race, ability, fortune, and others. But where the surrender to the Father is increasingly seen as anti-humanist, the assertion of the self to create itself out of nothing becomes an urgent necessity and thus human rights finds no solid ground to stand on. The church, with its gaze fixed adoringly, and thus transformingly, on the Father and the Father's election of the world, becomes a community of convocation. Here the world's enemies gather to feast together. Here human nature is fulfilled in an unguessable communion of the saints.

In the secular age, advances have been made as those formerly seen as the "enemy" or at least the lesser other, have been drawn into the community in ways that no Christian can disregard. Particularly one thinks of the new awareness within society of people with disabilities, of victims of abuse, of indigenous peoples trampled by colonial imperialism, and of sexual minorities. The equality of women in the secular age, though far from a fait accompli, has made significant advances. These strides, I would claim, are to some extent the residue of the unlimited election exposed in the church's contemplation of the cross. As such they can all be taken into the church (baptized first of course) and offered there as the conditions of divine apprehension.

And yet, do they finally match all that is indicated with God's love of his enemies? The ability of secularity to achieve true human solidarity is being sorely tested as non-secular people's immigrate into our societies and create a disturbing "other" who do not play by the rules of a liberal age.[76] What resources does secularity finally have when it meets a bona fide enemy? Can the church be content with merely "nonviolence"? What deeper fountains will nourish a church called to serve where no thanks is given? Where all the techniques, strategies, and therapies finally fail to turn the other into a friend? There is something about the cross that simply cannot be anticipated or mimicked by Pharaoh's magicians. Its embrace of the

---

[76]For a good recent diagnosis of this increasing failure of the liberal vision to achieve what it desires even within its own territory, see Ross Douthat, *The Decadent Society: How We Became the Victims of Our Own Success* (New York: Simon & Schuster, 2020).

enemy will always break open the church that has closed itself in on its own success.

Balthasar and Judgment

But a question might be asked of Balthasar: is the church, viewed as cruciform *solidarity* with the enemy merely a blanket, sociological collectivizing of the human race in salvation? Does it create this solidarity by abstracting away from the individual who may yet be a very particular, rebellious sinner? Was there not something about the presence of Jesus that singled out sinners and held them apart from the crowd in judgment? Is this solidarity, as we have described it, not prone to perpetuate the delusion that I as a sinner can hide behind the *massa damnata* and not come forth in authenticity before God? Here it is important to round out this discussion of the solidarity of the church with the enemy with some of Balthasar's words on judgment.

On the face of it, Balthasar is open to the criticism that his doctrine of the solidarity of Christ with the enemy presents a "blanket sociological covering" of the human race in salvation. We can note Balthasar's controversial views of eschatological hope. If all people are known through revelation as those whose curse and guilt have been borne by Christ, "dare we hope that all men be saved?"[77] Balthasar believed that such hope, though not an a priori certainty, was not only reasonable but demanded of the Christian. By extension, we might ask, does a gospel pacifism rooted in this incarnational, crucicentric unveiling of the Creator's horizon of election necessarily turn toward universalism? Likewise, does pacifism then tend to become only a general "reverence for life" that refuses violence based upon this enemy's membership in the human race? Finally, is gospel pacifism of this sort recused from all pointed judgment, the truthful denunciation of sin and the one who sins?

---

[77]Which is the title of his book on the issue. Hans Urs von Balthasar, *Dare We Hope: "That All Men Be Saved"? With a Short Discourse on Hell*, trans. David Kipp and Lothar Krauth (San Francisco, CA: Ignatius, 1988). For a description of Balthasar's views on the extent of final salvation as a contemplation of the theo-drama see Cameron Surrey, "Heaven Attracts and Hell Repels: A Dynamic Interpretation of Balthasar's Dare We Hope 'That All Men Be Saved'?" *Pro Ecclesia* 25, no. 3 (2016): 321–36.

Balthasar did not accept the term universalist for himself.[78] He rejected it because it was not contemplative of the theo-drama. It claimed a blanket certainty, a comprehensive a priori knowledge that, despite all dire warnings of the contrary possibility, all will be saved.[79] But neither, Balthasar insisted, do the scripture and the church's tradition make an a priori claim that, in fact, there will be people in hell. We can never know that any particular person is or will be in hell, not even Judas.[80] Neither of these two a priori certainties are truly contemplative and Christocentric.[81] Both are a gnostic rushing ahead of what has been revealed, asserting divine judgment for itself. As we have said at several points in this thesis, revelation for Balthasar has a relentlessly unguessable, unanticipatable quality to it. Balthasar believes this needs to extend to how we judge people in regard to how their present state relates to their final state.

What we do have in revelation are glimpses of the possibility of universal salvation coupled with the most severe warnings of the possibility of eternal loss. "What we have here are two series of [Scriptural] statements that, in the end, because we are *under* judgment, we neither can nor may bring into a synthesis."[82] The church must remain in a state of fundamental readiness or awareness to both series of statements. To be *under judgment* is to be a person for whom Christ has stood in his or her place. This places the person in both great hope and great peril. For Balthasar, this indicates that judgment is not a universal "collective" pronouncement but a fundamental personal crisis that every person is placed in before God by virtue of Christ's atoning work. I have no basis on which to damn anyone else; however, revelation places *me* in the unrelenting crisis of either revolt or consent.

Following from this, we might say two things in regards to judgment; first, the church has every basis on which to live and love according to the revealed truth that Christ has died for every brother and sister. In this sense, we can aspire to a nonresistant "universalist" practice of love. *Dare We Hope* was, after all, always

---

[78]He was, moreover, worried that Karl Barth had pressed too far in this direction. *Dare We Hope*, 94, 197.

[79]Balthasar, *Dare We Hope*, 20–1.

[80]Ibid., 19.

[81]Ibid., 208–10.

[82]Ibid., 22.

a book deeply rooted in the love of the church for its enemies. Hope must be maintained "under the presupposition that the solidarity with mankind expressed in the hope is practiced, struggled with and suffered through by Christians in a way similar to that manifested in the lives of the apostles."[83] In a discussion about an Augustinian, Calvinist, or Jansenist a priori "certainty" that there will in fact be those who have been consigned to damnation, Balthasar asks, "How, given an eternally valid bifurcation of mankind like this, simple human love of one's neighbour, or even love of one's enemy in Christ's sense, could still be possible?"[84] That is again to fall into the gnostic reduction of election, the unwillingness to believe that the cross exposes the church to Christ's breaking of all demonic, hubristic tribalisms. If we fall short of this hope, "the only thing of interest for us is that this hell is usually there 'for the others', for the sort, naturally, whom one can 'give hell to.' "[85]

But this practical, lived union with Christ's judgment of mercy on the enemy also exposes the believer to Balthasar's apocalyptic theo-dramatic law. The Christian must

> open his heart and allow himself to be most intimately affected, challenged, hurt. God in Christ went to the place of the loneliest sinner in order to communicate with him in dereliction by God. Christian community is established in the Eucharist, which presupposes the descent into hell (mine and yours). No flight into an abstract unity is permitted there. It demands the courage to penetrate into another's best defended fortress and, in the knowledge that it is, fundamentally, already conquered and surrendered, to contact its very center. That may provoke the other to the most savage resistance, and this must be endured. But it can only be done by completely humble faith in what God's love has already done, and without any kind of triumphalism, even of love.[86]

The church's judgment attuned to the solidarity of Christ is a nonresistant unwillingness to reckon with other persons on *their*

[83]Ibid., 213–14. Quoting Joachim Gnilka.
[84]Ibid., 196. It is clear that Balthasar would have no truck with a "limited atonement" in the Calvinist sense.
[85]Ibid., 193.
[86]Balthasar and O'Hara, " 'Communio'—a Program," 167–8.

terms, but rather a resolution to judge this person as Christ has taken their judgment on himself. Nonviolent love is in that sense a Christian judgment of sin in this instantiation and expression.

But then, second, a contemplative church will also enter into Christ's unique instantiation of that solidarity with each person. The church will become "co-judge" of the world with Christ, separating the spirits. In this the church participates with Christ in the Savior's ability, even with only his "presence" or his "word" to separate the spirits. "He and his disciples work as catalyzers."[87] Scriptures clearly warn about the real possibility of total loss and this possibility is placed before hearers with the greatest gravity and clarity by a church in union with the provoking Lord. In fact, the church in its crucicentric love of the enemy is a signal that hell, "a christological place"[88] is a real possibility. It is a place Christ has experienced for all and so is real. "Hell is no pedagogical threat, it is no mere 'possibility.'"[89] The church must always "remain at God's disposal"[90] in this matter as well. Christ confronts each sinner in radical solidarity, a confrontation that can elicit a "savage resistance." As the church acts in union with this confrontation it will need to endure this resistance as well.

In an essay titled "Persönliche Beichte überhölt?" Balthasar takes up the co-judging role of the church as its practice of confession and penance. He begins by showing the way in the Christian life

> every believer is personally placed before the demands of the gospel which separates "father and son, mother and daughter …" to the point that "the members of the household of each and every Christian" are "enemies".… The family of Christians is formed of real persons who are responsible to Christ.[91]

In the church, people become persons personally before God. It is this singling out process that establishes the necessity of personal confession which forms part of the act of the church's co-judgment with Christ. The church "has tried to imitate the conduct of Jesus

---

[87]Hans Urs von Balthasar, "Eschatology in Outline," in *Explorations in Theology*, vol. 4, *Spirit and Institution* (San Francisco, CA: Ignatius, 1995), 452.

[88]Ibid., 457.

[89]Balthasar, *Love Alone Is Credible*, 94.

[90]Balthasar and O'Hara, "'Communio'—a Program," 160.

[91]Balthasar, *The von Balthasar Reader*, 278. Translated as "Personal Confession."

from the beginning" and has tried to "discern the spirits and to forgive or (provisionally) retain sins with his authority."[92] The church in step with Christ and his judgment must practice confession. It does so as "the community founded by God for the world and filled with divine character and saturated with divine life."[93] "What is important is that someone who in thought, words, or deeds has offended seriously against the Spirit of the holy church of Christ must personally come forward and responsibly confess."[94] The need of the guilty person "to be rid of his or her guilt must be incarnated in an external deed, in an encounter with a fellow human being which secures punishment and forgiving reincorporation into the community—both at the same time."[95] Balthasar rarely discusses excommunication, but in his programmatic essay for *Communio* he says, "Consequently even exclusion from the visible communion of the Church (excommunication) can only be understood as an educative, temporary measure intended to help the guilty person (as Paul shows, 1 Cor 5:5; 2 Cor 2:6f)."[96] Thus we can see that the church as a community of solidarity with the enemy "incarnates" this judgment not by ignoring sin, or throwing a collective salvation over the *massa damnata,* but by being the voice of Christ to the sinner, extending judgment, inviting confession and repentance, announcing forgiveness of sin, and if need be, excommunicating from the church as an "educative, temporary measure." The key in all this is contemplation—not an a priori judgment but an active, real-time attentiveness to and participation in the solidarity of Christ with the enemy of the cross.

Gospel pacifism, I would argue, is a form of judgment. It is the Spirit-led ability of the church to conform its love to the brotherly solidarity of Christ with the enemy and to embody this solidarity existentially in the life of this particular Thou. Christ has loved this enemy and has made himself a brother to this enemy, setting this enemy in a crisis of decision. It was this very embrace of the enemy that exposed the world to the utter transparency of the Son to the Father in the extension of the election of God to creation's

---

[92]Ibid., 279–80.
[93]Ibid., 280.
[94]Ibid.
[95]Ibid.
[96]Balthasar and O'Hara, "'Communio'—a Program," 160–1.

boundaries. But within that solidarity, the presence of Christ (again mediated in part by the church) places each person in a crisis, a choice of either contemplative consent or violent revolt. Gospel pacifism, in order to retain its location in the theo-drama, must be both this unrestrained love and this induction into crisis. The church tethered contemplatively to the cross must also be the judgment of the world in this sense too, placing the enemy before the gospel message in all its merciful severity. Here the church must continue proclaiming not merely "nonviolence" but the judgment of God upon the world.

This solidarity in judgment (unity in difference) is the very figure of the New Testament church. In this sense, a gospel pacifism is seeking to enter the very furnace of the reconciliation between God and the world by the power of the Spirit, and to live there as a daily, earthy love in confrontation with evil. This convocation is what the church nourishes.

The Implications of the Church as the Convocation of Enemies

This then is the church as the convocation effected by the presence of the incarnation in world affairs as Christ's solidarity with sinners. Having described Balthasar's ecclesiology of enemy love in some detail, we can now pull this together and offer some reflections about where this points to in a theology of peace. What we have sought in this chapter from Balthasar is an emphasis in ecclesiology on a contemplative calibration of the church with the actions of God incarnate out of which enemy love can flow. The church is a loving company of enemies. That is its deepest truth as the incarnation of Christ's representative solidarity with the human community. "But now in Christ Jesus you who once were far off have been brought near by the blood of Christ" (Eph. 2:13). This is the work of the Holy Spirit, inspiring the church to transgress tribalistic boundaries that had been set in far too limited and gnostic a way and inducting the church into this love demonstrated in the sermons of mount and plain. The Spirit exposes the church to the dynamic of love and nonresistance between Jesus and the Father and further leads the church to become a community of judgment, expressing utter practical solidarity, but also mediating the provocative crisis that the incarnation sets upon the world.

There are several implications that this presents for churches seeking to live their unwillingness to kill as an outworking of their salvation. First, this is a pacifism deeply entwined with the prayer of the church. The church's wisdom on the relation between contemplation and action is ancient and Balthasar sought to restore the balance in favor of action flowing from a "kneeling theology." In prayer the church becomes *indifferent*[97] to the ways God intends to bring salvation to the world. Specifically, for Balthasar, in prayer the church becomes Marian, open to the mission of Christ and led to place herself within Christ's availability before the Father. It is prayer that nurtures a wise unity in difference with the world, not as a self-standing principle but as a daily contemplation of the theo-drama as it unfolds in the world before the eyes of the church. It is people who cultivate prayer in the church who can do their work in the world, alongside their fellow secularists, but nevertheless remaining in step with the gospel momentum in the world. It is not first the *kind* of work one does that sustains peacemaking as an ecclesial, gospel work in the world, but whether one is doing this work out of a contemplative, prayerful mingling with the Savior's mission. Here are Balthasar's words:

> *Prayer*, both ecclesial and individual prayer, thus ranks higher than all action, not in the first place as a source of psychological energy … but as the act of worship and glorification that befits love, the act in which one makes the most fundamental attempt to answer with selflessness and thereby shows that one has understood the divine proclamation. It is as tragic as it is ridiculous to see Christians today giving up this fundamental priority … and seeking instead an immediate encounter with Christ in their neighbor, or even in purely worldly work and technological activity. Engaged in such work, they soon lose the capacity to see any distinction between worldly responsibility and Christian mission. Whoever does not come to know the face of God in contemplation will not soon recognize it in action,

---

[97]An Ignatian term for an active disposal of oneself that ever seeks the Father's face for guidance to enter the mission of God. I like Sr. Gill Goulding's analogy of a tennis player dancing on the court baseline, anticipating the opponent's serve. The player's eyes are fixed on the opponent and the dancing is an *indifference*, a disposal of oneself to be wherever the serve goes. From an in-class lecture at Regis College.

even when it reveals itself to him in the face of the oppressed and humiliated.[98]

Second, a church contemplative of the descent of God into the world is aware that its obedience is a divinely given "epistemology" by which it can claim to know God. The church cannot know God except through its participation in the radiance of God's glory in the world as this glory is transposed in bidirectional nonresistance. This is earthly beauty, to care for the orphan and advocate for the oppressed in the solidarity of Christ. In this way, the church's worship and action become transparent to each other. The vision of God perceived in the church's prayer, scripture reading, and Eucharist, and the vision of God perceived in costly obedience in mission outposts, nourish together an understanding of beauty. It is the "ecstatic" appropriation of divine glory that leads to the costly expropriation, and costly expropriation leads to appropriation of God as he has given himself to be known. Theological aesthetics can reorient a pacifist church by an awareness of cruciform beauty.

What this divine epistemology opens is the possibility that a church can speak for God. As a church in step with the theo-drama in bidirectional nonresistance, it can be entrusted with the judgment of God. "Where two or three are gathered ... I am there among them" (Mt. 18:20), follows from "whatever you bind on earth will be bound in heaven" (Mt. 18:18). We return then to the early Anabaptist proportionality between church discipline and pacifism and understand (in hindsight) that where this proportionality is skewed by a church self-absorbed by the principle of its own purity, or by its own secular nonviolent principle, it will lose its incarnational unity in difference.

Third, this will be a church that lives by and with love. One would think it assumed that a church committed to pacifism would have a theology of love at its center. This cannot be assumed. In a secular age, wary of the abuse to which love is susceptible especially when coupled with religious fervor, it is tempting to place one's hope in themes such as "justice," "dignity," "sacredness of life," "human rights," or a democratic concern for "silenced voices." All of these themes can be integrated into love but one cannot assume they amount to love. Christian love is a human willingness, whether

---

[98]Balthasar, *Love Alone Is Credible*, 109.

carried out by reason, sentiment, or natural bonds, to regard another person as Christ regards them. It is deeply Christic in the most incarnational sense. It is personal without being sentimental. It is gentle without being flaccid. In all things it looks to the parables, teachings, and actions of Christ to attune its posture to Christ. It is born out of a personal experience of salvation through an encounter with the cross of Jesus. An ecclesial pacifism underpins a life of friendship within the world. The Mennonite emphasis on vigorous congregational friendship, camaraderie, and mutual aid is delightfully located to be a community of earthy love in its most incarnated form.

Fourth, a church contemplative of Christ will really be a nonresistant, nonviolent church. As it is conceivable that a church in a secular age may reduce love to "the politics of Jesus," so it is also tempting to speak much about love but little about how this relates to the structures and practices of violence in society. Balthasar has warned us that discipleship genuinely attuned to the Christ of the beatitudes is an exceedingly difficult pilgrimage, but this is exactly the set of problems a church obedient to the Sermon on the Mount must choose for itself. The Savior who set his life down in the place of his enemy as a transposition into human conditions of filial love for the Father is the very Lord who forbade his disciples killing and vengeance in the pursuit of justice. The more the church's pacifism is plunged into the Chalcedonian dynamics of salvation, the more its witness will become an inescapable inspiration and challenge to the broader church's ethics. Here the inner drama of the Christian gospel unfolds in the daily workings of the world.

Fifth, a church living an organic relation to the love and obedience of Christ on the cross to the point of suffering love has to be serious about ascesis, the practices by which human narcissism, egoism, and individualism are challenged and confronted. As Balthasar has shown us, to truly behold God in the manner in which he has revealed himself demands an expropriation of the self for the sake of the glory of God in mission. This is a church that expects and resources people to think about suffering and trials as a participation in the cross of Christ, the way in which he assumed sinful flesh and offered it to the Father as loving gift. The saints too receive the path of their lives in all its pain and joy and offer it to the Father through the Spirit. This refers not only to persecution and martyrdom but to a *Gelassenheit* in which the daily ordeals of life are understood as immersed in the suffering body of Christ in the world, partaking of his nonresistance to the Father and the world's wretched condition. It is in this availability that the resurrection and ascension too find their transposition in the lives of believers.

A secularization (or medicalization) of suffering is closely related to a secularization of pacifism. Suffering for the Christian cannot be "explained" satisfactorily as the failure of the welfare state to solve problems, class warfare in which certain segments of society are denied access to power, the repression of desires in a Freudian sense, or the failure of science to provide a cure for one's malady. Beneath all these legitimate occasions for suffering there is still always the hidden finger of God, providentially leading the world into the mystery of the cross. Where the hidden mystery of God's hand in the vexing trials of the world is denied, believers are robbed of a primal posture inherent in Christic nonresistance. The best society can do where this providence is denied is to either abolish suffering through scientific advance or assist in helping sufferers escape, even to the point of assistance in dying. In this too a secular age has failed finally to have resources for truly embracing the neighbor whose suffering is inescapable.

Finally, a church that seeks a contemplative simultaneousness with Christ in his solidarity with enemies is a church that offers judgment. Fraternal admonition, truth-telling, accountable leadership, and the practice of excommunication, when figured by the scriptures, can be ways in which Christ becomes visible in the world, taking genuine space in communities, without securing that space violently. Of course, church discipline can and has been practiced in worldly ways that seek to secure the church in safety within the world by a principle of a pure church. It will require a mighty sanctification for the church to become re-tethered in the theo-drama to such an extent that it can again offer judgment with confidence. I would argue that in order for pacifism to remain ecclesial it must rediscover (with lessons learned) forms by which the judgment of Christ borne in his wounds can discipline the church and offer critique and encouragement to the world. A church that no longer has the strength to offer a peaceful judgment on injustice, violence, and the whole catalog of human rebellion against the Lord will soon find itself offering a violent judgment. This is a church that can no longer claim a decisive union with Christ in being his provocative presence inciting the world to drama.

But all this an inch at a time in the cadence of the Lord who suffers his church and bears its burdens too. The church's faithfulness beyond a gnostic contraction of the horizons will necessarily be fitful and full of desire. Augustine's wisdom will be its guide:

> Our righteousness also, though true righteousness insofar as it is referred to the true ultimate good, is in this life only such as to consist in the forgiveness of sins rather than the perfection of virtues. This is borne out by the prayer of the whole City of God during its pilgrimage in the world, which cries out to God in the voice of all its members: "forgive us our debts, as we forgive our debtors."[99]

This calls for nothing less than a divine patience and tenderness *toward* the church even as the church is urged to turn its gaze into the fiery, purifying love of God in Christ.

---

[99]Augustine of Hippo, *The City of God Against the Pagans*, trans. R. W. Dyson (Cambridge: Cambridge University Press, 1998), sec. 19.27.

Conclusion: Christian Practices of Theo-dramatic Peacemaking

In this book, we have attempted to refigure nonviolence with the shape of God's descent into the world in Christ. The central problem this study has sought to address is the apparent reality that in secularity we can be good without God. When the gospel is lived as daily obedience "on the ground" a vexing optical illusion can appear. The more the church presses the gospel into the earthly rhythm of daily life, the more it appears to be merely that: earthly daily life. In secularity, where the world and God are ever-more intently held apart, the church must stay in step with the incarnation by insisting with more intensity on the mighty synthesis envisioned in the Chalcedonian definition. In the introduction, we stated that we sought a theological ethic that sought first to see what God was doing and then to act in tune with this vision. The definition, in its Neo-Chalcedonian, Maximian, Balthasarian form, positions the church to sink into a converting union with Christ and by this union hold together in one sanctity Christ's love for the Father and Christ's love for the world. That makes possible a genuinely theological ethic within a secular age.

Mennonites, in their history, serve as an example of a church that has labored with the tension between pacifism as union with Christ and pacifism as a cognate of modern attempts to create civility, order, and productivity. Mennonite pacifism survived in part because it was effective at developing the productive citizens states coveted. Recent relief and peacemaking efforts likewise make a good apologetic for the Mennonite way of life within secularity. But as society joins in

with these efforts for secular reasons, it is increasingly difficult to
see a confessional momentum in this endeavor. If all we want is the
ethics, we don't really need the confession. It is only if we have a
vision for ethics symbolizing and leading out to a deeper mystery
beyond ethics that ethicsw need to be immersed in the confession
of the church. And so the inherent connection between these good
works and this good confession must now be more consciously
asserted where earlier it seemed an organic relation. Christians
must now consciously do as a Christian vocation what others do
for secular reasons. This is a basic survival skill of faith in a secular
world. For this reason, I believe that as pacifist churches embrace the
dogmatic and spiritual vision of Chalcedon as Balthasar interpreted
it, and as this synthesis becomes not merely a structure, but a lens
to read scripture by, the church will be figured with an incarnational
unity in difference. Good works can be Christian sanctity, but only
when they emerge from a church that has learned to contemplate
the mystery glimpsed at Chalcedon.

We have seen Balthasar's Maximian, Chalcedonian Christology
and described how this gave Balthasar a foundation to ground the
ethical life in contemplation, attending to the posture of Jesus in his
ministry making hypostatic choices. Every decision, act of love, and
judgment in Christ's life, death, resurrection, and ascension was for
Balthasar a revelation of the inner-trinitarian dynamic of "letting
be," or nonresistance of Jesus to the Father. Christ actively allowed
himself to be begotten, receiving from the Father the power "to
have life in himself" (Jn 5:26). Thus, for Balthasar the daily actions
of Jesus, his "secular" life, to use the word in its ancient meaning,
is at each moment a transposition into human life of his eternal
divinity-as-Sonship. A key aspect of our argument has been that the
incarnation is not merely the unity of divinity and humanity, but
the unity of *Sonship* and humanity. In this unity there is no zero-
sum relation between divinity and humanity. Christology, mission,
and ethics come together as a union in Christ's nonresistance to his
Father. It is this reality that we participate in when we are converted
and sanctified by the Spirit. As we contemplate the works of Jesus
within this mystery, we become ethical people.

Balthasar also absorbed Maximus's Dyothelite emphasis. Christ
entered fully into the created nature of the human being, refusing
to violate the created direction and longings by which humans
were sent out to find their home in God. Christ took this to himself
even in the cursed state in which he found it. He embraced and

transposed the human fear of death and the human instinct of self-preservation (even self-defense) into an offering given on behalf of his Body, the church.

This amounts then to a bidirectional nonresistance, a refusal to violate either Sonship or humanity, even under the violent conditions of the human community. Christ shares this synthesis of heaven and earth with his Body, making the church analogously figured by Sonship and Christ's archetypal humanity. This we argued gives the church a *Gelassenheit* that does not violate human nature. It also does not violate the deeply divine origins of this height of love. As the church enters this ungraspable encounter between God and the world through its worship, preaching, prayer, acts of mercy, and mission, it becomes worldly in a divine way and divine in a worldly way, never losing its equipoise. The more it is immersed in this incarnational mystery the more bold and genuine can be its reach into the world.

We then entered the throes of history, noting how Balthasar understood the Book of Revelation to reveal the Christ-haunted existence of humanity in post-Christian realms. In Balthasar's view, many to whom the Lamb appears will writhe in rebellion, resisting the answer to humankind's deepest pathos revealed by the nonresistance of the Lamb. Humankind, in the wake of the Lamb's victory, erects all manner of disincarnating schemes, seeking to wrest fulfillment, immortality, and power from the One who has given it to them in the form of a nonresistance to the Father. This violence is the violence the saints are called to meet with love and forgiveness. When the love of saints caught up in the throes of their encounter with Jesus meets the vitriol of the world caught up in the throes of its attempt to solve human pathos apart from Christ, there we find a Christ-provoked Messianic woe. The enemy is not secularized but is known to be tangled in a fight to the end with the Lamb who holds out the offer of freedom—both the freedom of movement and freedom of ultimate dependence.

Finally, we argued that Balthasar's ecclesiology of solidarity with the Son's offering to the Father through the work of the Spirit understands the depths of the church's life to be an event of enemy love. It regards everyone it meets as "the brother for whom Christ died." Violation in the church is defined as treating someone in a manner that disregards the fact of Christ's present solidarity with this person. Christ stands in for this person now in sacrificial, loving exchange; the believer's attitude toward this person must be contemplative of how this person exists in Christ's great exchange.

We showed that each person's solidarity with Christ also becomes their judgment. As someone for whom Christ has died, each person is pressed to a decision, yielding either worship or revolt. The church's judgment must be contemplative of this reality as well. Its practices of confession, discipleship, admonition, boundary-setting, and excommunication must be rooted spiritually in what Christ is in fact doing with each person. This as opposed to the old Mennonite Gnosticism emerging in the principle of the pure church, or the new modern Gnosticism emerging in the principle of toleration, individual choice, or sentimental positivity.

Khaled Anatolios (borrowing from Jean-Luc Marion) provides the metaphor of a "saturated phenomenon" to describe the relation between trinitarian doctrine and the Christian life. I think this provides a helpful way to also understand the incarnation and its relation to sanctity and ethics:

> A saturated phenomenon involves an excess of presencing that so overtakes and overwhelms the knower that she cannot objectify the source of this saturation and enclose it within her cognitive grasp. Similarly, the meaning of trinitarian doctrine, or the apprehension of the trinitarian being of God, cannot be epistemically enclosed or objectified. Rather, we appropriate the meaning of trinitarian doctrine by learning to identify and interpret the various aspects of Christian existence precisely as saturated by the God who is Trinity; conversely, we learn to identify the God who is Trinity through the saturated phenomenon that is Christian existence as a whole and in all its aspects.[1]

The description of the incarnation as the presence of God in human flesh is an "excess" in that it cannot be comprehended or grasped by the knower or the doer. It is overwhelming in the infinite surplus of its depths of meaning. No act of human love, even if springing from a deified union with Christ, can adequately capture the meaning of Christmas, Good Friday, Easter, Ascension, and Pentecost. There is an infinite depth of love signed in these events that the church will never reach the bottom of. A human act will always fail at some

---

[1]Khaled Anatolios, *Retrieving Nicaea: The Development and Meaning of Trinitarian Doctrine* (Grand Rapids, MI: Baker Academic, 2011), 10.

level to be an appropriate manifestation of the incarnation. The act in itself will always seem too secular to be truly consonant with the divine love that elicits it. The church in its most radical and fulsome love will only dip its feet into the shallows of this unfathomable reality. This can be disconcerting and in a secular context tempts the church to close the veil on this mystery and engage with more manageable realities.

And yet, as Anatolios argues, while "trinitarian doctrine does not allow us to encompass the being of God within the confines of human knowing ... it does regulate our being and knowing so as to enable us to successfully relate ourselves to God, who is really Trinity."[2] Gospel pacifism figured by the incarnation, I have argued, is a saturated phenomenon. It is a human but no less deified articulation of the meaning of the incarnation as the reconciliation between God and the human community. It is a real-time prolongation of the incarnation that nevertheless cannot exhaust the mysterious depths inherent in its form. It really is the incarnation we are seeing when we witness these acts of sanctified and costly love. And yet these acts "do not allow us to encompass the being of God within the confines of human knowing."

In three aspects—incarnation, provocation, and convocation—we understand Christology to be not merely a "structure" or "scaffold" or "foundation" but a doorway through which the church approaches the mission of Christ from the Father. Christology, though a human science, is no less thereby a path to covenant, an icon of Christ, a sacrament by which the church touches its Savior. Christology in this perspective is a guidebook, leading the church by the hand to participate with Christ in his overcoming of evil with the love of the Father. It is a description of how God took the evil of the world to himself and "used" it to offer humankind's greatest gift to the Father in grateful love. It is a description of how this is not merely something God does *for* the human community, but a pentecostal reality the church is invited to participate in through baptism, Eucharist, church discipline, and costly sanctity in the world. By confessing along with the church in these ways, a believer is trained and brought "up to speed" with God's past, present, and future act of salvation.

---

[2]Ibid., 9.

In this perspective, dogma is alive and dynamic; it is given by God through the church to initiate the world into salvation, to bring the world into potent contact with the Christ who will not leave. Dogma unveils God and his manner of bringing about reconciliation. Dogma does not excuse the church from contemplating Christ's life and death, but is rather the Spirit-guided path directing the church ever farther into the mystery of Christ as he is revealed by the Father. It does not sever Christ from the gospels but deepens the church's glimpse of the love revealed there. It guards against any attempts to hive off the saving events into earthly constructions the church can manage on its own. Dogma serves to prevent salvation from becoming anticipatable. In this sense dogma keeps the church's confession nimble and ever-responsive to the living Christ revealed in scripture and in the life of the church.

What is needed for activists, peacemakers, mediators, politicians, conscientious objectors, and peace studies theoreticians is baptism, and the day-by-day contemplation of Christ as revealed in scripture as interpreted by the apostles. To attempt a peace witness that is not sustained by this day-to-day beholding of the glory of God is to risk a humanism that does not know its possibilities and limits. It will become a practice of peace that eventually disincarnates and becomes ugly. It will fail to manifest a divine proportion, or a genuinely *theological* aesthetic that deftly and effortlessly gets things just right; both individual and community, contemplation and action, human flourishing and martyrdom, involvement and withdrawal, freedom and dependence, blessing and judgment, effectiveness and faithfulness. A beautiful life emerges as a believer lives her days in step-by-step contemplation and solidarity with the living Christ as displayed in the church's scriptures. In obedience to his command, in imitation of his posture, in the strength and direction of his Spirit, and in the embrace of his Body, believers' lives become the Christ-figure in the world.

This book has delved into the dogmatic momentum surrounding ethical action in the Christian tradition. The connection between dogma and ethics is a daily spirituality of participation in the real-time actions of God in history. Christians desiring their work of peacemaking to be saturated with the incarnational submission of Christ to the Father and Christ to the world will need to invite the Holy Spirit to grant spiritual revival. This is the work of the Spirit in renewing the church and cannot be conjured, but the church can open itself to these winds of refreshment. How might this happen?

The practice of peacemaking needs to be linked directly, constantly, and personally to the worship of the congregation. Peacemakers need to be established, guided, and refreshed by the preaching of the church. The source of our action must be the announcement (alien, coming from outside oneself!) of the good news of Jesus Christ, his forgiving work of atonement, and the power of his Resurrection. This is the call to conversion by the announcement of the good news of Jesus springing from both the Old and New Testament spoken by our local pastor.

As those who hear the preaching, peacemakers must be baptized into Father, Son, and Spirit. Water and Spirit must pour as one baptism over believers inciting them to sweat in the labor of the body of Christ. Surely the first question that needs to be asked of peacemakers is, "did you receive the Holy Spirit when you became believers?" If the answer is no, then "Into what then were you baptized?" (Acts 19:1-7). Baptism is (as it was for the early Anabaptists) the act whereby a person consents to the call of the Holy Spirit. Vocation in the world has its source in the baptism of Christ.

Following baptism, the practice of peacemaking needs to be nurtured by the weekly practice of the Lord's Supper. The Lord's Supper is horizontal in mutual fraternal love because it is vertical, hosted and guaranteed by our Savior Jesus Christ. It is the regular edible sign that points into the mystery whereby the body and blood of Jesus have become the daily source of our salvation and the ever-needed justification and forgiveness of our work.

The Lord's Supper, as this gracious, divine synthesis of the divine into the human, must be figured, sustained, and promoted by a scriptural church discipline. The church must discover ways to reintegrate its judgment into the real-time dialogue of Christ with each member. As we confess our sins to one another and receive the forgiveness of Christ in the words of a sister or brother, we are poised now to work for peace. Peacemaking demands the ability to extend judgment, a word dividing truth from lies and judging the thoughts and intentions of the heart. If this is to be a gracious, Christic judgment, it must spring from the church's own practice of discipline among its own members.

This then is a peacemaker immersed in the daily, weekly rhythms of the church's life. And all this covered in prayer. Following from this will be a blurring of the lines between church and parachurch. The parachurch organization has emerged in modern times as a way to slightly orphan the work of the church from the confession of the church. It is often the church's own inability to resolve its conflicts that has driven the creation of parachurch organizations who are not hobbled by the church's disunity. Believers who might not worship together or recognize each other's baptism can nevertheless do the church's work together in parachurch organizations. Parachurch agencies and churches need to resist the secularity that is tempting when the church's work is done apart from the church's worship. This need not be the end of the parachurch, but rather the incentive to fresh and creative partnerships between them. Pastors can become the chaplains of the parachurch, churches can provide board members and regular funding to the parachurches, and parachurches can demand that workers participate in the church's preaching, baptism, Lord Supper, and church discipline.

Finally, if this still needs to be said in the twenty-first century, the old divisions between evangelism, church planting, social justice advocacy, scripture distribution, relief, and development can be transcended. As we have shown, unless the work of pacifism is evangelistic in its intent it falls short of the glory of Christ's own actions. Gospel peacemaking seeks not only to love enemies, but to lead enemies toward the deification by which they become partakers in the divine nature and realize in an existential way the solidarity Christ established with them on the cross. In my own observation, it is especially agencies devoted to relief and development that still maintain these divisions with the clearest focus. But these divisions are a species of secularity.

These divisions are not merely overcome by agencies, say, choosing to do both church planting and social justice advocacy. It happens as workers in their *person* surrender to the bidirectional nonresistance of Christ. As each worker becomes contemplative of Christ's work across the pages of scripture, as each worker is baptized into the mission team of the Trinity, as each worker discerns for themselves what place Christ is leading them to work, and as each worker then offers each day's task to the Father, the work itself will cease to be neatly divided by these distinctions. When the division is erased in the soul of the worker it will also be erased in the work of the worker.

We leave now with a last word from Balthasar:

The entire futility and decay of earthly existence can, as such, be transformed into fruitfulness, if it understands itself as the "pangs" of the new aeon and as a sharing in Christ's sufferings. It follows that everything that human endeavour achieves in respect of the commission given at creation—the struggle against injustice, hunger, sickness, need and depravity, and the struggle for better conditions of life, education, wages, etc.—acquires a positive significance in view of what God has done in Christ and of the help of the Holy Spirit, and that nothing of this will be lost ultimately. God assumes that his creature will be at work, even when he reserves to his own sovereign synthesis to determine how the contributions of his creature are applied. The convergence of human achievement and the coming of God as the omega is absolutely incalculable ... but this does not make it any less certain.[3]

---

[3]Balthasar, *Glory of the Lord,* 7:519

BIBLIOGRAPHY

Primary Sources Written by Hans Urs von Balthasar

Balthasar, Hans Urs von. *A Theological Anthropology*. New York: Sheed and Ward, 1967.

Balthasar, Hans Urs von. *A Theology of History*. New York: Sheed and Ward, 1963.

Balthasar, Hans Urs von. *Cosmic Liturgy: The Universe According to Maximus the Confessor*. Translated by Brian E. Daley San Francisco, CA: Ignatius, 2003.

Balthasar, Hans Urs von. *Dare We Hope: "That All Men Be Saved"? With a Short Discourse on Hell*. Translated by David Kipp and Lothar Krauth. San Francisco, CA: Ignatius, 1988.

Balthasar, Hans Urs von. *Engagement with God: The Drama of Christian Discipleship*. Translated by R. John Halliburton and Margaret Turek. San Francisco, CA: Ignatius, 2008.

Balthasar, Hans Urs von. "Eschatology in Outline." In *Explorations in Theology*, Vol. 4, *Spirit and Institution*, 423–67. Ignatius, 1995.

Balthasar, Hans Urs von. *Explorations in Theology*. Vol. 4. *Spirit and Institution*. Translated by Edward T.Oakes. San Francisco, CA: Ignatius, 1995.

Balthasar, Hans Urs von. *Explorations in Theology*. Vol. 5. *Man Is Created*. Translated by Adrian Walker. San Francisco, CA: Ignatius, 1989.

Balthasar, Hans Urs von. *Heart of the World*. Translated by Erasmo S. Leiva. San Francisco, CA: Ignatius, 1979.

Balthasar, Hans Urs von. *Love Alone Is Credible*. Translated by D. C. Schindler. San Francisco, CA: Ignatius, 2004.

Balthasar, Hans Urs von. *My Work: In Retrospect*. San Francisco, CA: Communio, 1993.

Balthasar, Hans Urs von. *Mysterium Paschale: The Mystery of Easter*. Translated by Aidan OP Nichols. San Francisco, CA: Ignatius, 1993.

Balthasar, Hans Urs von. *Prayer*. Translated by Graham Harrison. San
  Francisco, CA: Ignatius, 1986.
Balthasar, Hans Urs von. *The Christian and Anxiety*. Translated
  by Dennis D. Martin and Michael J. Miller. San Francisco,
  CA: Ignatius, 2000.
Balthasar, Hans Urs von. *The Glory of the Lord: Seeing the Form*. Edited
  by Joseph Fessio and John Riches. Translated by Erasmo Leiva-
  Merikakis. Vol. 1. San Francisco, CA: Ignatius, 1982.
Balthasar, Hans Urs von. *The Glory of the Lord: The New Covenant*.
  Edited by John Riches. Translated by Brian McNeil Vol. 7. San
  Francisco, CA: Ignatius, 1989.
Balthasar, Hans Urs von. *The Glory of the Lord: The Realm of
  Metaphysics in the Modern Age*. Edited by BrianMcNeil and John
  Riches. Translated by Oliver Davies, Andrew Louth, BrianMcNeil,
  John Saward, and Rowan Williams. Vol. 5. San Francisco,
  CA: Ignatius, 1991.
Balthasar, Hans Urs von. "The Fathers, the Scholastics, and Ourselves."
  Communio 24 (1997): 347–96.
Balthasar, Hans Urs von. *The von Balthasar Reader*. Edited by
  MedardKehl and Werner Loeser. Translated by Robert J. Daly and Fred
  Lawrence. New York: Crossroad, 1982.
Balthasar, Hans Urs von. *Theo-Drama: Dramatis Personae—Man
  in God*. Translated by Graham Harrison. Vol. 2. San Francisco,
  CA: Ignatius, 1993.
Balthasar, Hans Urs von. *Theo-Drama: Dramatis Personae—Persons
  in Christ*. Translated by Graham Harrison. Vol. 3. San Francisco,
  CA: Ignatius, 1992.
Balthasar, Hans Urs von. *Theo-Drama: Prolegomena*. Translated by
  Graham Harrison. Vol. 1. San Francisco, CA: Ignatius, 1989.
Balthasar, Hans Urs von. *Theo-Drama: The Action*. Translated by Graham
  Harrison. Vol. 4. San Francisco, CA: Ignatius, 1994.
Balthasar, Hans Urs von. *Theo-Logic: The Spirit of the Truth*.
  Translated by Graham Harrison. Vol. 3. San Francisco,
  CA: Ignatius, 2005.
Balthasar, Hans Urs von. *Theo-Logic: Truth of God*. Translated by Adrian
  J. Walker. Vol. 2. San Francisco, CA: Ignatius, 2004.
Balthasar, Hans Urs von. *Tragedy Under Grace: Reinhold
  Schneider on the Experience of the West*. Washington,
  DC: Ignatius, 1997.
Balthasar, Hans Urs von, and W. J. O'Hara. "'Communio'—A Program."
  Communio 33, no. 1 (2006): 153–69.
Ratzinger, Joseph, Hans Urs von Balthasar, and Heinz Schurmann. "Nine
  Propositions on Christian Ethics." In *Principles of Christian Morality*.
  San Francisco, CA: Ignatius, 1996.

Secondary Sources on Hans Urs von Balthasar

Barrett, Melanie Susan. *Love's Beauty at the Heart of the Christian Moral Life: The Ethics of Catholic Theologian Hans Urs Von Balthasar.* Lewiston, ME: Edwin Mellen, 2009.

Bauerschmidt, Frederick C. "Theodrama and Political Theology." *Communio* 25 (Fall 1998) 532–52.

Beattie, Tina. "Sex, Death and Melodrama: A Feminist Critique of Hans Urs Von Balthasar." *The Way* 44, no. 4 (October 2005): 160–76.

Daley, Brian E. "Balthasar's Reading of the Church Fathers." In *The Cambridge Companion to Hans Urs von Balthasar*, edited by Edward T. Oakes and David Moss, 187–206. New York: Cambridge University Press, 2004.

Gross, David. "The Religious Critique of Culture: Paul Tillich and Hans Urs Von Balthasar." *Philosophy Today* 54, no. 4 (2010): 392–400.

Healy, Nicholas J. *The Eschatology of Hans Urs Von Balthasar: Eschatology as Communion.* New York: Oxford University Press, 2005.

Kilby, Karen. "Balthasar and Karl Rahner." In *The Cambridge Companion to Hans Urs von Balthasar*, edited by Edward T. Oakes and David Moss, 256–68. New York: Cambridge University Press, 2004.

Kilby, Karen. "Perichoresis and Projection: Problems with Social Doctrines of the Trinity." *New Blackfriars* 81, no. 957 (November 1, 2000): 432–45.

Long, D. Stephen. *Saving Karl Barth: Hans Urs von Balthasar's Preoccupation.* Minneapolis, MN: Fortress, 2014.

Martin, David. *Pentecostalism: The World Their Parish.* Hoboken, NJ: Wiley-Blackwell, 2002

Martin, David. *Tongues of Fire: The Explosion of Protestantism in Latin America.* Hoboken, NJ: Wiley-Blackwell, 1993.

Martin, Jennifer Newsome. "The 'Whence' and the 'Whither' of Balthasar's Gendered Theology: Rehabilitating Kenosis for Feminist Theology." *Modern Theology* 31, no. 2 (April 1, 2015): 211–34.

McInroy, Mark. *Balthasar on the "Spiritual Senses": Perceiving Splendour.* Oxford: Oxford University Press, 2014.

McIntosh, Mark A. *Christology from Within: Spirituality and the Incarnation in Hans Urs Von Balthasar.* Notre Dame, IN: University of Notre Dame Press, 2000.

Mongrain, Kevin. *The Systematic Thought of Hans Urs Von Balthasar: An Irenaean Retrieval.* New York: Crossroad, 2002.

Nichols, OP, Aidan. *Divine Fruitfulness: A Guide through Balthasar's Theology beyond the Trilogy*. Washington, DC: Catholic University of America Press, 2007.

Nichols, Aidan. *No Bloodless Myth: A Guide through Balthasar's Dramatics*. Washington, DC: Catholic University of America Press, 2000.

Nichols, Aidan. *The Word Has Been Abroad: A Guide through Balthasar's Aesthetics*. Washington, DC: Catholic University Press, 1998.

Oakes, Edward T. *Pattern of Redemption: The Theology of Hans Urs von Balthasar*. London: Bloomsbury Academic, 1997.

Papanikolaou, Aristotle. "Person, Kenosis and Abuse: Hans Urs von Balthasar and Feminist Theologies in Conversation." *Modern Theology* 19, no. 1 (January 1, 2003): 41–65.

Patterson, Patrick D. M. "By Thine Agony and Bloody Sweat: Dogmatic Description of the Double Agency of Christ—A Modest Proposal." ThD thesis, Wycliffe College, 2012.

Pitstick, Alyssa Lyra. *Light in Darkness: Hans Urs Von Balthasar and the Catholic Doctrine of Christ's Descent into Hell*. Grand Rapids, MI: Eerdmans, 2007.

Pitstick, Alyssa Lyra, and Edward T Oakes. "Balthasar, Hell, and Heresy: An Exchange." *First Things* 168 (December 2006): 25–32.

Sherwood, Polycarp. "Survey of Recent Work on St. Maximus the Confessor." *Traditio* 20 (1964): 428–37.

Steck, Christopher. *The Ethical Thought of Hans Urs Von Balthasar*. New York: The Crossroad, 2001.

Surrey, Cameron. "Heaven Attracts and Hell Repels: A Dynamic Interpretation of Balthasar's *Dare We Hope 'That All Men Be Saved'?*" *Pro Ecclesia* 25, no. 3 (2016): 321–36.

Snyder-Belousek, Darrin. "God and Nonviolence: Creedal Theology and Christian Ethics," *MQR* 88, no. 2 (April 2014): 233–69.

Walatka, Todd. "Theological Exegesis: Hans Urs von Balthasar and the Figure of Moses." *Pro Ecclesia* 19, no. 3 (2010): 300–317.

Walatka, Todd. *Von Balthasar & the Option for the Poor: Theodramatics in the Light of Liberation Theology*. Washington, DC: Catholic University of America Press, 2017.

Waldron, Stephen. "Hans Urs von Balthasar's Theological Critique of Nationalism." *Political Theology* 15, no. 5 (September 2014): 406–20.

Yeago, David S. "Literature in the Drama of Nature and Grace: Hans Urs von Balthasar's Paradigm for a Theology of Culture." *Renascence* 48, no. 2 (1996): 95–110.

Yenson, Mark L. *Existence as Prayer: The Consciousness of Christ in the Theology of Hans Urs Von Balthasar*. Bern: Peter Lang, 2014.

Other Sources

Anatolios, Khaled. *Retrieving Nicaea: The Development and Meaning of Trinitarian Doctrine.* Grand Rapids, MI: Baker Academic, 2011.

Aquinas, Thomas. *Summa Theologica.* Translated by the Fathers of the English Dominican Province. New York: Benziger Bros. edition, 1947.

Bainton, Roland H. "The Left Wing of the Reformation." *The Journal of Religion* 21, no. 2 (1941): 124–34.

Bathrellos, Demetrios. *The Byzantine Christ: Person, Nature, and Will in the Christology of Saint Maximus the Confessor.* Oxford: Oxford University Press, 2004.

Barth, Karl. *Church Dogmatics: The Doctrine of Reconciliation.* Vol. IV/3.2. New York: T&T Clark International, 2004.

Bender, Harold S. "The Anabaptist Vision." *Mennonite Quarterly Review* 18, no. 2 (1944): 67–88.

Bender, Harold Stauffer. "The Pacifism of the Sixteenth Century Anabaptists." *Mennonite Quarterly Review* 30, no. 1 (1956): 5–18.

Blough, Neal. *Christ in Our Midst: Incarnation, Church and Discipleship in the Theology of Pilgram Marpeck.* Kitchener, ON: Pandora, 2007.

Blough, Neal. "The Uncovering of the Babylonian Whore: Confessionalization and Politics Seen from the Underside." *Mennonite Quarterly Review* 75, no. 1 (2001): 37–55.

Blowers, Paul M. *Drama of the Divine Economy: Creator and Creation in Early Christian Theology and Piety.* Oxford: Oxford University Press, 2012.

Blowers, Paul M.. "Theology as Integrative, Visionary, Pastoral: The Legacy of Maximus the Confessor." *Pro Ecclesia* 2, no. 2 (1993): 216–30.

Braaten, Carl E. *That All May Believe: A Theology of the Gospel and the Mission of the Church.* Grand Rapids, MI: Eerdmans, 2008.

Burkhart, Irvin E. "Menno Simons on the Incarnation [1]." *Mennonite Quarterly Review* 4, no. 2 (1930): 113–39.

Burkhart, Irvin E. "Menno Simons on the Incarnation [2]." *Mennonite Quarterly Review* 4, no. 3 (1930): 178–207.

Burkholder, J. Lawrence. *The Limits of Perfection: Conversations with J. Lawrence Burkholder.* Edited by Rodney Sawatsky and Scott Holland. Waterloo: Institute of Anabaptist-Mennonite Studies, 1993.

Burkholder, John Richard, and Barbara Nelson Gingerich. *Mennonite Peace Theology: A Panorama of Types.* Akron, OH: Mennonite Central Committee Peace Office, 1991.

Bush, Perry. *Two Kingdoms, Two Loyalties: Mennonite Pacifism in Modern America.* Baltimore, MD: Johns Hopkins University Press, 1998.

Called Together to Be Peacemakers: Report of the International Dialogue between the Catholic Church and Mennonite World Conference, 1998-2003. Kitchener, ON: Pandora, 2005.

Carter, Craig A. "The Legacy of an Inadequate Christology: Yoder's Critique of Niebuhr's Christ and Culture." *Mennonite Quarterly Review* 77, no. 3 (2003): 387–401.

Carter, Craig A. *The Politics of the Cross: The Theology and Social Ethics of John Howard Yoder.* Grand Rapids, MI: Brazos, 2001.

Charles, J. Daryl. "Protestants and Natural Law." *First Things* 168 (December 2006): 33–8.

Coakley, Sarah. "What Does Chalcedon Solve and What Does It Not? Some Reflections on the Status and Meaning of the Chalcedonian "Definition." In *The Incarnation: An Interdisciplinary Symposium on the Incarnation of the Son of God*, edited by Stephen T. Davis, Daniel Kendall, and Gerald O'Collins, 143–63. New York: Oxford University Press, 2004.

Cochrane, Arthur C. *The Mystery of Peace.* Elgin, IL: Brethren Press, 1986.

Collins, Adela Yarbro. "Political Perspective of the Revelation to John." *Journal of Biblical Literature* 96, no. 2 (June 1977): 241–56.

Covington, Sarah. "Jan Luyken, the Martyrs Mirror, and the Iconography of Suffering." *Mennonite Quarterly Review* 85, no. 3 (2011): 441–76.

Davis, Kenneth R. *Anabaptism and Asceticism: A Study in Intellectual Origins.* Scottdale, PA: Herald, 1974.

Davis, Stephen T., Daniel Kendall, and Gerald O'Collins. *The Incarnation: An Interdisciplinary Symposium on the Incarnation of the Son of God.* New York: Oxford University Press, 2004.

Diefenthaler, Jon, ed. *The Paradox of Church and World: Selected Writings of H. Richard Niebuhr.* Minneapolis, MN: Fortress, 2015.

Dintaman, Stephen F. "On Flushing the Confessional Rabbit out of the Socio-Ecclesial Brushpile." *The Conrad Grebel Review* 24, no. 2 (2006): 33–49.

Dintaman, Stephen F. "The Spiritual Poverty of the Anabaptist Vision." *Conrad Grebel Review* 10, no. 2 (1992): 205–8.

Driedger, Leo, and Donald B. Kraybill. *Mennonite Peacemaking: From Quietism to Activism.* Scottdale, PA: Herald, 1994.

Dyck, Cornelius J. *Spiritual Life in Anabaptism.* Scottdale, PA: Herald, 1995.

Epp, Frank H. *Mennonites in Canada, 1786–1920.* Toronto: Macmillan of Canada, 1974.

Epp, Frank H. *Mennonites in Canada, 1920–1940: A People's Struggle for Survival.* Toronto: Macmillan of Canada, 1982.

Finger, Thomas N. "Anabaptism and Eastern Orthodoxy: Some Unexpected Similarities?" *Journal of Ecumenical Studies*, December 1, 1994.

Finger, Thomas N. *Christian Theology: An Eschatological Approach.* Vol. 2. Scottdale, PA: Herald, 1989.

Finger, Thomas N. "Did Yoder Reduce Theology to Ethics." In *A Mind Patient and Untamed: Assessing John Howard Yoder's Contributions to Theology, Ethics, and Peacemaking.* Edited by Ben C. Ollenburger and Gayle Gerber Koontz, 318–39. Telford: Cascadia, 2004.

Finger, Thomas N. "Post-Chalcedonian Christology: Some Reflections on Oriental Orthodox Christology from a Mennonite Perspective." In *Christ in East and West,* 155–69. Macon, GA: Mercer University Press, 1987.

Finger, Thomas N. *Self, Earth & Society: Alienation & Trinitarian Transformation.* Downers Grove, IL: InterVarsity, 1997.

Finger, Thomas N. "The Way to Nicea: Some Reflections from a Mennonite Perspective." *Journal of Ecumenical Studies,* March 1, 1987.

Fiorenza, Elisabeth Schüssler. *The Book of Revelation: Justice and Judgment.* Minneapolis, MN: Fortress, 1998.

Francis, E. K. "The Mennonite Commonwealth in Russia, 1789–1914: A Sociological Interpretation." *Mennonite Quarterly Review* 25, no. 3 (1951): 173–82.

Friedmann, Robert. "Anabaptism and Pietism I." *Mennonite Quarterly Review* 14, no. 2 (1940): 90–128.

Friedmann, Robert. *The Theology of Anabaptism: An Interpretation.* Scottdale, PA: Herald, 1973.

Friesen, Duane K. *Artists, Citizens, Philosophers: Seeking the Peace of the City: An Anabaptist Theology of Culture.* Scottdale, PA: Herald, 2000.

Friesen, Duane K. "Toward a Theology of Culture: A Dialogue with John H Yoder and Gordon Kaufman." *Conrad Grebel Review* 16, no. 2 (1998): 39–64.

Friesen, Layton Boyd. "Seditions, Confusions and Tumult: Sixteenth Century Anabaptism as a Threat to Public Order." Regent College, 2001.

Goertz, Hans-Jürgen. "The Confessional Heritage in Its New Mold: What Is Mennonite Self-Understanding Today?" In *Mennonite Identity: Historical and Contemporary Perspectives.* Edited by Calvin Wall Redekop and Samuel J. Steiner, 1–12. Lanham, MD: University Press of America, 1988.

Goosen, Rachel Waltner. "'Defanging the Beast': Mennonite Responses to John Howard Yoder's Sexual Abuse." *Mennonite Quarterly Review* 89, no. 1 (2015): 7–80.

Gray, John. "Steven Pinker Is Wrong about Violence and War." *The Guardian,* Accessed May 29, 2017. https://www.theguardian.com/books/2015/mar/13/john-gray-steven-pinker-wrong-violence-war-declining.

Grillmeier, Alois. *Christ in Christian Tradition*. New York: Sheed and
    Ward, 1965.
Grimsrud, Ted. *Compassionate Eschatology: The Future as Friend*.
    Eugene, OR: Wipf & Stock, 2011.
Harder, Leland. *The Sources of Swiss Anabaptism: The Grebel Letters and
    Related Documents*. Scottdale, PA: Herald, 1985.
Harder, Lydia Marlene. *Obedience, Suspicion and the Gospel of
    Mark: A Mennonite-Feminist Exploration of Biblical Authority*.
    Waterloo: Wilfrid Laurier University Press, 1998.
Hardin, Michael. "Mimesis and Dominion: The Dynamics of Violence
    and the Imitation of Christ in Maximus Confessor." *St Vladimir's
    Theological Quarterly* 36, no. 4 (1992): 373–85.
Hart, David Bentley. "God and Nothingness." In *I Am The Lord Your
    God: Christian Reflections On The Ten Commandments*. Edited by
    Carl E. Braaten and Christopher R. Seitz, 55–76. Grand Rapids, MI:
    Eerdmans, 2005.
Hart, David Bentley. *The Beauty of the Infinite: The Aesthetics of
    Christian Truth*. Grand Rapids, MI: Eerdmans, 2004.
Hart, David Bentley. "The Precious Steven Pinker." *First Things*. Accessed
    October 29, 2015. http://www.firstthings.com/article/2012/01/
    the-precious-steven-pinker.
Hauerwas, Stanley. *A Community of Character: Toward a Constructive
    Christian Social Ethic*. Notre Dame, IN: University of Notre Dame
    Press, 1981.
Hauerwas, Stanley. *Against the Nations: War and Survival in a
    Liberal Society*. Notre Dame, IN: University of Notre Dame
    Press, 1992.
Hauerwas, Stanley. "Peacemaking: The Virtue of the Church." In *Doing
    Right and Being Good: Catholic and Protestant Readings in Christian
    Ethics*. Edited by David Oki Ahearn and Peter R. Gathje, 25–32.
    Collegeville, PA: Liturgical Press, 2005.
Hauerwas, Stanley. *The Hauerwas Reader*. Edited by John Berkman and
    Michael Cartwright. Chapel Hill: Duke University Press, 2001.
Hauerwas, Stanley. "The Humanity of the Divine." *The Cresset* XXXV,
    no. No. 8 (June 1972): 16–17.
Hauerwas, Stanley. "Why War Is a Moral Necessity for America or How
    Realistic Is Realism?" *Seminary Ridge Review* Spring 2007.
Hauerwas, Stanley. *With the Grain of the Universe: The Church's Witness
    and Natural Theology*. Grand Rapids, MI: Brazos, 2001.
Hays, Richard. *The Moral Vision of the New
    Testament: A Contemporary Introduction to New Testament Ethic*.
    New York: HarperCollins, 1996.
Healy, Nicholas M. "Ecclesiology." In *The Cambridge Dictionary
    of Christian Theology*. Edited by Ian A. McFarland, David A. S.

Fergusson, Karen Kilby, and Iain R. Torrance. Cambridge: Cambridge University Press, 2011.

Healy, Nicholas M. *Hauerwas: A (Very) Critical Introduction*. Grand Rapids, MI: Eerdmans, 2014.

Heidebrecht, Paul C. "A Prescription for the Ills of Modernity? Understanding A. James Reimer's Approach to Theology." *Mennonite Quarterly Review* 80, no. 2 (2006): 229–48.

Hershberger, Guy F. (Guy Franklin). "Biblical Nonresistance and Modern Pacifism." *The Mennonite Quarterly Review* 17, no. 3 (1943): 115–35.

Hershberger, Guy F., Albert N. Keim, and Hanspeter Jecker. "Conscientious Objection." Accessed August 7, 2014. http://gameo.org/index.php?title=Conscientious_Objection&oldid=103534.

Hershberger, Guy Franklin. *War, Peace, and Nonresistance*. Scottdale, PA: Herald, 2009.

Historical and Theological Essays Presented at the International Catholic-Mennonite Dialogue 1998–2002. Winnipeg, 2002. Unpublished manuscript.

Huebner, Chris K. *A Precarious Peace: Yoderian Explorations on Theology, Knowledge, and Identity*. Scottdale, PA: Herald, 2006.

Huebner, Chris K. "Mennonites and Narrative Theology: The Case of John Howard Yoder." *Conrad Grebel Review* 16, no. 2 (1998): 15–38.

Huebner, Harry J. *An Introduction to Christian Ethics: History, Movements, People*. Waco, TX: Baylor University Press, 2012.

International Theological Commission. "Select Questions on Christology." Accessed May 30, 2017. http://www.vatican.va/roman_curia/congregations/cfaith/cti_documents/rc_cti_1979_cristologia_en.html.

"Is God Nonviolent?" *The Conrad Grebel Review* 21, no. 1 (2003).

Jantzen, Grace M. "Roots of Violence, Seeds of Peace." *Conrad Grebel Review* 20, no. 2 (2002): 4–19.

Jeschke, Marlin. "Getting Christ Back Out of Christmas." *Concern* 16 (November 1968): 9–13.

Johns, Loren L., ed. *Apocalypticism and Millennialism: Shaping a Believers Church Eschatology for the Twenty-First Century*. Kitchener, ON: Pandora, 2000.

Johns, Loren L.. *The Lamb Christology of the Apocalypse of John: An Investigation into Its Origins and Rhetorical Force*. Eugene, OR: Wipf and Stock, 2014.

Johnson, Darrell W. *Discipleship on The Edge: An Expository Journey Through The Book Of Revelation*. Vancouver: Regent College Publishing, 2004.

Kasdorf, Julia. "Mightier than the Sword: Martyrs Mirror in the New World." *Conrad Grebel Review* 31, no. 1 (2013): 44–70.

Kauffman, Ivan J. "Mennonite-Catholic Conversations in North America: History, Convergences, Opportunities." *Mennonite Quarterly Review* 73, no. 1 (1999): 35–60.

Keim, Albert N. *Harold S. Bender, 1897–1962.* Scottdale, PA: Herald, 1998.

Kelly, J. N. D. *Early Christian Doctrine: Revised Edition.* New York: HarperCollins, 1978.

Kerr, Nathan R. *Christ, History and Apocalyptic: The Politics of Christian Mission.* Eugene, OR: Wipf and Stock, 2008.

Klaassen, Walter, ed. *Anabaptism in Outline: Selected Primary Sources.* Kitchener, ON: Herald, 1981.

Klaassen, Walter. "'Gelassenheit' and Creation." *Conrad Grebel Review* 9, no. 1 (1991): 23–25.

Klaassen, Walter. "Investigation into the Authorship and the Historical Background of the Anabaptist Tract Aufdeckung Der Babylonischen Hurn." *Mennonite Quarterly Review* 61, no. 3 (1987): 251–61.

Klassen, William, and Walter. Klaassen, eds. *The Writings of Pilgram Marpeck.* Kitchener, ON: Herald, 1978.

Koontz, Ted. "Grace to You and Peace: Nonresistance as Piety." *Mennonite Quarterly Review* 69, no. 3 (1995): 354–68.

Koop, Karl, Jeremy M. Bergen, and Paul Doerksen, eds. *Creed and Conscience: Essays in Honour of A. James Reimer.* Kitchener, ON: Pandora, 2007.

Koop, Karl Peter. *Anabaptist-Mennonite Confessions of Faith: The Development of a Tradition.* Kitchener, ON: Pandora, 2004.

Kraus, C. Norman. *God Our Savior: Theology in a Christological Mode.* Eugene, OR: Wipf and Stock, 2006.

Kraus, C. Norman. *Jesus Christ Our Lord: Christology from a Disciple's Perspective.* Eugene, OR: Wipf and Stock, 2004.

Kraybill, J. Nelson. *Apocalypse and Allegiance: Worship, Politics, and Devotion in the Book of Revelation.* Grand Rapids, MI: Brazos, 2010.

Krehbiel, H. P. *War, Peace, Amity.* Self-published, 1937.

Kreitzer, Beth. "Menno Simons and the Bride of Christ." *Mennonite Quarterly Review* 70, no. 3 (1996): 299–318.

Kroeker, Travis P. "Hauerwas: A (Very) Critical Introduction." *Modern Theology* 32, no. 2 (April 2016): 300–302.

Liechty, Daniel. *Early Anabaptist Spirituality: Selected Writings.* New York: Paulist Press, 1994.

Loewen, Howard John. *One Lord, One Church, One Hope, and One God: Mennonite Confessions of Faith in North America: An Introduction.* Elkhart, IN: Institute of Mennonite Studies, 1985.

Loewen, Howard John. "Reply to A. J. Reimer, 'The Nature and Possibility of a Mennonite Theology.'" *Conrad Grebel Review* 1, no. 2 (1983): 56–8.

Mangina, Joseph L. *Karl Barth: Theologian of Christian Witness*. Louisville, KY: Westminster John Knox, 2004.

Mangina, Joseph L. *Revelation*. Grand Rapids, MI: Brazos, 2010.

Marpeck, Pilgram. *Later Writings by Pilgram Marpeck and His Circle*. Translated by John D. Rempel, Walter Klaassen, and Werner O. Packull. Kitchener, ON: Pandora, 1999.

Martens, Paul. "How Mennonite Theology Became Superfluous in Three Easy Steps: Bender, Yoder, Weaver." *Journal of Mennonite Studies* 33 (2015): 149–66.

Martens, Paul. *The Heterodox Yoder*. Eugene, OR: Wipf and Stock, 2012.

Martens, Paul. "With the Grain of the Universe: Reexamining the Alleged Nonviolent Rejection of Natural Law." *Journal of the Society of Christian Ethics* 32, no. 2 (2012): 113–31.

Martin, David. *The Breaking of the Image: A Sociology of Christian Theory and Practice*. Vancouver: Regent College Publishing, 2006.

Martin, Dennis D. "Nothing New under the Sun: Mennonites and History." *Conrad Grebel Review* 5, no. 1 (1987): 1–27.

McFarland, Ian A. "The Theology of the Will." In *The Oxford Handbook of Maximus the Confessor*. Edited by Pauline Allen and Bronwen Neil, 516–32. Oxford: Oxford University Press, 2015.

McGuckin, John Anthony. *St. Cyril of Alexandria: The Christological Controversy: Its History, Theology, and Texts*. Yonkers: St. Vladimir's Seminary Press, 2004.

Meyendorff, John. *Christ in Eastern Christian Thought*. Washington, DC: Corpus, 1975.

Moltmann, Jürgen. *The Trinity and the Kingdom: The Doctrine of God*. Minneapolis, MN: Fortress, 1981.

Moskos, Charles C., and John Whiteclay Chambers. *The New Conscientious Objection: From Sacred to Secular Resistance*. Toronto: Oxford University Press, 1993.

Nation, Mark Thiessen. *John Howard Yoder: Mennonite Patience, Evangelical Witness, Catholic Convictions*. Grand Rapids, MI: Eerdmans, 2006.

National Conference of Catholic Bishops. *The Challenge of Peace: God's Promise and Our Response*. St. Paul, MN: St. Paul Editions, 1983.

Neufeld, Thomas R. Yoder. *Killing Enmity: Violence and the New Testament*. Grand Rapids, MI: Baker Academic, 2011.

Niebuhr, H. Richard. "The Doctrine of the Trinity and the Unity of the Church." *Theology Today* 3, no. 3 (October 1946): 371–84.

Niebuhr, Reinhold. *An Interpretation of Christian Ethics*. Louisville, KY: Westminster John Knox, 2013.

Nygren, Anders. *Agape and Eros*. Louisville, KY: Westminster, 1953.

Nylrod, Henderson. "Nasty Noel." *Concern* 16 (November 1968): 2–3.

Parrella, Frederick J. "Paul Tillich's Life and Spirituality: Some Reflections." *Revista Eletrônica Correlatio* 6 (November 2004): 1–31.

Penner, Carol. "Mennonite Silences and Feminist Voices, Peace Theology and Violence against Women." PhD dissertation, University of St. Michaels, 1999.

Peterson, David, and Edward S. Herman. "Steven Pinker on the Alleged Decline of Violence." Accessed September 2, 2014. http://zcomm.org/znetarticle/steven-pinker-on-the-alleged-decline-of-violence-by-edwards-herman-and-david-peterson/.

Pinker, Steven. *The Better Angels of Our Nature: Why Violence Has Declined*. New York: Penguin, 2011.

Regehr, T. D. *Mennonites in Canada, 1939–1970: A People Transformed*. Toronto: University of Toronto Press, 1996.

Reimer, A. James. "God (Trinity), Doctrine Of." Accessed February 12, 2016. http://gameo.org/index.php?title=God_(Trinity),_Doctrine_of.

Reimer, A. James. "How Modern Should Theology Be? The Nature and Agenda of Contemporary Theology." In *The Church as Theological Community: Essays in Honour of David Schroeder*. Edited by Harry Huebner, 171–98. Winnipeg: CMBC Publications, 1990.

Reimer, A. James. *Mennonites and Classical Theology: Dogmatic Foundations for Christian Ethics*. Kitchener, ON: Pandora, 2001.

Rempel, John D. "Critically Appropriating Tradition: Pilgram Marpeck's Experiments in Corrective Theologizing." *Mennonite Quarterly Review* 85, no. 1 (2011): 59–75.

Rempel, John D. *The Lord's Supper in Anabaptism: A Study in the Christology of Balthasar Hubmaier, Pilgram Marpeck, and Dirk Philips*. Scottdale, PA: Herald, 1993.

Riches, Aaron. "After Chalcedon: The Oneness of Christ and the Dyothelite Mediation of His Theandric Unity." *Modern Theology* 24, no. 2 (n.d.): 199–224.

Riches, Aaron. *Ecce Homo: On the Divine Unity of Christ*. Grand Rapids, MI: Eerdmans, 2016.

Riedemann, Peter. *Peter Riedemann's Hutterite Confession of Faith*. Translated by John J. Friesen. Scottdale, PA: Herald, 1999.

Rose, Matthew. "Theology and the Limits of Ethics." *Pro Ecclesia* 23, no. 2 (May 1, 2014): 174–94.

Roth, John D. "Pietism and the Anabaptist Soul." In *The Dilemma of Anabaptist Piety: Strengthening Or Straining the Bonds of Community?* Edited by Stephen L. Longenecker and Ronald C. Arnett. Bridgewater, MA: Forum for Religious Studies, Bridgewater College, 1997.

Roth, John D., ed. *Constantine Revisited: Leithart, Yoder, and the Constantinian Debate*. Eugene, OR: Wipf and Stock, 2013.

Roth, John D. "The Complex Legacy of the Martyrs Mirror among Mennonites in North America." *Mennonite Quarterly Review* 87, no. 3 (2013): 277–316.

Roth, John D. "The Significance of the Martyr Story for Contemporary Anabaptists." *Brethren Life and Thought* 37, no. 2 (1992): 97–106.

Roth, John D., Conrad Kanagy, and Elizabeth Miller. *Global Anabaptist Profile: Belief and Practice in 24 Mennonite World Conference Churches.* Goshen, Egypt: Institute for the Study of Global Anabaptism, 2017.

Rummel, Erika, ed. *The Erasmus Reader.* Toronto: University of Toronto Press, 2015.

Sawatsky, Rodney James. *History and Ideology: American Mennonite Identity Definition through History.* Kitchener, ON: Pandora, 2005.

Schlabach, Gerald W. "Continuity and Sacrament, or Not: Hauerwas, Yoder, and Their Deep Difference." *Journal of the Society of Christian Ethics* 27, no. 2 (2007): 171–207.

Schlabach, Theron F. "Reveille for Die Stillen Im Lande: A Stir among Mennonites in the Late Nineteenth Century: Awakening or Quickening, Revival or Acculturation?" *Mennonite Quarterly Review* 51, no. 3 (1977): 213–26.

Schönborn, Christoph. *God's Human Face: The Christ-Icon.* San Francisco, CA: Ignatius, 1994.

Schwager, Raymund. *Must There Be Scapegoats? Violence and Redemption in the Bible.* Leominster, MA: Gracewing, 1987.

Sharing Peace: Mennonites and Catholics in Conversation. Collegeville, PA: Liturgical Press, 2013.

Shearer, Tobin Miller. "A Prophet Pushed Out: Vincent Harding and the Mennonites." *Mennonite Life* 69 (2015) https://mla.bethelks.edu/ml-archive/2015/a-prophet-pushed-out-vincent-harding-and-the-menno.php

Sider, J. Alexander. "Mennonites and Classical Theology: Dogmatic Foundations for Christian Ethics." *Mennonite Quarterly Review* 76, no. 1 (January 1, 2002): 137–9.

Sider, J. Alexander, and Jonathan R. Seiling, trans. "Theologian in Contradiction: An Interview with Hans-Jürgen Goertz on John Howard Yoder's Radical Pacifism." *The Conrad Grebel Review* 33, no. 3 (2015): 375–83.

Simons, Menno. *The Complete Writings of Menno Simons: c. 1496–1561.* Translated by Leonard Verduin. Scottdale, PA: Herald, 1966.

Slater, Peter. "Tillich on the Ambiguity of Spiritual Presence: More Protestant Principle Than Catholic Substance?" *Toronto Journal of Theology* 31, no. 1 (July 24, 2015): 105–22.

Smith, James K. A. *How (Not) to Be Secular: Reading Charles Taylor.* Grand Rapids, MI: Eerdmans, 2014.

Smucker, Donovan E. "The Theological Basis for Christian Pacifism." *Mennonite Quarterly Review* 27, no. 3 (July 1, 1953): 163–86.

Snyder, C. Arnold. *Anabaptist History and Theology: An Introduction.* Kitchener, ON: Pandora, 1995.

Snyder, C. Arnold. "The Monastic Origins of Swiss Anabaptist
    Sectarianism." *Mennonite Quarterly Review* 57, no. 1 (1983): 5–26.
Staples, John R. "Johann Cornies, Money-Lending, and Modernization
    in the Molochna Mennonite Settlement, 1820s-1840s." *Journal of
    Mennonite Studies* 27 (2009): 109–27.
Staples, John R. "'On Civilizing the Nogais': Mennonite-Nogai Economic
    Relations, 1825–1860." *Mennonite Quarterly Review* 74, no. 2
    (2000): 229–56.
Stassen, Glen H., D. M. Yeager, and John Howard Yoder, eds. *Authentic
    Transformation: A New Vision of Christ and Culture.* Nashville,
    TN: Abingdon, 1996.
Stauffer, Ethelbert, and Robert Friedmann. "The Anabaptist Theology of
    Martyrdom." *Mennonite Quarterly Review* 19, no. 3 (1945): 179–214.
Stayer, James M. *Anabaptists and the Sword.* Lawrence, KS: Coronado, 1972.
Stone, Ronald H. *Paul Tillich's Radical Social Thought.* Louisville,
    KY: John Knox, 1980.
Studer, Gerald C. "A History of the Martyr's Mirror." *Mennonite
    Quarterly Review* 22, no. 3 (1948): 163–79.
Stutzman, Ervin R. *From Nonresistance to Justice: The Transformation
    of Mennonite Church Peace Rhetoric, 1908–2008.* Scottdale,
    PA: Herald, 2011.
Swartley, Willard M., and Cornelius J. Dyck, eds. *Annotated Bibliography
    of Mennonite Writings on War and Peace, 1930–1980.* Scottdale,
    PA: Herald, 1987.
Taylor, Charles. *A Secular Age.* 1st ed. Cambridge, MA: Belknap Press of
    Harvard University Press, 2007.
Taylor, Charles. "The Myth of the Secular, Part 2." CBC Radio.
    Accessed March 22, 2017. http://www.cbc.ca/radio/ideas/
    the-myth-of-the-secular-part-2-1.3143513.
Thiessen, David Almon. "The Church in Mission: Factors That
    Contributed to the Sixteenth Century Anabaptists Being a Missionary
    People." MCS Thesis, Regent College, 1980.
Toews, John B. "Origins and Activities of the Mennonite Selbstschutz
    in the Ukraine, 1918–1919." *Mennonite Quarterly Review* 46, no. 1
    (1972): 5–40.
Toews, Paul. *Mennonites in American Society, 1930–1970: Modernity and
    the Persistence of Religious Community.* Scottdale, PA: Herald, 1996.
Toews, Paul. "The Long Weekend or the Short Week: Mennonite Peace
    Theology, 1925–1944." *Mennonite Quarterly Review* 60, no. 1
    (1986): 38–57.
Urry, James. *Mennonites, Politics, and Peoplehood: 1525 to 1980.*
    Winnipeg: University of Manitoba Press, 2011.
Van Braght, Thieleman J. *The Bloody Theater or Martyrs Mirror of the
    Defenceless Christians: Who Baptized Only upon Confession of Faith,*

and Who Suffered and Died for the Testimony of Jesus, Their Saviour, from the Time of Christ to the Year A.D. 1600. Translated by Joseph F. Sohm. Scottdale, PA: Mennonite Publishing House, 1951.

Vogt, Virgil. "Marginalia." *Concern* 16, no. November, 1968 (n.d.): 22–24.

Volf, Miroslav. *Exclusion and Embrace: A Theological Exploration of Identity, Otherness, and Reconciliation.* Nashville, TN: Abingdon, 1996.

Volf, Miroslav. "'The Trinity Is Our Social Program': The Doctrine of the Trinity and the Shape of Social Engagement." *Modern Theology* 14, no. 3 (July 1998): 403–23.

Wandel, Lee Palmer. *The Reformation: Towards a New History.* Cambridge: Cambridge University Press, 2011.

Weaver, Alain Epp. "Missionary Christology: John Howard Yoder and the Creeds." *Mennonite Quarterly Review* 74, no. 3 (2000): 423–39.

Weaver-Zercher, David. *Martyrs Mirror: A Social History.* Baltimore, MD: Johns Hopkins University Press, 2016.

Weaver, J. Denny. "Christology in Historical Perspective." In *Jesus Christ and the Mission of the Church: Contemporary Anabaptist Perspectives.* Edited by Erland Waltner, 83–105. Newton, MA: Faith and Life, 1990.

Weaver, J. Denny, ed. *John Howard Yoder: Radical Theologian.* Eugene, OR: Wipf and Stock, 2014.

Weaver, J. Denny. *Keeping Salvation Ethical: Mennonite and Amish Atonement Theology in the Late Nineteenth Century.* Scottdale, PA: Herald, 1997.

Weaver, J. Denny. "Perspectives on a Mennonite Theology." *Conrad Grebel Review* 2, no. 3 (1984): 189–210.

Weaver, J. Denny. "Renewing Theology: The Way of John Howard Yoder: Musings from Nicea to September 11." *Fides et Historia* 35, no. 2 (2003): 85–103.

Weaver, J. Denny. *The Nonviolent Atonement.* Grand Rapids, MI: Eerdmans, 2011.

Weaver, J. Denny. *The Nonviolent God.* Grand Rapids, MI: Eerdmans, 2013.

Webb, Stephen H. *Jesus Christ, Eternal God: Heavenly Flesh and the Metaphysics of Matter.* New York: Oxford University Press, 2012.

Wenger, J. C. *Introduction to Theology.* Scottdale, PA: Herald, 1954.

Wenger, J. C. "The Schleitheim Confession of Faith." *Mennonite Quarterly Review* 19, no. 4 (1945): 243–53.

Wiebe, Dallas E. "Can a Mennonite Be an Atheist." *The Conrad Grebel Review* 16, no. 3 (1998): 122–32.

Wood, Ralph C. *Flannery O'Connor and the Christ-Haunted South.* Grand Rapids, MI: Eerdmans, 2005.

Yeago, David S. "Jesus of Nazareth and Cosmic Redemption: The Relevance of St Maximus the Confessor." *Modern Theology,* April 1, 1996.

Yeatts, John R. *Revelation*. Scottdale, PA: Herald, 2003.

Yoder, John Howard. "Anabaptist Vision and Mennonite Reality." John Howard Yoder Digital Library. Accessed October 16, 2015. http://replica.palni.edu/cdm/ref/collection/p15705coll18/id/3618.

Yoder, John Howard. "How H. Richard Niebuhr Reasoned: A Critique of Christ and Culture." In *Authentic Transformation: A New Vision of Christ and Culture*, edited by Glen H. Stassen, D. M. Yeager, and John H. Yoder, 31–89. Nashville, TN: Abingdon, 1996.

Yoder, John Howard. *Nevertheless: The Varieties and Shortcomings of Religious Pacifism*. Scottdale, PA: Herald, 1971.

Yoder, John Howard. "On the Meaning of Christmas." *Concern* 16 (November 1968): 14–19.

Yoder, John Howard. *Preface to Theology: Christology and Theological Method*. Grand Rapids: Brazos, 2002.

Yoder, John Howard. "The Anabaptist Dissent: The Logic of the Place of the Disciple in Society." *Concern* 1 (June 1954).

Yoder, John Howard, ed. *The Legacy of Michael Sattler*. Scottdale, PA: Herald, 1973.

Yoder, John Howard. *The Original Revolution: Essays on Christian Pacifism*. Scottdale, PA: Herald, 1977.

Yoder, John Howard. *The Politics of Jesus*. Grand Rapids: Eerdmans, 1994.

Yoder, John Howard. *The Priestly Kingdom: Social Ethics as Gospel*. Notre Dame, IN: University of Notre Dame Press, 1984.

Yoder, John Howard. *The War of the Lamb: The Ethics of Nonviolence and Peacemaking*. Grand Rapids, MI: Brazos, 2009.

Zeman, Jarold K. "Anabaptism: A Replay of Medieval Themes or a Prelude to the Modern Age?" *Mennonite Quarterly Review* 50, no. 4 (1976): 259–71.

Zimmerman, Earl. "Beyond Secular and Sacred: An Anabaptist Model for Christian Social Ethics." *Conrad Grebel Review* 25, no. 2 (2007): 50–67.

Zizioulas, Jean. *Being as Communion: Studies in Personhood and the Church*. Yonkers: St. Vladimir's Seminary Press, 1985.

INDEX